BLACK BIRD

BLACK BIRD

ONE MAN'S FREEDOM HIDES IN ANOTHER MAN'S DARKNESS

JAMES KEENE with HILLEL LEVIN

ST. MARTIN'S GRIFFIN
NEW YORK

Published in the United States by St. Martin's Griffin, an imprint of St. Martin's
Publishing Group

www.stmartins.com

The Library of Congress has cataloged the hardcover edition as follows:

Keene, James, 1963–
    In with the devil : a fallen hero, a serial killer, and a dangerous bargain for
redemption / James Keene with Hillel Levin.—1st ed.
        p.   cm.
    Includes bibliographical references.
    ISBN 978-0-312-55103-2
    1. Keene, James, 1963–   2. Hall, Larry DeWayne.   3. Serial murder investigation—
United States—Case studies.   4. Serial murderers—United States—Case
studies.   5. Informers—United States—Case studies.   I. Levin, Hillel.   II. Title.
    HV6529.K44 2010
    364.152'32092—dc22

                                                                      2010021661

ISBN 978-1-250-87949-3 (trade paperback)
ISBN 978-1-250-87950-9 (ebook)

Previously published as *In with the Devil*

Second St. Martin's Griffin Edition: 2022

10   9   8   7   6   5   4   3   2   1

Authors' Note

This is a true story, though some names have been changed.

Dedicated in loving memory to my Dad,

JAMES KEENE, SR.,

for always standing by my side

no matter what.

For believing I could move mountains.

In loving memory of

Robert "Robbie" Varvel

Contents

Acknowledgments

This book is due to the many people who, through their loyalty and contributions to my life, have helped make it what it is today.

I would like to thank all of the following, with a special thanks to Timothy "Timmy" Keene, my brother and partner in life through the good and the bad. My mother, Lynn, of whom I am very proud for overcoming all her setbacks and obstacles in her life and for standing by me in my darkest time. My sister, Terri Keene, for all the help and support she gave me throughout my whole ordeal. My grandmother, for her love and support throughout my life. My niece Sarina Keene.

Jeffrey Steinbeck, my attorney and personal friend, who handled, set up, and negotiated the arrangements for the situation described in this book. Lawrence Beaumont, the assistant U.S. attorney who handled my case, made me this incredible offer for redemption, and now is a close personal friend. Edward Eckhaus, for introducing Hillel and me. Kathy Psikos, for all her loyalty and support through everything. Brenda Kelleher, for always being there for me. Film producer and my close personal friend Alexandra Milchan, for whom I have immense respect and owe gratitude for believing in me and all I could be. Scott Lambert, for all his moral support. Oscar-winning producer Graham King, who saw the great potential in my story and is now making it into a Hollywood motion picture. Nat Sobel, my literary agent, of Sobel Weber and Associates, for so passionately believing in my story. Joel Gotler of Intellectual Property Group, who I have great respect for and who was a very integral part of my story becoming a book and movie. Rob Wilson, Lee Froehlich, the editors at *Playboy*, and the entire *Playboy* organization for seeing this as a great story, and for all the creative design and editing they did to present this story in their magazine. Sally Richardson, president and publisher; John Murphy, vice president and director of publicity; Charlie Spicer, executive editor; Yaniv Soha, associate editor; Allison Caplin, assistant editor; and the entire St. Martin's Press staff for all their creative design and additional feedback in the process of creating my book. Paul Desmarteau, Kevin Corrigan, Mark Capriotti, Steve Themer, Scott Themer, Carol Sperry, Michael Keegan, Robbie Wilson, Johnny Olshefski, and Jimmy Olshefski. The best friends a guy could ever ask for.

Last, but not least, Hillel Levin, for all of his superior research and expert developmental skills in making my book possible. I have great admiration for Hillel and immense respect for his skill as well as his character.

—James Keene

This book was the result of generous contributions from dozens of people to whom I am most grateful. I offer my sincere thanks to each of the following:

First and foremost to Jimmy Keene, who brought me his amazing story and was willing to share some painful memories in getting it told; Ed Eckhaus and Jeffrey Steinback for introducing us; my literary agent Nat Sobel of Sobel Weber Associates, who instantly saw the potential of Jimmy's story for a book and for Hollywood; Joel Gotler of Intellectual Property Group who got us the best possible audience with film makers, and to producers Graham King and Alexandra Milchan, who responded so enthusiastically; Lee Froehlich and the editors at *Playboy* who provided the first platform for Jimmy's story, which itself led to other major developments for our book; St. Martin's executive editor Charlie Spicer for his patience and critical assistance with the manuscript, and to the assistant editor, Yaniv Soha, who also gave me valuable feedback and suggestions; Donna and Garry Reitler for their incredible kindness to me and for their willingness to reopen the darkest chapter of their lives; Gary Miller for his time and the guided tour of Georgetown; Lawrence Beaumont for setting Jimmy's mission in motion; court reporter Toni Judd for her help in tracking down transcripts; the Rauh family for their introduction to Wabash and, in particular, to Ron Woodward, the town historian, who provided indispensible help with local history; former Iron Brigade reenactor Micheal Thompson for his memories and assistance in finding photographs, court records and old newspaper articles; former Wabash City policemen Ron Smith, Jeff Whitmer, and Phil Amones; the childhood friends of the Hall twins, Ron Osborne and Ross Davis; the excellent and thorough reference librarians at the Marion Public Library and the Springfield-Greene County Library; Randy Greer for his book, *Echoes of Mercy*, which provided me with important background on the Medical Center for Federal Prisoners from the perspective of its guards; criminologist Steven Egger for his writing on serial murder and reference to other research in the field; Marc Winkelman, Marc Brown, Wendover Brown, Mike Brown, and my coworkers at Calendars.com who helped me make the transition from business executive to full-time writer; Mark Coe and Coe-Truman Technologies for the technical help in designing and supporting the Web site InWithTheDevil.com; my friend artist Tony Fitzpatrick for the inspiration, each day, to get behind the mule and plow; my brothers Jay, Jonathan, and Wayne, for their constant support and encouragement; and finally, to my most important contributor, my wife, Mary Jo, who helps make everything possible, and to my sons Adam (always my best reader), Aaron, and Gabe, who all manage to put up with me.

—Hillel Levin

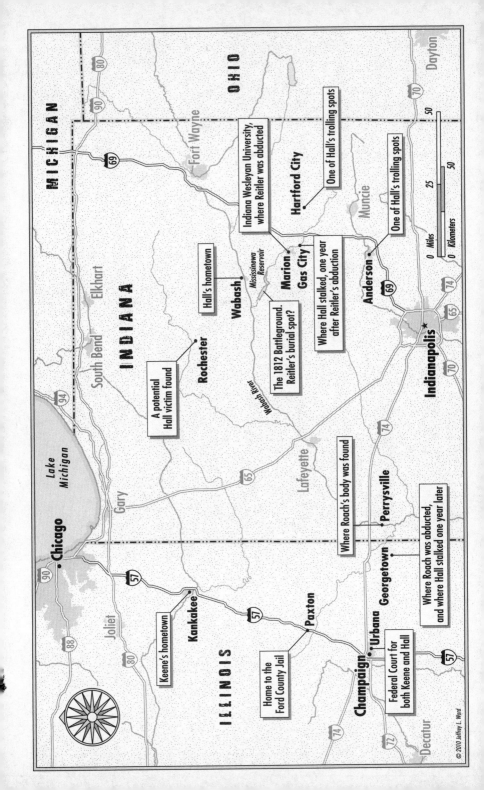

INTRODUCTION

The Victims' Pageant

IN LIFE, PEOPLE CAN TAKE a few wrong turns that destroy them. I'm one of those people. But I was given a second chance—not only to save myself but to redeem society for the wrong choices I made.

If you had shown up in my hometown of Kankakee, Illinois, and asked about me in the early nineties, most people would have told you that Jimmy Keene could do no wrong. I was considered to be some golden child with a handsome, heroic father, who had been both a police officer and a firefighter, and a beautiful mother, who had her own popular restaurant. In high school I lettered in three sports and was the star running back when our football team went all the way to the state championship game. The caption for an article about one victory read, "Keene in control." As far as everyone was concerned, I was just as successful when I got out of college. After my father retired from the fire department, we ran a bunch of businesses together, ranging from trucking and construction to frozen food. Besides the house I built for myself in Kankakee, I had a couple of others in Chicago, including one in the ritzy area they call the Gold Coast. Wherever I stayed, the latest corvette was always in the driveway, with a crotch rocket and a Harley in the garage and a hot girl in the bedroom.

But all my good fortune was never as good as it seemed. My parents may have looked great together, but actually they never got along well, and their divorce, when I was eleven, put an end to my happy childhood. While I was in high school, they struggled with their finances, too, more than anyone else knew, and it was rough keeping up with the fast crowd I was hanging with. But back then I discovered a way to put more money in my pocket than the richest kids had—selling drugs. I was kind of a natural for it with the charm I inherited from my parents, and the fearlessness that I felt from my experience in sports and martial arts. Instead of going to a big-name university where I could play football, I went to a community college in a suburb of Chicago where I could keep expanding my business. I stopped going to class after two years so I could deal full-time. I had all the cash you could ever want—to buy stupid stuff, but also to help my dad when he got into financial trouble. He never wanted to know where all my money was coming from, but the businesses we started together were also a way for me to earn a legitimate income. Only those businesses never worked out the way we hoped. In fact, they lost money, which put me back on my dealer treadmill, running that much harder to stay in place—until the Feds came "knocking" in 1996. Along with my front door, they shattered every dream I ever had, and every dream my dad had, too.

I took a plea, not knowing I would get a sentence of ten years to life in return. After ten months I had just started to settle down to do my time in a Michigan federal prison when I got yanked back to Illinois again. Now my prosecutor was ready to make me an offer. It was strange beyond belief and it would change my life more than any prison sentence.

The Ford County jail was an unlikely place for Jimmy Keene to find deliverance. Located in Paxton, barely a smudge of a city in the great expanse of central-Illinois farmland, it sat practically hidden behind the squat courthouse. The jail dated back to the nineteenth century, but more recent renovations were practically a monument to indifference, grafting two mismatched brick buildings to the original limestone structure with as much thought to design as a pile of toddler's blocks. On the inside, the hodgepodge design continued through a warren of cramped, oddly shaped cells that stank of urine and body odor. For Keene, any time he spent in the jail was a special kind of torture. "I'd rather be in a hard-core prison and have to worry about getting stabbed," he says, "than be confined in that little, nasty ancient-history shit hole."

Unfortunately for him, Ford County jail was somewhat centrally located on his road to ruin. An hour up the highway in one direction was his hometown of Kankakee, where he was busted for conspiracy to distribute cocaine. Down the highway from Ford County in the other direction was the U.S. courthouse in Urbana, where he took a plea on the drug charge and was sentenced to ten years. Then he was held at the jail a few days longer until he was transferred to the custody of the U.S. Bureau of Prisons. He did not relish returning to Ford County yet again in 1998, even though he would be closer to family and friends, and he certainly didn't look forward to seeing Lawrence Beaumont, the assistant U.S. attorney who had summoned him from his federal prison in Michigan.

He blamed Beaumont most for his crushing sentence. The prosecutor had worn a full beard then—shot with gray—and Jimmy remembered how he stared down on him in the courtroom from a terrible height, like some Old Testament prophet, eyes blazing and voice booming. When Keene's lawyer, Jeff Steinback, told him that Beaumont was ready to talk about a deal for an early release, Jimmy says, "I immediately thought it was some kind of trap."

Keene had not been any small-time dealer. In the fifteen years before his arrest, he had built one of the biggest independent drug empires in the Chicago area. Along the way, he had dealt with a tempting array of targets for the Feds. His suppliers included a Mexican drug lord and Chicago-area mafiosi. Among his customers were porn stars, yuppies, cops, doctors, lawyers, club owners, and the adult children of prominent politicians. After his arrest, some narcotics detectives even asked him to give up damaging information about his father—also named James Keene and known as Big Jim—a popular former ranking officer in the Kankakee police and fire departments who had influential friends in the highest reaches of state and local government. "They wanted me to cooperate in the worst way," Jimmy says, "but I always refused to testify against anyone in court, and I wasn't going to start, no matter how many years they kept me locked up."

For the meeting with the prosecutor, a sheriff's deputy put Keene in handcuffs and shackles, then marched him into the jail's tiny, windowless conference room, where his lawyer, Steinback, was waiting. Although Keene was cuffed, sheriff's deputies still crammed in around the table to watch over him. Soon the prosecutor himself entered and stared down at him again. Only this time he was accompanied by Ken Temples, a benign, balding FBI agent Jimmy hadn't seen before. Beaumont then sat opposite Keene and, with a typical dramatic flourish, slid a fat legal file across the table.

Jimmy nonchalantly grabbed it with his cuffed hands and lifted up the flap, putting on his best poker face to mask his reaction to whatever he saw inside. Still, nothing could have prepared him for the first glossy photograph he pulled from the folder. This was not a picture of a drug dealer or local big shot. Instead, he saw the battered naked body of a young woman, sprawled between rows of standing corn. Her skin was torn and discolored. As best he could with the cuffs, Jim turned over photo after photo of the grisly scene, first thinking, "Are they trying to pin this on me, too?"

He looked up expecting to see a scowl from Beaumont. But the prosecutor's gaze was no longer as hard or even accusing. Keene continued through the file. One photograph was of a second naked victim in a ditch, but other pictures were of smiling, attractive young women. They could have come from high school yearbooks. The file also included terse police reports from Indiana, Michigan, Wisconsin; even states as far away as Utah. Some of the teens had been found dead and, like the girl in the cornfield, with signs of strangulation. Others were still missing.

The pageant of beaming victims finally stopped with a man's mug shot. Notations at the bottom of the photo indicated that he'd been booked in an Indiana county jail back in 1994, but his cherubic face— framed by slick strands of hair, a trimmed mustache, and bushy mut- tonchop sideburns—could have been snapped a century earlier. His strangely placid eyes stared off into the distance as though stuck in an interminable pose.

His name was Larry DeWayne Hall. Beaumont had prosecuted him as well, and he explained to Keene that Hall was serving a life sentence for abducting the girl in the cornfield. Pointing to the thick folder, Beaumont added, "We think he's responsible for more than twenty other killings."

Hall's bizarre grooming was a key element that tied him to many of his suspected victims. Their abductions coincided with "reenact- ments" at nearby historic battlefields. A dedicated Civil War buff, Hall traveled throughout the country to portray a Union foot soldier and even appeared as a period extra in two films. His muttonchops, emulating those of a Union general, were intended to make his face look as authentic as his uniform and rifle.

Although Beaumont and the FBI were convinced that Hall was a serial killer, he had been convicted for killing just one victim, Jessica Roach, the girl in the cornfield, and it took two trials to do it. The guilty verdict from the first was overturned on appeal, and now an appeal was pending on the second conviction. A basis for both appeals was that Hall's confession had been coerced by wily investigators. If the government lost the second appeal, Beaumont would have to try Hall yet again and he might go free.

Still stunned, Jimmy stared at the photos of the girls and listened to Beaumont talk about Hall, barely absorbing the details. Finally he blurted out, "What does this have to do with me?"

Beaumont was prepared to make Keene a deal. He would transfer Jimmy undercover to the maximum security penitentiary and psychiatric hospital in Springfield, Missouri, where the federal Bureau of Prisons kept its most mentally ill inmates. There Hall had been serving a life sentence as a model prisoner, attending to the building's boiler room and carving finely crafted falcons in the arts-and-crafts shop. Only the warden and chief psychiatrist would know Jimmy's objective—to befriend the serial killer. If Jimmy could get him to confess to his crimes and disclose details that had not previously been publicized, then the prosecutor would have Keene testify the next time he tried Hall. In return, Beaumont would ask the judge to give Keene an early release.

Jimmy was still confused. Why did the prosecutor want *him* to go undercover? "Why don't you take some FBI guy and send him in?" he asked.

"Hall would smell him a mile away," Beaumont replied. "He'd be too polished, and Hall would sense that and clam right up. But you're perfect. You can mix with anyone—from the street level to the board level." As the prosecutor described Jimmy's qualifications for the job, Keene realized that during all the years that they had tried to put him away, Beaumont and the narcotics squads had observed Keene's social skills with grudging admiration. He says, "It seemed like a dream. One minute, I'm sitting in Michigan on the hot dime of a ten-year sentence with a long way to go. Then Beaumont pops up out of nowhere with this serial-killer thing and like tomorrow I could be out."

Keene desperately wanted to get out of prison, but to the surprise of everyone in the conference room, he closed the folder and pushed it back at Beaumont. "I can't do this. I don't have any experience with serial killers or anything like that."

"No, no, no," Beaumont pleaded. "That doesn't matter." Suddenly, the man who had argued so loudly to put him away was begging for Jimmy's consideration and added, "I'm willing to make it worth your while." Although Keene could appreciate that irony, he couldn't help but be suspicious of the Feds, especially Beaumont. But then Steinback, who was shoved in next to Jimmy at the table, elbowed him in the side and held up his hand. "Mr. Beaumont, I'd like to talk to my client out in the hallway."

Steinback was not the original lawyer in Keene's case. A balding man with a powerful stature but a soft voice, Steinback is not just known for his work as a trial lawyer. His specialty is in the court of last resort—the various proceedings that come *after* a guilty verdict or plea. His clients have ranged from mobster hit men to media mogul Conrad Black. But never had he seen a deal like the one Beaumont offered Keene. Once Steinback had Jimmy in the hall outside the conference room, he hissed, "You have to do this. If you succeed, it will be a total wash on everything: your sentence, your fine, even your parole."

"And what if I fail?" Keene asked. "I'll be stuck in a penitentiary with lunatics."

"Jim, please, just for me," Steinback begged. "No matter what happens, this will give me a reason to go back to the judge, and we'll get something extra for your effort. I promise."

Keene and Steinback then returned to the conference room and Jimmy broke the news: "I'll go ahead and give it a try."

Beaumont, Keene remembers, was ecstatic, practically reaching across the table to hug him: "That's great. Great."

Once again, Beaumont and the FBI agent deluged Jimmy with background information on Hall. He listened, still in a daze. However, as they kept talking, he realized that Hall's story was more complicated than it had first sounded. Beaumont most wanted Hall to confess to *another* killing—one of the most famous missing-person cases of the nineties. They suspected that Hall had abducted this young woman right from her college campus, but the local police disputed who was responsible for her disappearance. If Hall told Keene where he buried her and they found the body, then there would be no doubt about Hall's guilt. This was to be Keene's objective in addition to obtaining a confession. "If you don't get us the location of that body," Beaumont told him, "you don't get released. No body, no release."

Any confidence Keene felt about accomplishing Beaumont's crazy mission suddenly melted away. *No body, no release?* It was one thing to hear Hall confess. It was quite another to get inside his head and get him to reveal a burial place that he may have repressed or even forgotten. It all seemed so impossible—like capturing the witch's broomstick in *The Wizard of Oz.*

Still in handcuffs and leg shackles, Keene was pulled to his feet, and then, with a few claps on the back, he was returned to his putrid jail cell with Larry Hall's fat legal folder tucked under his arm. Again and again over the next few weeks, Jimmy would have second thoughts about Beaumont's mission. At one point, he even told his lawyer that he was ready to back out. It would take a harrowing personal tragedy two weeks later before he would fully commit to the bizarre criminal investigation, not just for himself but for his family. In the process, he would learn as much about his own inner demons as Hall's—an experience that would sear his soul far more than a lengthy sentence— and help him emerge from prison a truly changed man.

1

Fathers & Sons

IT'S THE JUDGMENT OF THE COURT *that the defendant be committed to the custody of the attorney general of the United Sates or her authorized representative for the minimum guideline term of one hundred twenty months.*

When Jimmy Keene first heard the judge pronounce his sentence in July of 1997, he says, "The life went right out of me." It was exactly the term that prosecutor Larry Beaumont had recommended, and when Keene went before the bench to make a presentencing statement, he told the judge, "I know I did something wrong, but not to ruin my whole life. Ten years will ruin my life."

But only moments later, with sickening finality, he would hear those words—"one hundred twenty months"—from the judge's own lips. Jimmy was hollow and numb. It was, he thought, like hearing a doctor's diagnosis of terminal cancer. He felt helpless and hopeless in a way that he'd never felt before.

The worst was yet to come. His mother sobbed hysterically somewhere behind him, but when the marshals grabbed his arms to lead him out of the court, he first scanned the spectators to find his father— his idol and his best friend. A tall, brawny man with a mustache and full head of dark hair, Big Jim looked a decade younger than his sixty years. But now, upon hearing the sentence, he, too, was stunned, his face pale and eyes unfocused. "Like he was lost," Jimmy says.

As soon as Big Jim could, he went to see his son at Ford County jail. They looked at each other through the thick bulletproof glass of the visiting room, and Jimmy says, "We cried like babies."

It was not the first time that they had been in jail together. As a thirteen-year-old in 1976, Jimmy tagged along with his father, then a police officer, when he was called to the Kankakee station house to deal with an unruly prisoner in the holding cells. "As soon as we walked in the station, we heard screaming and yelling. It sounded like a riot. When we went into the cellblock, we could see this huge, crazy black guy whipping everyone into a frenzy. All the guards seemed scared to death, but my father knew him and called him by name. He walked right up to his cell and very calmly said, 'Choo Choo, you've got this whole cellblock out of hand. If I have to unlock that cell door and get in there with you, it won't be a pretty thing.' And Choo Choo said, 'I don't want no problems with you, man,' and then completely settled down. It was like watching Superman. When we left the station, the desk sergeant said to me, 'That's what we love about your dad.'"

Big Jim's bravery did not stop with the police. He also joined the fire department and, for five years, was a ranking officer in both forces. Jimmy has a favorite newspaper clipping that shows Big Jim rushing a frail little girl into the back of an ambulance. He had passed her burning house on his way home, heard the cries of her mother on the sidewalk, and rushed inside without a helmet or any other gear. Another time, when Jimmy was a teenager, he and some friends had pped their car by a burning building when they saw his father on roof. "Just then we heard *kaboosh,* and we watched the whole building collapse. Everyone on the roof dropped down inside and they were trapped there for hours. A few of them even died. But somehow, my dad got out alive."

Big Jim was larger-than-life. He had the macho magnetism that drew both men and attractive women. At the age of twenty-six, he married one of those women, a raven-haired beauty named Lynn Brower. Jimmy arrived the next year, with a face that had both his father's Irish square jaw and his mother's blue eyes. Although Big Jim never rose above the rank of lieutenant in either the police or fire department, he still hung out with some of the most important people in town: Kankakee's longtime mayor, Tom Ryan, who was his best friend, and Tom's older brother, George, who would go on to become governor and—like two of his predecessors—would also end up in prison. But such was the Kankakee pedigree of power and corruption, dating back to the days of Al Capone. Scarface made the riverside town—an hour south of downtown Chicago—his summer getaway and kept most of the local politicians firmly in his pocket.

In many ways, when Jimmy was born in 1963, he embodied his hometown's moral ambiguity: Big Jim may have been in law enforcement, but Jimmy's maternal grandfather was a driver for Capone. Keene grew up listening to his Italian grandmother's tales of the fancy supper clubs and the fast guys who ran them. "She was a high-fashion mink-stole lady," Jimmy says, "with some serious Mafia connections."

His father had no reservations about meeting with his in-laws' friends. One Mafia princess even became Jimmy's godmother. It all added to Big Jim's aura as a man who worked both sides of the street. But his political friends were no different and were shameless in exploiting their clout. When Jimmy tagged along to his father's bull sessions with the local big shots, he heard them dole out government contracts like chips in a poker game. To cash in on these connections, Big Jim started a construction business on the side. Meanwhile Lynn saved the money to finally open her own bar and grill. In addition to Jimmy, they also had another son and a daughter, living just outside of town where they could afford a large house on a big lot. From all appearances, the attractive couple led a storybook lifestyle.

But behind closed doors, a completely different plot played out for Jimmy. Like the song "Jumping Jack Flash," he says, "I was born in a cross-fire hurricane." His parents argued constantly—mostly about money. Despite Big Jim's side businesses, he could not give Lynn all the trappings of wealth to keep up with their fancy friends. Then there was Lynn's nighthawk lifestyle. "My dad had an old-world mentality," Jimmy remembers. "He wanted his wife in the kitchen with dinner on the table. She never went along with that." Sometimes she was still not home when Big Jim was ready to start his morning shift. He would jump back in the squad car and tear over to the restaurant, where the two would empty the bar with their screaming. But nothing bothered him more than her flirting. "She was always a glamour queen," their son says. "Guys would flock to her, and as far as my father was concerned, she was too nice to them."

Big Jim's worst suspicions ultimately panned out when he caught Lynn outside a motel in a car with one of his business partners. His parents divorced when Jimmy was eleven, in 1974, and his childhood came to an abrupt end. Not only did he lose the father he idolized, but a few months after the separation he was forced to live in the same house with the man who had torn his family apart and married his mother.

Sports became Jimmy's escape from this domestic turmoil. He had grown into a compact version of his father with both strength and blazing speed. Against his mother's advice, he enrolled in Kankakee's Eastridge public high school just so he could stick with the football players he had grown up with. Their team ultimately went all the way to a state championship game with Keene as the star running back. He would also letter in wrestling and track. His father never missed a game or a meet.

Although Jimmy was one of the few white students in a tough inner-city school, Big Jim never worried about his safety. He had sent his son, from the age of five, to martial arts schools, where he would earn black belts in karate, kung fu, and tae kwon do. Ironically, Jimmy faced as much danger in his mother's house as on the streets. One night after wrestling practice, the fifteen-year-old returned home to find Lynn and his stepfather drinking in the kitchen. Words with *her* quickly escalated into a fistfight with *him*. "He came barreling after me," Keene remembers. "When he took a swing, I ducked out of the way and punched him in the face." Jimmy didn't stop punching until he had his stepfather on the floor, with two black eyes.

If nothing else, the fight gave him an excuse to live with his father, but just then Big Jim was settling into bachelor life. When women came to visit, they were surprised to find his teenage son knocking about. Keene says, "I could tell it was cramping his style and mine, too." He returned to his mother's house, doing his best to stay confined to the basement and away from his stepfather.

With his good looks and limited parental supervision, Jimmy was sleeping with multiple girlfriends by the time he was fifteen. It was the late seventies, an era still on the cusp of AIDS awareness, and sex had never been more casual. He can drive through most neighborhoods in town and point to a home where one of his conquests had lived—from the tightly packed bungalows to the mansions by the river. His athletic success in high school had brought admiration from the boys, but so did his willingness to fight anyone at any time. His experience in both martial arts and wrestling made for a lethal combination. His one-man rumbles against three or four assailants at a time became school legend. He was often in demand as much for protection as companionship at the wild parties hosted by Kankakee's wealthiest kids. If their parents were out of town, their keggers could last all weekend.

Increasingly, as Keene ran with the rich crowd, he became self-conscious about his own comparatively modest means. "My buddy would show up to a party with a brand-new Ford Bronco. At the dock behind his house, he had matching jet boats—red and white—that his parents gave him for his sixteenth birthday. And then here is Jimmy with his junky little Toyota Celica. The only thing I had was sports."

He felt that stigma grow when Big Jim was suddenly dragged into a well-publicized drug sting. Big Jim and some friends did nothing more than listen to a paid informant boast that he could arrange for a shipment of cocaine to Kankakee, but the state's attorney still brought charges against them. Although the case was thrown out before it ever came to trial, the stain remained on Big Jim and, by extension, his sons. No amount of fighting could stop the whispers. "My mom was losing her restaurant and my dad was going broke on a fireman's salary," Keene recalls, "and everybody thought I was the godfather's kid."

As high school students kept approaching Jimmy for dope, he started to wonder if it would be such a bad thing to oblige them. Kankakee's depressed industrial economy had already made it a hotbed for drug dealing and other criminal activity. "It was a way for me to make money," he says, "but it was also a reason for me to keep hanging with the rich kids. The fact that I could be the guy with the sources and connections to get them their party goods made me the man of the hour."

Keene himself had little use for drugs or alcohol because of their effect on his athletic performance, but he had several pot-smoking friends who introduced him to their local sources. Jimmy quickly realized that he was perfectly suited to build a "sales" network. He could recruit his buddies who were wrestlers and football players as dealers. They were fearsome on their own, but if they encountered any tough customer who refused to pay, Jimmy was their ultimate enforcer. Everyone in school knew about his black belts, and those who had seen his fights were terrified of him. Quickly his sales force reached into the community beyond just high school students, and

Keene was dealing directly with Kankakee's biggest pot supplier, a Mexican who lived in a big house on the river and had a matching set of $40,000 jet boats.

When it came time to graduate in 1982, most Eastridge High School football fans thought Jimmy Keene would soon be a running back for a major university. Instead, he chose to attend Triton, a community college in a suburb of Chicago. The football program was locally renowned but was nothing on the national radar. He explained to Big Jim that he wanted to remain close to Kankakee.

In fact, he was making too much money and having too much fun to leave his drug operation behind, and it clicked into high gear once he hit the Windy City. Before long, Keene says, "My mind was straying from sports and school." He continued to recruit fellow football players and wrestlers to join his other "team," but he was more careful to insulate himself from direct contact with the customers. Instead, he concentrated on the "connections" who could supply the drugs to his burgeoning sales force. To pay them off, he'd set up meetings, always careful to use pay phones instead of his home phone. He would casually walk into a restaurant with a briefcase packed with cash, take a seat opposite the supplier's courier, then just as casually leave the briefcase behind when he got up to go.

The heaviest connections soon valued Jimmy as much as he did them. "Being a drug dealer is a bigger job than anyone thinks," he explains. "Everything is high risk. You have the cops breathing down your neck. You have to meet people living in areas that could be detrimental to your health. You have to collect money from some customers who don't want to pay. It's the kind of job nine out of ten people would fail at."

For a time, his biggest suppliers were an Italian father-and-son team deeply involved with Chicago's mob. They owned several legitimate businesses in Cicero as fronts to launder cash. They quickly picked up on Keene's Italian roots, and the father, who had experience as a barber, loved cutting his thick black hair. Afterward, they would all sit down to a home-cooked Italian meal.

The son talked Jimmy into extending his product line into cocaine. "I don't know why you fuck with the pot," the son told him. They had to haul in truckloads of marijuana to equal the street value of a few suitcases of coke. Keene discovered he could sell the powder to many of his existing customers. After he had lucked into meeting a real Mexican drug lord, he became the Cicero mobsters' supplier.

With a crew of eight dealers, his total sales exceeded a million dollars a year, and he was netting as much as $400,000 of it. "I realized I could put the college education on hold," Keene says, "and become a millionaire very quickly." He had already left the football team, and by 1984, after his sophomore year, he'd stopped attending classes,

He had too much cash to safely deposit in a bank without getting reported to the Feds, so instead he spent it on "stupid shit" that he didn't really need. "Everything was in excess," he remembers. "One motorcycle or Corvette wasn't enough, I had to have two. I had hundreds of leather jackets. If I wanted a music collection, I'd go into a record store and buy everything in sight. If I went to a restaurant or bar, I'd buy a bunch of booze for everyone there."

With all of his party connections, Keene was invited onto the Chicago set of *The Color of Money* when it was filmed in 1985. He instantly hit it off with Tom Cruise, who maybe saw a little of himself in Jimmy—or the more macho, muscular self he wanted to be. They hung out and even went shopping for cars together. Jimmy was an extra in a few scenes, and before he left town, director Martin Scorsese told him that he could have a career in Hollywood. It was something Big Jim never let him forget. *He could have been a star.* But for Jimmy, even movie money seemed like chump change compared to that of his booming business. He would buy another stash house on Chicago's Gold Coast that had a lakefront view, as well as a vacation home back in Kankakee.

Never for a moment had Keene been tempted to use any of the merchandise he sold. He says, "I don't think I ever understood what people meant when they talked about having addictions to dope or alcohol or gambling. But the money was something different for me. Once I saw all that cash coming in—rooms full of it—that became my addiction."

Nothing made Keene feel better about his newfound wealth than helping Big Jim. His father had retired around the time that Jimmy had left college. Big Jim had always fancied himself to be an entrepreneur and decided to devote himself full-time to his myriad business ventures. But it didn't take long for all of his deals to crumble around him. Once impossibly boyish, he now wore a full beard that had gone completely gray. He had become like a hulking Hemingway in winter. One day in 1986, Jimmy stopped by the house his father owned on a hill overlooking the river. He found him hunched over some papers on the kitchen table, sobbing. It broke Jimmy's heart. Superman wasn't supposed to cry.

Big Jim was on the verge of eviction. His treasured Corvette, Chevy 4×4, and Harley had already been repossessed. Worse yet, if all of his assets were liquidated, it could raise questions about the other notes he had signed. To add to the humiliation, his ex-lover was telling everyone in town that her new boyfriend was about to buy Big Jim's things from the sheriff's auction. The next morning, Keene arrived at his father's door with a big bag. Inside was $350,000 in cash. First, they paid the entire mortgage on the house, then they reclaimed everything that had been repossessed. All Jimmy wanted in return was that his father not ask any questions.

This was the first of many cash infusions into Big Jim's affairs—a sort of reverse trust fund. Big Jim trusted that the source of money wasn't too bad. The son trusted that his father could somehow leverage the ill-gotten gains into a legitimate moneymaking enterprise.

Jimmy had tried on his own, investing in an adult-video company with a male childhood friend who had become a porn star. Along the way, as a fringe benefit, Keene had a brief fling with Samantha Strong, then the reigning XXX queen. They met when he happened to sit next to her at a party. "First," Keene says, "she asked, 'Um, what movies are you in?' and then I told her, 'Well, I haven't been in any movies.' We just hit it off from there and ended up having our own little private party later that night. For a while, we were seeing quite a bit of each other. She'd fly me out to Vegas while she did all her shows. She wanted me to be her travel companion, but I was just too busy for that kind of relationship between all my legitimate businesses and the crooked business." Meanwhile, his partner proved too flaky to run the adult-video business. As Jimmy remembers, "All he wanted to do was party, party, party." Keene ended up losing more than $300,000 before he shut the business down.

If nothing else, Jimmy's capital investment put the life back into Big Jim. He shaved off his beard of woe and was once again riding high with an attractive new lady on his arm. They had season tickets to Bears games and regular nights out at Chicago's finest restaurants. Keene himself wasn't living so large, but he never begrudged Big Jim his expensive tastes. "My dad was everything to me," Jimmy explains. "I would have done whatever I had to do to make his life better and more enjoyable for him. It pushed me that much harder on the street."

Big Jim never intended to force his son into selling drugs, but every legitimate place where he sunk Jimmy's money proved to be a dry hole, from trucking to real estate to—most improbably—a line of Italian frozen food. "He was spending it as fast as I could make it," Keene says. "It was like I was on a treadmill."

If Big Jim had any illusions about the real source of his son's wealth, they were surely dispelled in 1992 when both Jimmy, now almost thirty, and his younger brother, Tim, were busted as they drove two vans packed with 150 pounds of pot. The deal had been set up by Tim, who was making his own bones in the trade. Although it looked as if he had a reliable source, he had been snared by a sting instead. Jimmy helped engineer the deal and pushed to complete it when Tim became suspicious about his connection. The older brother even offered to help drive at the last minute. After the arrest, the Keenes were hauled to the county jail, but when directed to a pay phone to make his one call, Jimmy did not dial up his lawyer. Instead, he called his live-in girlfriend. As quietly as possible he said, "I'm not going to be coming home tonight." When she asked what had happened, he replied, "It is what we've always worried about." Then, just as calmly, he told her how to lift up the floorboard in the laundry room where he had stashed six kilos of cocaine and $150,000. "Put what you find in the laundry basket and cover it with a bunch of clothes," he told her, "and get the hell out of there."

As the girlfriend pulled out of the driveway, she was convinced an undercover cop was already following her. Once she lost him in the little side streets of their neighborhood, she stopped the car and sprinkled the cocaine among the evergreens in someone's backyard. She then drove over to Big Jim's house. When he opened the door to greet her, she said, "Listen, Jimmy's in a lot of trouble, and he told me to give you this." She then shoved the laundry basket into his arms and left him standing there, dumbstruck. By the time she had returned home, the cops had already burst through the front door of their house.

With the sons' arrests, all the fissures that had cracked up the Keene family in the first place came to the surface again. Most of Lynn's anger was directed at Jimmy for dragging his brother into drug dealing and using her van for part of the haul, although Tim protested that it was just as much his idea. She also lit into her ex-husband for the leniency he had shown the boys through the years. True to form, Big Jim couldn't help but be concerned for Jimmy. As usual, he partly blamed himself for his son's behavior. "I always had an idea of what was going on," he told Jimmy, referring to the seemingly bottomless "trust" funds. "Now I know for sure. I shouldn't have remained silent. But this is serious now. You need to get away from all this before they try to put you away forever." Still, despite the lecture, Big Jim never did tell Jimmy what he did with all the money in the laundry basket.

Ultimately, the brothers took a plea on possession of cannabis with intent to deliver. They served no more than probation because the local narcotics squad did not properly search and seize the vans. Still, despite the lucky break, Jimmy could not get off the dealing treadmill. His goals, he says, were modest by drug-dealer standards. "I wanted five million dollars that I could bury in a hole. Then I'd start a normal life. It's not like I had dreams of big mansions, private jets, and stuff like that. I just wanted enough money to give me and my dad some peace of mind. Then we could have gone fishing or rode motorcycles together and done whatever we wanted to do with no pressure to get up and have to work a stupid nine-to-five job with menial pay. That's what my poor dad struggled with his whole life. Suddenly I came of age and I tried to do it for both of us. And I came close. I really did."

To further that plan, Jimmy completed his college degree, but Big Jim's wheeling and dealing—especially with the frozen food—was burning through the money faster than Jimmy could make it. "Looking back," he says, "it's amazing what I spent to come clean."

One day when Jimmy Keene's drug dealing was at its height, he received a call from a man we will call Hector Gonzales—a narco trafficker in a northern-Mexican state who had become Jimmy's major supplier of cocaine and marijuana. "Hello, Jimmy, my friend," he said in English that had only the slightest accent.

"What's going on?" Keene asked. Hector was not the sort of connection who called just to chat.

"Oh, nothing. Nothing much at all—except that I've got your friend here."

"My friend?"

"Yes," Hector answered. "Your little, skinny hippie party friend. The one we can't trust. The one you and I need to get rid of."

Hector then clicked on the speakerphone and Keene heard the sobbing voice of Nick Richards, one of his oldest friends. "Jimmy, you got to save me," he cried. "These guys are going to kill me. They're going to kill me for real, man."

By all rights, Keene should have let Nick die. A pretty boy, with the looks and flowing locks of rocker Rick Springfield, Richards liked cocaine as much as their most degenerate customers. "When Nick had the party goods and some girls to impress," Keene says, "he was just a talking, snorting fool." Jimmy let none of his other dealers get away with such conspicuous consumption, but he always cut some slack for Richards. Their relationship dated back to the days when they both played peewee hockey. Nick was the first close friend to help Jimmy sell drugs. But Keene paid dearly for his loyalty. Although Nick had led Keene to Hector, he had previously introduced Jimmy to another "supplier" in Phoenix who tried to kill Keene when he arrived with a cash payment. Keene barely escaped in a dash through the desert that summoned every ounce of his running-back prowess— all while he balanced a duffel bag on his shoulder with a million dollars inside. After that close call, Keene took the next plane home, went directly to Nick's home, and punched him in the nose.

Hector was not so forgiving. When he discovered that Richards had poached three kilos—worth hundreds of thousands of dollars— from a large shipment of cocaine, he snatched him from his condo in Phoenix and smuggled him down to Mexico to dispense a drug lord's justice. Hector shouted over the speakerphone to Keene, "Let me blow the motherfucker's head off right now and do us both a favor. He'll get us all busted one of these days."

No matter how much Richards had screwed up through the years, Jimmy was not about to hear him whacked on the other end of a phone line. "You just can't kill one of my guys," Jimmy argued. "That's not fair. Just put him on ice and I'll come down there tomorrow so we can talk about it." Of course, once inside Hector's lair, Jimmy would be as much a prisoner as Nick, but he didn't think of those consequences. He never thought of the consequences.

The next day, Keene flew to Tucson and, as usual when he visited Hector, rented a sports car for the ninety-minute drive into Mexico. He remembered the first time he ever made that trip—to deliver a suitcase filled with a million dollars. Although Hector was as short and round as a bowling ball, he still looked every inch the Latin drug lord. His long black hair was slicked back and his mustache and goatee neatly trimmed. He wore diamond rings on his manicured fingers and thickly braided gold bracelets dangled from his wrist. He was always impeccably dressed in tailored suits or silk shirts and linen pants. But no matter how stylish his appearance, he could still be as ruthless and brutal as the most bone-chilling thug. When Jimmy put the suitcase on a table between them, Hector's eyes flashed before Jimmy opened it. Hector asked, "Gringo, what's to stop me from turning you around right now and blowing your head off?"

"Nothing," Keene replied. As he knew too well, Hector had paid off all of the local politicians and Feds. Meanwhile nobody even knew Jimmy was in Mexico. He could be dead and buried along some desert road and no one would ever be the wiser. "You can kill me, rip me off, do whatever you want," Jimmy said as he snapped open the suitcase. "But then you'll get just *one* of these from me. Do the deal like you promised and it won't be long before I'm back here with another suitcase and then another one after that."

Hector closed his eyes into little slits, leaned right across the table, and then burst out in a big hearty laugh. "I like you, amigo. You're smart and that's why we're going to get very rich together."

Hector's home was a pink Moorish-style mansion that took up much of a mountaintop. Visitors approaching on the winding roads could be seen for miles by the guards. They wore sunglasses and wandered the grounds shirtless with cartridge belts and semiautomatic rifles slung over their shoulders. Jimmy drove up to the wrought-iron entry gates at the bottom of Hector's mountain and announced his arrival through the intercom.

Typically when Keene visited, he found the hacienda in full party mode. Naked strippers lounged by the pool, and laughing guests lapped up the cocaine or sumptuous spreads of food inside. But the day he came for Richards, he found a much more surreal atmosphere than usual. Only Hector's steady girls were in attendance. Instead of greeting Keene, they turned their heads and skittered out of his way. The guards were so coked up, they twitched. Everyone cringed with each keening shriek that came from somewhere inside the house. Jimmy followed the sound to the kitchen—as big as any in a restaurant with stainless steel counters and appliances—where he found Nick tied to a chair. His face looked like a Kabuki fright mask, his hair wild and tangled and both eyes black. Rivulets of blood ran down from his nose and mouth against his powdery-white skin.

Behind him, Hector paced the floor. Although he was neatly dressed in a shirt and tie, his forehead glistened and his eyes were feverish as though he, too, were high on something. His fury even unsettled the entourage of guards who hung around him. They, too, looked away from Keene as he approached.

"I've been making your friend smoke dope for three days." Hector laughed. He grabbed Richards by the hair. "Show your friend how you like to smoke dope," he commanded. "That's all you want to do, you partying piece of shit." Turning to Keene, Hector said, "I say we do him right now, Jimmy. We'll bury him here and nobody will ever know what happened."

At first, Jimmy didn't know how to reply, but if he didn't move quickly, he would soon see Nick's brains splattered on the stainless steel counters. Somehow he had to find a way to save Richards without challenging the drug lord's authority. As everyone watched, Jimmy strode right up to Nick and slapped him twice across the face. Richards yelped—as much in shock as pain—but then sobbed even louder. Hector and the guards were as stunned as Nick, but then erupted with laughter.

"You stupid fuck," Keene yelled at Richards. "You fuck up everything." Jimmy turned to Hector. "I halfway don't blame you for wanting to do this. He's a complete fuckup."

Then Jimmy took a few breaths and got close enough to the drug lord to speak softly. "But you have to understand something, Hector. I've grown up with this kid. I don't want him to get killed. Besides, no matter where you bury him, people in my organization will figure out what happened. That won't make me look too good."

Hector dismissed the argument with a swat of his pudgy hand, but he started to soften. "Come on, Jimmy. You baby this fucking guy too much."

"You're right. I totally agree with you, but let me handle it. I promise I'll get him out of the organization, so you never have to deal with him again."

At last Hector relented with another dismissive swat. "If you don't know who your real friends are, Jimmy, I'm not going to tell you."

As soon as the ropes were untied, Keene hustled Richards to the rental car. Other than his sniffles and his whimpers, Nick didn't say a thing until they crossed the border. Only then did he break out in a huge smile and sob, this time for joy, "Thank you, Jimmy. Thank you. I owe you my life, man. I owe you everything."

Somehow that debt would not be great enough to keep Richards's mouth shut just a few years later.

Ever since he'd started dealing drugs in high school, Jimmy Keene had been in the sights of local narcotics agents. He had always frustrated surveillance and stings by speeding away from tails or using buffers to make his deals. But after the pot bust, he became the prime target of a regional task force that included investigators from every level of government and as far away as Chicago. It was only a matter of time—four years—before they found a way to infiltrate his organization, and no snitch would be more valuable to them than Nick Richards.

One evening in November 1996, Jimmy grabbed something to eat in his kitchen and was walking with a tray to the living room when he noticed the knob on his front door start to jiggle. "At first I thought it was just my imagination," he says, "and then boom—the whole door blew off the hinges." Eleven agents stormed into the house, wearing black uniforms, crash helmets, and goggles. "One guy came lunging right at me, but I sidestepped and just lay flat on the ground so no one had an excuse to shoot me. Still, it seemed like they all had their guns pointed at my head and one said, 'Just move, motherfucker, and we'll blow your fucking head off.' I kept asking for some kind of identification, and finally they pulled me up and put handcuffs on me. This guy fumbled around trying to get his wallet out and then stuck it in my face and said, 'DEA, that's who we are, fucker.'"

For a while, the agents tore through the house as though it were the first time they had searched it. Then one, with his cell phone in hand, went directly to the master bathroom. Jimmy had personally built it with two of his closest friends when he added on to the house a few years before. By pushing a button behind the toilet, the wall would open. Behind it, he had a safe between the floorboards. The only person who had ever seen the setup was an old girlfriend whom he had paid to clean the house. The Feds had flipped her and, Keene suspected, probably snuck into the house before the raid to figure out how it worked. Inside the safe, the DEA agents found small bags of coke and weed along with an electronic scale. They also found two pistols in the nightstand by his bed and cash in an attic safe that could be tracked to another informant who had used marked bills to buy cocaine. It was all icing on the cake.

These were not Keystone Kops like the ones who had busted him and his brother for pot. These were the Feds, and they were as cocky as Keene himself, always acting as if it were a just a matter of time before they had his ass behind bars. It started the night of the raid. For nearly the next twenty-four hours, they held him prisoner in his own home, handcuffed to the kitchen chair, seeing what information he'd be willing to trade before his lawyer showed up. When they finally did leave, they had Jimmy's Chevy pickup truck in tow. Because they found drugs on the premises, they could impound anything on wheels as a potential means for transporting the controlled substance.

It took another few weeks before they came back to his front door to arrest him and then haul him downtown, where he would be paraded in front of the media along with a raft of gangbangers and low-level dealers. They had been swept up in another investigation completely different than the one that had caught Keene, but the association couldn't have been more humiliating for Jimmy or his family.

Larry Beaumont was the assistant U.S. attorney assigned to his case, and Keene found him as smug as the DEA agents. Unlike most other federal prosecutors, he had local roots, having previously served as an assistant state's attorney for central Illinois. Early in their first meeting, Beaumont revealed his familiarity with the cast of Kankakee characters, but then stunned Jimmy by adding cryptically, "And we know all about your father."

Rather than risk a trial and even more humiliation for his family, Keene decided to take a plea, believing his sentence would be based on the minimal amount of drugs found in his house. But in the presentencing report, Beaumont insisted on charging Keene with the additional amounts that the informants alleged he had sold to them. What Richards alone said he bought from his childhood friend was enough to boost Jimmy's sentencing guidelines from a few years to ten years and nearly twenty years. For added effect, during the sentencing hearing, Beaumont referred the judge to the guns and electronic scale that had also been found in the house and argued, "We are not talking about a casual dealer here."

Jimmy's lawyer tried lamely to portray Keene as no bigger a dealer than the informants who had turned him in, but there was no sweet-talking Judge Harold A. Baker. Then sixty-eight, he had sat on the federal bench for nearly two decades. He looked down on Keene with a stern gaze framed by dark glasses and a shock of white hair. He fully believed the testimony about the additional hearsay amounts of drugs sold, and even though the gun charges were dropped, he further augmented the mandatory sentence because of the pistols found in Jimmy's nightstand. "It's well-known," he said, "that people who traffic in drugs carry guns for their own protection and the protection of their merchandise." He then invoked his sentence of ten years with no chance for parole.

Jimmy heard later that his father stayed behind in the courtroom. He asked for a few words with Beaumont and even introduced himself to the court reporter, hoping she might be a back door to the judge. His son, he assured them, would do whatever was necessary to reduce his sentence.

Big Jim knew that the government was always interested in using prisoners to make cases against their former associates. Jimmy also had a cunning, hard-edged girlfriend, Tina, who was more than willing to rope other dealers into the Feds' net if it would help cut his sentence. But as they quickly learned, these deals could trim a few months here and there at most. Law enforcement had spent years trying to catch Keene, and they weren't about to let him go anytime soon.

When Big Jim came to visit, he tried to keep up a brave front, but as soon as his son would appear in the jail's orange jumpsuit, he would lose his composure and sob, "Son, this is the last place I wanted to see you." Big Jim had always been so proud of him—for his success at sports and his toughness with other males; for the wide circle of friends and beautiful girls he had attracted growing up; for the industriousness he'd shown with legitimate projects such as home construction. But Big Jim blamed himself, too, for taking Jimmy's money and ignoring its source—even after the pot bust. For too long the Keenes had nurtured the mutual fantasy that they could somehow transform drug money into a legitimate fortune. Now, as he spoke to his son through the phone in the visiting room of the jail, Big Jim wondered whether the example of his political friends and their cronies hadn't thrown off Jimmy's moral compass. "It's my fault," Big Jim said. "If only you hadn't been raised around so much corruption."

2

On the Banks of the Wabash, Far Away

WHEN FIFTEEN-YEAR-OLD JESSICA ROACH disappeared one afternoon in September of 1993, the only evidence left behind was her cherished mountain bike—tossed on its side in the middle of a gravel road. If not for the height of the corn, her family's trailer home would have been visible just fifty yards away.

She was a beautiful young woman, with a short, athletic build, big doe eyes, and long brown hair. As she had set out on her bike, she told her older sister that she was going to help prepare a float for the high school homecoming parade. Her sister drove past her when she took the family car to pick up groceries. Since the family lived in a sea of cornfields—miles from town or much of anything else—the bike was especially precious to Jessica. When the sister found it abandoned on her return home, she knew something was wrong.

Their father immediately called the police from nearby George-town, Illinois (population 3,628), and a search soon began—complete with dogs to pick up Jessica's scent. After a few hours, when the police still couldn't find her, they called for help from Pat Hartshorn, the county sheriff.

Vermilion County sits like a domino in the midsection of Illinois, flush on the border of Indiana—two hours south of Chicago and two hours west of Indianapolis. It is mostly rural and relatively bucolic, except for a gritty pocket around Danville, the county seat. When teenagers go missing, they usually turn out to be runaways. But Hartshorn—a detective before he was elected sheriff—could quickly see that Jessica's disappearance was an exception. When he called his chief investigator, Gary Miller, he told him, "There is something really wrong here."

Miller, then a twenty-year veteran of the sheriff's department, had snuck out of work early to watch his son play baseball, but left before the game was over and arrived at the Roach home as the sun was setting. The Georgetown patrolmen continued to comb the cornfields with their yelping dogs. Hartshorn sat inside the trailer home with the distraught Roach family: Jessica's parents, her older sister, and younger brother, all of whom were shaken and in tears. Nothing about the girl suggested any spontaneous act of youthful protest. She had no boyfriend or recent argument with parents or siblings. If anything, she couldn't wait for the homecoming parade that weekend. As Miller later learned, the parents were Jehovah's Witnesses and hewed closely to the sect's sober lifestyle, so most of Jessica's social life outside of church revolved around her school activities.

Before it was dark, Miller and Hartshorn got into a car and drove a few miles in each direction to acquaint themselves with the area. The immediate vicinity was as flat as a pool table and covered with cornfields. The Indiana border was literally up the road, but once they crossed the state line and made a quick turn, the road descended into a different world, where the even farmland tore open into some sort of Midwest Middle-earth, complete with jagged, wooded ravines and river gorges. Looking over the edge of one bluff, Miller saw a drop of one hundred feet to the whitecapped Wabash River below. "That gal didn't have to go too far to get into all kinds of trouble," he thought.

Miller, then forty-five, is a garrulous man with a barrel chest and a slight Southern twang. He easily breaks into a hoarse, deep-throated laugh. But his easygoing manner masks a steely persistence that saw him through a stint in the Marines dismantling bombs and proved just as valuable in detective work.

At first, Miller had his hands full just chasing down the leads about Jessica that flooded into the police tip lines. Meanwhile, he had to proceed on the typical path of a police investigation, moving out in tight concentric circles from the victim, starting first with her family. Jessica's father had been napping in the trailer while his oldest daughter was out with the family car. Miller says, "It's always difficult dealing with the parents at the beginning of an investigation. They feel you can never do enough. And what made this even more difficult was their beliefs as Jehovah's Witnesses, which to my understanding don't foster great trust in the arms of government. But the father was one of the last one to see her, and it's just basic police work to ask that person for a polygraph. Somehow we got through that with him and he came out okay, but I'm sure there were hard feelings."

Although Jessica had no real boyfriends, she did have typical crushes, and these unsuspecting young men had to be interviewed. Some elders of the Jehovah's Witness Assembly Hall had contact with her and were questioned as well. Miller then pushed the circle out farther, beyond those with personal acquaintance, to individuals in the vicinity with a history of rape or sexual abuse charges.

Only after exhausting all of the usual suspects did Miller consider the outermost circle: a total stranger from beyond the community randomly lighting down on Jessica—in other words, a serial killer. "That idea of someone from the outside coming in to commit a crime just goes against the grain of every local investigator," Miller explains. "You really want to believe it's in your control to figure out what happened."

Miller knew that the FBI had a database that supposedly linked missing persons and unsolved cases with serial killers, so he reached out to a local FBI agent, Ken Temples, for help. Together, from Temples's office, they called Quantico, Virginia, to speak to one of the bureau's vaunted profilers. They answered a few questions about Jessica and the circumstances surrounding her disappearance, then listened to the expert clack away at a computer until he confidently concluded, "She's a runaway."

Miller could only scoff, "This gal in no way had the desire or street smarts to take off on her own."

If there was any question about Jessica's whereabouts, it would be put to rest by an Indiana farmer. While shearing through a field of corn, six weeks after her disappearance, he saw a dark object between the uncut rows and climbed down from his combine for closer inspection. To his horror, he found a badly decomposed naked body, nearly skeletal in some places. Another piece of farm equipment had rolled over it, so the head lay a few feet from the torso.

Because the corpse was recovered in Indiana, it went to a medical examiner in Terre Haute. He quickly determined that the remains could not have been those of a fifteen-year-old. Miller was incredulous. "It had to be Jessica. The location was just too close, and the decomposition was in line with the time that she was missing." Before the report became public, Miller says, "I drove as fast as my squad car would go to get to Jessica's parents and I told them, 'He's saying it's not Jessica. I disagree. I understand that I'm disagreeing with a doctor, but I'm telling you I disagree.'"

Miller then probed to see if they had any information that could be used to identify their daughter. She had not been to a dentist, so the most reliable forensic marker—a dental chart—was missing, but years before, the parents said, when she was still in grade school, a deputy sheriff visited the class and had the students put their fingerprints on a card. That deputy had been Miller himself, and Jessica's mother still had the card. The medical examiner could only pull one print from the remaining fingertips, but when that was sent to the FBI lab in Washington, it was a positive match with a print from Jessica's card. Only then, Miller says, did the Indiana pathologist step back from his earlier conclusion and agree that the remains belonged to Jessica Roach. It was the first of many occasions when Miller questioned the competence and professionalism of legal authorities "on the other side" of the state line.

But even after the body had been identified, Miller still had little to go on. The autopsy suggested strangulation as the cause of death and that her jaw had been broken first, but there was no other physical evidence. A local resident came forward a few months later to claim that on the night of her abduction he had seen a man step out from the cornfield where her body was later found. He also remembered that a van was parked by the side of the road. But he could give no detailed description of the suspect or the van.

As months passed, no other leads surfaced. Still, Miller could not let go of the investigation—maybe because it was the first kidnap murder he had ever handled or maybe because his own son was Jessica's age. "Every day when I woke up in the morning," he remembers, "the first thing that occurred to me was the Jessica Roach case."

In his greatest act of desperation, Miller even brought in the *America's Most Wanted* TV show, the Hail Mary pass that police make only when they feel all other options have been foreclosed. It was another painful ordeal for the publicity-shy Roach family, but at least they now had full faith in the county investigator's intentions to turn over every possible stone.

When the big break in the investigation finally came—nearly a year after Jessica's abduction—it did not come from a TV show or FBI database, but good old-fashioned police work, fueled no doubt by Miller's obsession with the case. Each week he thumbed through police reports in his county, and he came across one about a man in a van who had harassed two fourteen-year-old girls riding their bikes down a Georgetown street. After they escaped through an alley too narrow for a van, one told her father, who drove around town with the girls until they spotted the vehicle. He took down the license number and reported it to the local deputy sheriff. When Miller checked the number, he discovered that the plate had been called up three times by other local police departments—something they tend to do if they catch an out-of-state vehicle aimlessly cruising the streets or suspiciously parked on them. The van was registered to a Larry D. Hall, and to find him, Miller could have done no more than traced the Wabash River, which raged near Jessica's home, coursed north along the state line, and then veered east through the heart of Indiana to the city of Wabash, three hours away.

On a hunch, with only the license-plate information, Miller called the Wabash police department to ask about the van's owner. He was ultimately connected to Detective Sergeant Jeff Whitmer, who not only knew Larry Hall, but readily admitted that he grew up with him. Miller filled him in and asked, "Can you think of any reason he would be in this area?" Whitmer replied, "Do you have Civil War reenactments over there? He travels all over going to those."

Miller didn't have a clue. He next called the county parks department and was told that they did not host Civil War reenactments, but just as he was about to hang up, Miller remembers, "The guy said, 'You know we did have a Revolutionary War reenactment.'" It was held a year before at the Forest Glen park just outside Georgetown—and on the weekend preceding the Monday when Jessica disappeared.

Moments later, Miller was back on the phone with Jeff Whitmer in Wabash, who told him something else about Hall. Although Whitmer considered him a "harmless weirdo," Hall had been a suspect in another missing-person case, that of Tricia Reitler, a nineteen-year-old girl who had apparently been abducted six months earlier from her college campus in Marion, just down the state highway from Wabash. Miller was familiar with the case because it had made the national news, and because a few missing-person flyers had crossed his desk with Reitler's photo.

But Whitmer was quick to minimize Hall's involvement with Reitler. "They might have looked at him," he told Miller, "but they're tied into another suspect. I think they know who did theirs."

Still, whatever Hall's role in the Reitler case may have been, Miller says, "A lot of things were coming together. With that reenactment, I had a reason to place Hall close to where Jessica Roach was abducted, and for some reason he's back in Georgetown a year later. That created enough interest for me to interview him."

When Miller asked if Hall would submit to an informal interview, Whitmer assured him that he would. The department's other detective had known the Hall family and had a good relationship with Larry. "He'll get him to come in and talk to you."

The Miami, the native tribe that once dominated their namesake state of Indiana, called the river Wah-Bah Shik-Ki—"pure white" or "bright"—to describe the sun reflecting off its limestone banks. For French trappers, the first European interlopers in the territory, it was known as Oubache, and that became Wabash for the English speakers. It is the longest river east of the Mississippi and so closely identified with Indiana that the state's official song remains "On the Banks of the Wabash, Far Away"—a maudlin hit tune from a hundred years ago.

Despite the sentimental attachment, the Wabash has brought as much grief as gain to its mother state. Unlike the Mississippi, it never had the predictable currents or, in some stretches, the depth that commercial shipping required during the westward expansion of the mid-nineteenth century. Politicians decided instead to build a canal alongside it that would ultimately link up with the Erie Canal to the north and the Mississippi to the south. It was to be Indiana's internal

Suez Canal, but it became one of the greatest public works boon-doggles in American history, literally bankrupting the state and then, for good measure, driven into early obsolescence by the transcontinental railroad system. Ever since, Indiana, compared with other states, has tended to frown on statewide initiatives or regional authorities. Nothing exemplifies that spirit of disunity more than the state's strange time-zone map, where counties in the northwestern and southwestern corners observe central time ("Chicago time," as the locals say) and more than twenty counties between them observe eastern time.

As Gary Miller drove the three hours from his office to Wabash, a crazy-quilt pattern of industrial development and agriculture flashed by his car window. Flat, geometric farms were interspersed with untended woodland and sudden outcroppings of smokestacks and manufacturing complexes. For Miller, Indiana police departments were as patchwork as the countryside. "A detective one week is a patrolman the next," he says. "Nobody seems to get the time or training on the job to become a professional investigator."

Wabash was not unlike Danville, the tired factory town that served as Vermilion's county seat. Driving through Wabash, Miller passed streets packed tight with working-class bungalows that gave way to blocks with massive factories—many now shuttered with desolate, empty parking lots. The downtown sprawled up a little hill from the Wabash River. At the top was the beaux arts, brick-and-limestone county courthouse, easily the most prominent structure in city. The other buildings, mostly drab brick, rose no higher than a few stories.

Police headquarters were in a squat, dilapidated station house that would soon be vacated for more modern facilities. Sergeant Whitmer greeted Miller in the lobby, then introduced him to his partner, Phil Amones—the Hall family friend—who hovered protectively over Larry. At first, Miller didn't know what to make of the stocky, little man, with his greasy hair and funny sideburns. Hall spoke in a meek, almost robotic voice, and Miller says, "The guy never wanted to look you in the eye."

Miller expected to be ushered into an interrogation room for the interview, but instead Whitmer led them out of the police station and across the street to a conference room in City Hall, where they were joined by two more policemen—detectives from the Marion police department.

Miller was incredulous. He had wanted an intimate, little Q-and-A with Hall—usually the best way to elicit an admission that might later blossom into a confession. But now he had an audience of other detectives, and from the tense looks on their faces, they seemed as nervous as the suspect about what he would ask. As they all sat around the oversize conference table, Miller placed himself next to Hall at the head of the table.

Miller's conduct during that first session with Hall would be much debated over the next few years, but in his mind he did nothing intimidating. "Any investigator worth his salt would have immediately picked up how timid Larry was," he says. "He was not going to open up to me if I was aggressive."

Miller asked first about the most recent stalking incident and says Hall calmly read the police report. While he admitted to driving the van that day, he added in his quiet, little voice, "I've never been in Georgetown, Illinois."

Miller asked if he had ever traveled out of Indiana in his van, and Hall replied that he did drive to Civil War reenactments, although he couldn't name all the places he had been. Miller pulled a road atlas from his briefcase and slid the map of Illinois in front of Hall, who stayed hunched down in his chair, his hands limp in his lap.

Miller put his finger on Georgetown. "Were you anywhere near here?"

Hall glanced briefly at the map and agreed that he could have been in the area looking for an old Dodge Charger. Now Miller pressed him for more details on where he did go; if he couldn't remember names, Miller suggested, he could identify landmarks. Hall then recalled a small town with a traffic light and a Hardee's hamburger stand and remembered stopping a few times to talk to girls, "just because I like to talk to people." He said he would ask their names and ages and whether they wanted a ride in his van.

"But did you chase anyone?" Miller asked.

"No, sir, I did not," Hall replied. "And if I did, it would just be in fun."

Suddenly, one of the Marion detectives broke in. At first Miller was annoyed at the interruption because he felt that he was on a roll, but he was stunned when he heard the question.

"Larry," the detective said, "why don't you tell him about your dreams."

After an eerie silence, Hall, his eyes still downcast, told Miller, "Sometimes I dream about killing women. But I think it's just a dream."

"Tell him where you are in those dreams."

"I kind of leave my body and look down on myself."

"Can you remember what you're doing?" Miller asked.

"I can't tell you exactly. I only remember that it's something bad."

Miller reached into his briefcase again, but this time pulled out a glossy photograph and laid it in front of Hall. It was a picture of Jessica Roach—with her radiant smile, doelike eyes, and long brown hair. As Miller later wrote in his notes, Hall "flinched" and looked away, holding up a hand as though to shield his eyes from a blinding light.

3.

Lost in the System

PRISON MAY HAVE BEEN THE LAST PLACE where Big Jim wanted to see his son, but at least he passed on to Jimmy both his charm and physical aggressiveness—two somewhat countervailing assets—that helped Keene survive and sometimes thrive behind bars. Beating other convicts in fights was essential, but having the personal skills to avoid them would prove even more important.

Still, in the first few weeks of his incarceration, Jimmy wanted no part of diplomacy. Instead, his fearlessness mixed with his seething anger to make a combustible brew. It was shaken even further by the claustrophobic conditions of Chicago's federal lockup, the Metropolitan Correctional Center, an architecturally distinctive skyscraper from the outside with sharp angles and narrow slotted windows, but a relentlessly dehumanizing birdcage on the inside with towering tiers of tightly packed two-man cells and dayrooms. It held both antsy convicts—stuck in a holding pattern until permanent placement could be found in federal facilities—and local flight risks waiting to be tried. Volatile gangbangers bumped up against much more passive illegal immigrants and white-collar criminals.

Few areas in the MCC incubated more tension than the tiny phone room, where prisoners stood in line waiting their turn to talk on the phones mounted to the wall. Jimmy's daily chats with friends and family became his island of sanity in the sea of MCC chaos, and he clung tenaciously to conversations with any friend or relative who took his collect call. But one day as he was on the phone talking, three Mexican gangbangers clustered close around him. He remembers, "They were right next to me and speaking real loud to make me get off the line. Finally I had enough of it. I said to the guy closest to me, 'You want the phone? You want the phone?' and I took the receiver and busted him over the head with it." Keene then punched out the other two Mexicans before the guards pulled him off and took him away.

Ordinarily he would have been charged him with an infraction. "But they were lenient," Keene says, "because they could see I was a new fish. Everyone is a little high-strung and pissed off when they get to the MCC. If you're a white guy and levelheaded, they will reason with you, but they told me, 'If this shit happens again, you're in big trouble.'"

But it almost happened again, this time in the bathroom near his cell. He had just brushed his teeth and spit into the sink. A black prisoner in his late fifties, who was called with strange formality Mr. Green by the younger gangbangers, waited in line behind him. He told Jimmy to rinse out the sink before he finished. In a fury, Keene shouted back at him, "Don't you tell me what to do," and immediately Keene was surrounded by what seemed to be dozens of black gangbangers. Mr. Green, he says, "could see I was ready to fight, but he held up his hand and waded through the crowd to calm me down." His full name, as Jimmy later learned, was Charles Green, and he had been a founder of El Rukns, a black street gang from the South Side of Chicago with tentacles into many other U.S. cities.

When Green got Keene to sit down on the bunk in his cell, he asked, "What they got you in here for, boy?"

"Some bullshit conspiracy," Jimmy replied.

"Well, I got sentenced to four life sentences, so I think I know what you're going through."

Green then gave Jimmy his first tutorial on prison survival skills. Being a hothead, he explained, would not get Keene any more respect from other inmates. It would only get him killed or, at the least, singled out by the guards. Instead, if he showed respect to the right people, he would get it in return.

Keene listened to the advice and started off by showing "Mr. Green respect." Jimmy was soon invited to Green's cell to share in the contraband food that the gang had smuggled into the MCC. Once, as they ate, Green laughed and said, "We belong together. You're Keene and I'm Green."

One of Green's codefendants in his racketeering trial was then fifty-five-year-old Noah Robinson Jr., the younger half brother of the Reverend Jesse Jackson. After a few weeks, MCC authorities made him Keene's cellmate. A lighter-skinned version of his brother, Robinson had been an MBA graduate of the Wharton School of Business and a successful operator of Wendy's franchises, but he saw control of the South Side drug world as a bigger opportunity than fast food and enlisted El Rukns to be his muscle. Along the way, according to the government's charges, he also had them try to kill a former business partner, so he, too, was sentenced to life. The disgrace Keene felt for himself and his family couldn't compare to Robinson's fall and the publicity it received in the national press. "He was very clean-cut and very sophisticated," Keene says. "You would not expect him to be a hard-core killer. To hear him talk, you would have thought he was mayor of the South Side of Chicago." He claimed to have personally bankrolled Jesse Jackson's presidential campaigns in 1984 and 1988. This came as no surprise to Keene. He knew many public figures had a darker side, from the shady backroom deals that went down for Big Jim's friends in Kankakee, but also from the tales he heard from his grandmother about the influence that mobsters had had over Illinois politics.

Jimmy's other roommate at the MCC was Malcolm Shade, another African-American from a middle-class background. A roly-poly computer whiz with thick glasses, he had been convicted of multiple counts of identity theft. Still, Keene says, "He was ready to do it again as soon as they released him. He always tried to teach me how to do it, too. That's the one thing about prison: you can get the best education in the world at being a criminal."

Still, after three months, Jimmy couldn't wait to get out of the sweaty MCC and was grateful that he received placement at the Federal Correctional Institution in Milan, Michigan, forty-five miles south of Detroit and a four-hour drive from Kankakee. The prison's low-rise buildings sprawl over several acres in a setting not much different from a college campus—absent the razor wire and wall. Inmates walk outdoors from their cellblock to the cafeteria. There's also an elaborate gym building complete with basketball court, boxing ring, and a well-equipped weight room. For Keene, it was all a welcome contrast to his cooped-up, high-tension high-rise back in Chicago.

If his previous jail experience had been like a kindergarten education in working the system, Jimmy leaped to graduate school with Milan, quickly developing a life that could be as comfortable as possible within the confines of a federal correctional facility. An important contributor to his comfort level was his ability to avoid the drudgery of daily work in the prison factory. Because of his various allergies, he had received a letter from medical doctors that exempted him from exposure to the fumes and other substances of a manufacturing environment. He was instead assigned to a cushy chair in the law library, where he worked alongside Frank Cihak, who had another twenty years to serve for embezzling tens of millions from a Houston bank. Cihak's large frame had become stooped and aged beyond his fifty-five years, and he had a fringe of white hair on the top of his head. With misty eyes, he remembered the days when he flew on private jets to fancy restaurants and fine resorts. Cihak used his library job and considerable intelligence to become an accomplished jailhouse lawyer. "He was one hundred percent convinced he was going to beat his case, and he was constantly filing appeals," Jimmy remembers. "Guys just flocked to him for advice."

Jimmy started his own library of sorts by getting friends and relatives to send him pornographic magazines. In exchange for a "date" with a title in his collection, he won all sorts of favors throughout the system. Probably most valuable to Keene were the fresh fruit and vegetables that the kitchen staff would help sneak into his cell—the gloppy prison food was one of his biggest beefs with institutional living. One connection took a special liking to a magazine and, in return for a weekend date, gave him a whole turkey. "Me and my buddies had it with rice and a side of vegetables," Keene remembers. "Everything was mixed up in a way that would make no rhyme or reason in the regular world, but it was an absolute feast in prison."

For his own sexual release, Keene had regular visits from his girlfriend, Tina, who would stay at a nearby hotel for a few days twice a month. Like the other women he was attracted to, she had a dark complexion and lithe body. He says, "There were times in the visiting room that she managed to slip her hand under my drawers when the guards weren't looking. One day I said to her, 'I just can't wait to get out of here and look between those legs again.' And she said, 'Well, I'll be right back. I have to go to the bathroom.' When she came back, she hiked up her skirt and spread her legs, so I could see that she had cut a big section out of her panties. She let me look down there for the rest of the afternoon."

After a few weeks, Keene settled into a fairly tolerable routine. He had to be up at five thirty with the other prisoners, but every morning, without fail, he would first call Big Jim. "We'd talk for a half hour or so," Jimmy remembers. "Always he tried to be upbeat, telling me, 'Don't worry, Son. We're still working for you out here. Your lawyer's making a lot of progress.' Finally, I had to cut him off before they closed the chow hall." Jimmy had a kitchen friend slip him eight fresh pancakes for breakfast—usually his best meal of the day. Around his job at the law library, he could hit the gym at least twice a day, lifting weights and occasionally working out on the speed bag by the prison's elaborate boxing ring. For a while, Jimmy even had a cell to himself, perched on the top tier of the residential building, but he soon learned the danger of that luxury.

One day, three black gangbangers stopped by the library while Keene was alone on duty. "These were big, giant weight-lifting guys with their hair in long braids and tattoos all over them," Keene says, "and they were all arguing with each other already." The three, who were always together, used letters of the alphabet as their names: B, C, and L. B had a stutter and took a while to ask his question—about the difference in weight between muscle and fat. Jimmy thought they were joking and first replied with a chuckle. But it was no joke, and looking back, Keene realizes that B thought Jimmy was laughing at his stutter. When Jimmy did answer the question, he appeared to side with C and L. Now these two started laughing at B. One of them said, "You don't know shit, man." Before he left, B gave Keene a hard stare, but he thought nothing of it.

A little later, after lunch, Jimmy returned to his empty cell. Having turned up his nose at the cafeteria's Polish sausage, he decided to dine instead on a can of tuna he'd bought from the commissary. As he bent over his desk to crank a homemade opener, he felt a little gust of air as his door flew open. A fist followed, punching him squarely in the side of the head. Reflexively, Keene, with both hands, grabbed his assailant's wrist and flipped him into the cell. It was B. Still wearing his heavy winter boots, Keene launched a karate kick that struck B in the face, then grabbed the pigtail braids on either side of his head and flung him into the corner of the bottom bunk bed. As he started to punch B, L burst into the room and jumped on Jimmy's back. Keene reached back to grab his braids and flipped him into the bunk with B. "Because of my wrestling experience," Keene says, "I could use my legs to lock them both down on the bed and pound their faces as fast and hard as I could until they were just a bloody mess."

Out of the corner of his eye, he could see C in the doorway. He had probably been the lookout for the other two. When Keene sprang from the bunk, C ran away, but Jimmy was not finished with the alphabet. "I was so pissed at B," he says, "I grabbed him by his pigtails and dragged him out of my cell and started stomping his head on the third-floor tier where everyone could see us." Keene didn't stop until someone pulled an alarm that went off throughout the whole prison. L had stumbled off on his own, so Keene closed the door to his cell and followed the rest of the prisoners to wait outside in the cold and snow. When the alarms stopped ringing, he stamped around a little longer before he went back inside, but by the time he had reached his cell, the guards were waiting for him. They put him in handcuffs and marched him down to the Special Housing Unit, where they had the solitary-confinement cells. Once they had him in the interrogation room, the guards took off his handcuffs, and they were all joined by the lieutenant who supervised the cellblock. He assured Jimmy that they were on his side. B, C, and L had assaulted others. It was three against one, so clearly *they* attacked *him* in his cell, but Keene was not about to cooperate. "I don't know what you're talking about," he said. "Nothing happened."

The lieutenant told him to hold up his hands, palms turned inward. His hands were chafed different shades of red, and his own blood still ran from his knuckles. "Okay," the lieutenant said, "then tell me how you got those fresh cuts all over your hands?" Keene replied that he must have pinched his knuckles when he put the dumbbells back in the weight-room rack.

Even after the lieutenant threatened to throw him in the hole,

Jimmy would still not talk. "So, you want to be a stand-up guy, you want to take this all on your own?" the lieutenant asked. "Well, guess what? You're not going to get any special protection. See how you like that."

When he got back to his cell, a young guard he called Surf popped in to see him. He enjoyed chatting with Keene, especially during those idle hours when other prisoners were at work in the factory. Surf said, "I heard about your problem, but don't worry. I got your back. I'm going to make sure nobody comes around your cell who don't belong here."

But Keene couldn't stay in his cell all day. He certainly didn't want to stop going to the gym. Before long, word went out that a hit had been put on Keene by the D.C. Blacks, a street gang from Washington, D.C., with members in prisons across America. He could tell as soon as he entered the weight room, which was practically a clubhouse for all the black gangs. "Everyone in there gave me the hard-guy stare." At one point, when he went to pick up a barbell plate, one of the bigger weight lifters in the room screamed, "Don't get in my way, white motherfucker." Keene went nose to nose with him. "Yeah?" he yelled. "What are you going to do about it?" The weight lifter screamed back, "I want you to just hit me. That's all I want you to do. Just hit me once, so I can tear you up."

Keene replied, "You ain't tearing nobody up, punk." The two stood staring at each other, but by this time their shouting had drawn a few guards. Finally, the weight lifter backed away and Jimmy backed off, too.

The whole experience with the alphabet crew was a wake-up call for Keene. No matter how soft Milan seemed, he always had to stay on guard. Keene explains, "Most prison fights are over stupid shit and that's totally unexpected." A few weeks later, for reasons that were never explained, B, C, and L were thrown into solitary and then shipped to different prisons around the country. Keene still had to watch his back around black gangbangers, but he had also become friendly with the leader of the prison's Black Muslims, which may have afforded him some added protection.

Since being alone no longer seemed like such a privilege, Keene welcomed the arrival of a cellmate even though he was old enough to be his father. At sixty, Frank Calabrese Sr. had the stocky build and bulldog look of a graying Tony Soprano, but unlike James Gandolfini, he was the real thing, considered by federal prosecutors to be among the most vicious killers in the homicidal history of Chicago's Mafia, known as the Outfit. Keene saw a very different side to Calabrese and says, "He was very mellow. An easygoing guy, kind of jolly and fun." Calabrese loved that Jimmy had an Italian grandmother and practically treated him like a nephew, dispensing advice and offering to buy him food in the commissary. At night, they would sit around their hot plate with the commissary snacks and vegetables that Jimmy had rustled from his friends in the kitchen. "I taught him a few recipes I learned to cook in prison, and he showed me a few, too," Keene remembers. "We made some goofy concoctions, just talking and hanging out."

Calabrese did not brag about the murders he had committed, but he didn't deny them either. "He'd say, 'So we had to whack the guy.' But in his mind it was justified for the sake of the organization because they caught the guy stealing money from them. It was the price you paid for being in the mob." Usually, Calabrese didn't divulge any of the details of the hits, except in the case of Tony Spilotro, the Outfit's out-of-control enforcer in Las Vegas. He was played with foaming-at-the-mouth fury by Joe Pesci in Martin Scorsese's *Casino,* but the movie's portrayal of Spilotro's execution—along with that of his brother—was wrong, Calabrese told Keene. "Everybody thinks they were killed out in that cornfield. But they were really killed in a basement in Bensenville and then *buried* in a cornfield." They were not buried well and were found by a farmer a few days later. Calabrese's younger brother confessed that he killed the mobster who botched the burial.

A few months after Calabrese became Jimmy's cellmate, his son, Frank Jr., also arrived in Milan. He, too, started hanging out with Keene in the prison yard and the dining hall. A younger, bigger version of his father, with a little more hair on his bald pate, Junior did not seem to be as tough as the other mob guys. From Frank Jr.'s perspective, Keene was not like the other prisoners, either. "You're more like the guys I hung around in college," he told Jimmy. "Guys who were always going to parties and chasing girls."

As Keene and Frank Jr. began spending more time together, Frank Sr. suggested that his son become Keene's cellmate instead. But it was Jimmy—not the big-time mobsters—who had to make the new arrangements happen. "There's a myth about the clout that mobsters have inside federal prison," Keene says. "Even though there were a lot of Chicago mobsters in Milan, none of them got shit." Jimmy went to Surf, the guard he had befriended, and he switched Frank Jr. for Frank Sr. in Keene's cell.

In time, Jimmy got to know the mild-mannered son as well as he did his tough-talking father and felt as close as a member of the family to them. They even offered him a job in one of their restaurants when he got out. Despite the contrasts between father and son, Keene never saw any friction between the two men. "They were perfectly good friends," he remembers. "We all hung around in the same group out on the prison yard. We'd walk the track together for hours and hours."

Much of the time, Keene says, the Calabreses discussed how they could get Frank Jr. out of prison. "They knew that the old man was going down for a long, long time, and nothing was more important for the father than seeing that his son didn't do that time with him. The plan was for Junior to roll on his dad."

A decade later, in a Chicago courtroom, Frank Jr. did indeed testify against Senior in a celebrated federal case known as Family Secrets. Among other charges, Calabrese was accused of participating in eighteen contract killings—most notably Spilotro. Frank Jr. and other witnesses, including Frank Sr.'s younger brother, testified that the father often beat his son as he was growing up and forced him into crime. For some of the media covering the trial, Junior's testimony was an oedipal act of betrayal, and they reported that Senior responded to it with contempt and red-faced fury. But as far as Keene is concerned, it was all an act. "He absolutely loves Junior, and he was doing what any good father would do for his son. My father would have done the same for me."

For the time that Jimmy was in Milan, *his* father somehow managed to remain a constant presence in Jimmy's life. Big Jim would visit two or three times a month, usually making the four-hour trip himself, but sometimes bringing Jimmy's brother or sister for company. "Once he came up and didn't arrange for the visit the way you're supposed to," Keene remembers, "so he went right to the warden and told him how he used to be a cop, and the next thing you know, they had me see him that day in a private conference room—something that almost never happens."

While Keene's mother might speak to him once a week, he usually talked to Big Jim three times a day. "Sometimes other inmates would be waiting for the phone and they would get mad at how much time I was taking. I would tell them I was talking to my attorney, so they'd cut me a little slack." But the phone company didn't cut any slack for his father. Big Jim's toll for all the collect calls could be as high as $1,000 a month. "We better get you out of there soon," he'd say to Keene, "because these phone bills are killing us."

Despite Big Jim's obsession with getting his son out of prison, surprisingly he did not think Jimmy should accept Beaumont's deal. After ten months at Milan, when Keene was summoned back to the Ford County Jail, he was not supposed to tell anyone about the secret mission. However, it proved impossible for him to keep his father in the dark. He swore him to secrecy and broke the news. Instead of being overjoyed, Big Jim was terrified. "Once you go down there," he said, "they'll own you. They could shoot you up with a drug and then say you tried to kill a guard. They write it down in your file and the next thing you know, they tack ten more years onto your sentence. It happens all the time. Guys go in those places for a few years and they never come out. They get lost in the system."

As always, Big Jim's concerns struck home with Jimmy and were compounded by a delay in the processing of his transfer to Springfield. The problem, Beaumont explained, was that no federal prisoner had ever requested a transfer from a lower-security facility to the highest-security prisons known as U.S. Penitentiaries. "You tell a prison inmate that he's going to a penitentiary," Keene says, "and you might as well tell him he's going to a hellhole."

Although some of the prisoners Keene met at Milan had long sentences, few had a life sentence.* But a penitentiary was full of lifers who had little to lose. Although Keene had been jumped in Milan, it was probably more likely to happen in Springfield, and the legal consequences for winning a fight might be worse than the physical consequences for losing it.

As Keene's doubts grew, the alternative of returning to Milan did not seem so bad, especially compared to the wretched conditions he was then experiencing in his temporary jail cell. "Ford County," Keene says, "was like solitary confinement for six people." Each pod, as they called it, had three tiny cells with two metal bed slabs hanging from the wall and an exposed toilet. "If the other guy took a shit while you were sleeping," Keene says, "you literally woke up gagging with the smell." The cells shared a dayroom less than twenty feet long with an exposed shower to one side. Making matters worse, his

---

*After the Family Secrets trial, Frank Calabrese did get sentenced to life.

roommates tended to be illegal immigrants, most of whom were Mexicans and, in one case, a Cuban. Camaraderie was nonexistent. Their rudimentary English and Jimmy's rudimentary Spanish did not make for long conversations and, in the case of the Cuban, led to incomprehensible games of Scrabble. "He'd put the most screwed-up words on the board, and I'd go, 'Carlos, that is not a word, man,' and he'd go, 'It's a word. It's a word,' and I'd say, 'Okay, but you don't get points for it.'"

The pod left literally no place for privacy. Whenever Keene picked up the accordion folder with the material about Hall, he says, "One of the guys would be looking over my shoulder, asking, 'What do you got? What do you got?'" His only time for study came at night, when he could read the file by the light from the hall that shone into his cell. The more he studied Hall, the stranger the case seemed to him. Keene put a lot of stock in his ability to win people over, but he wondered what he would have in common with this odd janitor from Indiana. Also, the FBI agent had placed all these conditions on approaching Hall, even demanding that Keene wait six months before talking with him. Six months could be a lifetime in Springfield.

Keene finally decided to heed Big Jim's advice. He would turn down Beaumont's offer and return to Milan. But when he called his father to tell him about his decision, there was no answer. He left message after message and couldn't get through to his brother, Tim, either. Finally, a call was picked up by his stepmother, whom Big Jim had married a year before. In a halting voice, she told Jimmy that Big Jim had had a stroke, but he didn't want Jimmy to hear the news over the phone. He wanted to get out of the hospital first so that Jimmy could see he was okay.

A few days later, Tim wheeled Big Jim into the visiting room. "Even thinking about it now makes me want to break down and cry," Keene says. "The whole left side of his face drooped, especially the corner of his mouth. His eye was almost closed and the left side of his body was slumped over. Here was Superman hurt worse than I ever could imagine, and I knew it was a direct result of what I had done to him—all the worry and all the aggravation. We both just sat there for a while, looking at each other through the glass and crying. And I said, 'Dad, I am so sorry. I'm going to get out of here.'"

Then Big Jim spoke in a weak slur that was a sickening contrast to the deep, commanding voice he had once had. "Son, it's not your fault. It's my fault that you never got out of that life. I know you did it to help me. But someday, I'm going to find a way to help you get everything back."

"There he was practically dying in front of my eyes," Keene says, "and what was his last wish? To help me." Despite all of Big Jim's financial reversals, he had always seemed physically indestructible. Now Jimmy wondered if his father would still be alive by the time he got out of prison.

When Jimmy returned to his cell, he says, "All I had in my mind was that vision of my father slumped in the wheelchair. I couldn't concentrate on the serial killer stuff or anything else, but finally I realized that this wasn't just about me anymore. It was about him, too. I had to do everything in my power to get out of prison as soon as I could." The next morning, he called his lawyer, Jeff Steinback. "I was very determined, like I was on a mission. I said, 'Jeff, get this whole deal straightened out with Beaumont. Even if he doesn't promise us what you want. I'm ready to go to Springfield.'"

For Jimmy Keene, those few hours of passage from the Ford County jail to Springfield, Missouri, floated by like a dream. A team of three U.S. marshals retrieved him just as the sun was setting on a hot, humid day in August of 1998. It had taken Beaumont three months to get the necessary approval from the Bureau of Prisons and his higher-ups at the Department of Justice in Washington, D.C. Keene was led from the jail in the usual handcuffs and shackles, but once inside the van, to his amazement, the restraints were all removed and the marshals handed him a set of civilian clothes. Then, stunning him even further, they stopped at a nearby family restaurant and all went inside for a meal. While they ate, Keene remembers, "the marshals tried to school me. They kept saying, 'Remember what Beaumont and the FBI agent told you. Don't approach this guy too quickly.'"

But Jimmy was only listening with half an ear. He couldn't help but look around at the other diners, chatting or just eating their food, immersed in the humdrum of their daily unfettered lives. No one observing the four men at his table would have suspected that one was a prisoner and the others his guards. He says, "It made me feel like I was free again."

After dinner, they got back in the van and drove a few hours to an airport. They arrived just before midnight. When Keene had previously flown as a prisoner, he was chained inside a ratty old Con Air cargo plane. But this time, his ride was a sleek corporate jet with eight plush leather seats and carpeted walls. On board, the marshals served him snacks and soda. For much of the ninety-minute flight, he forgot about the danger and uncertainty that awaited him. It was almost as though his mission were already over.

They landed at a little airport where a van with two other marshals was waiting for them. It was not yet dawn, so they still had some time to kill and drove around aimlessly for a few hours, stopping for some fast food. After they ate, they drove down tree-lined country roads. As daylight started to break, Jimmy could look out the window and see verdant green farmland to each side and moisture rising from it like steam. Once again, a warm feeling welled up inside him, and as he chatted and joked with the marshals, he says, "I felt like a normal guy again."

Most of the marshals didn't look that much different from Jimmy. They were roughly his age and, like him, were fitness fanatics with big arms and tapered torsos. But when he actually tuned in to their conversation, "it started to bother me," he says. "They had all these other things going on in their lives with family and career. They didn't have to worry about going back to prison and dealing with some serial killer. In my mind we were all the same kind of guys. I could have been one of them. How did I end up on the other side?"

All the reveries and regrets about his past life were suddenly wiped away when the van turned a corner and headed up a parklike drive. In the distance, jagged blocks of redbrick buildings rose incongruously from the Missouri plain, glowing in the early-morning haze. As they drove closer, he could see guard towers and fences of razor wire, all illuminated by shafts of light, sweeping back and forth.

"This sure ain't no Milan," Keene murmured under his breath. Although built in a Depression-era institutional style with a white steeple topping off the central structure, the lighting and fences cloaked it in an ominous aura. "It was like some creepy medieval castle," he remembers, "in the middle of nowhere."

The marshals had stopped talking, and when Jimmy brought his gaze back inside the van, he realized all eyes were on him. The driver executed an abrupt U-turn. "They could see how nervous I was getting and said they had to drive around a little more for me to relax." But finally, at five o'clock, they circled back toward the entrance road. The marshal in charge solemnly announced that the time had come for Jimmy's entrance.

But as he stared again at the glowing redbrick complex, Keene had a serious case of cold feet. "Look, man," he said, "I can't do this. I can't. This whole thing's off. Let's just go back."

All of the marshals chimed in to change his mind. "They were actually pleading with me," Jimmy remembers. "They were saying, 'Please, please give it a try.'"

But Keene now focused on his worst-case scenario. "What if Beaumont backs out?" he asked. "Then I'll be stuck here."

The marshals insisted just as vociferously that Beaumont would not back out; that no matter how tough the prosecutor seemed, they could vouch that he was always good for his word. Now the marshals glanced anxiously at their watches, too. They had a narrow window for his delivery, just as the guard shifts changed—so there wouldn't be too many questions about the transfer—and just before the early morning alarm rang to wake the prisoners.

Finally, the supervising marshal took charge. He had a buzz cut and was slightly older than the others. He had also met with Jimmy a few times before the pickup to prepare him for the transfer. "We can't wait any longer," he said firmly. "We've all put a lot of time and effort into this operation; me especially. If you're going to do this for anyone, do it for me. I assure you it will be in your own best interest."

Seeing the aggravation in the marshal's face, Keene realized that the Feds—and Beaumont in particular—would not soon forgive him for a last-minute scrub. There really was no backing out. "Okay," Jimmy said. "Then let's do this."

The driver used a card to buzz them through a sliding mesh gate. As they got closer, Keene could see other five-story buildings behind the central one, all joined by walls that circled a vast prison yard. They stopped at the prisoner intake dock, but as they climbed out of the van, one of the marshals put a hand on Keene's shoulder and said, "Sorry, Jim, but we got to put you back in cuffs now." As Keene felt the metal click into place around his wrists, his little dream of freedom popped like a soap bubble. The door to the prison opened, and Keene says, "From that second, I was just another scumbag prisoner again."

He was shoved to the side while a correctional officer asked, "So what do we got?"

The marshals acted as if they didn't even remember Keene's name, he was just some guy they had to transport. They handed over his file, then joked around with the guards. Had he really been taken for such a sucker? Only as they turned to leave, when the guards had their heads turned, did one of the marshals look directly at Jimmy and sneak him a quick thumbs-up. This was to be his one shred of consolation as the guards shouted at him to remove his clothes and bend over for the strip search.

After the intake guards had issued Keene his bed kit and toiletries, they took him directly to his cell. To move between buildings, they walked downstairs to a network of submerged, humid tunnels. Jimmy was shocked at how old everything looked, from the plaster walls and pillars to the battleship-linoleum floors. The only light came from recessed ceiling fixtures that cast a dim yellow haze. At last they surfaced in "9 building," and a ward that looked more like a hospital floor than a prison, but with doors of solid, vaultlike metal.

Inside, the cell was slightly bigger than the ones at Milan, but the added space made the furnishings look even sparser—an open toilet, a metal slab bed that pulled down from the wall, and a galvanized-steel locker, desk, and bookshelf unit common to all federal prisons. Keene was just starting to set up his toiletries when a loud, reverberating buzzer sounded through the ward. Still in a daze—he hadn't slept for a day—he wandered outside his cell and was immediately caught up in a crush of convicts surging down the hall. Keene figured they were going to breakfast, but compared with the orderly procession to the mess hall at Milan, he says, "This was like mass hysteria: guys running, shouting, and shoving." They all wore green shirts, camouflage pants, and shiny black boots—like a bizarre army. Most disturbing for Keene were the ones who shuffled forward with blank expressions like zombies in what looked to be some drug-induced stupor.

He followed the crowd to a cavernous dining hall with cathedral windows, where noises—clinking plates, strange chatter, and shouts— echoed even louder. The tables were bolted to the floor in row after

row, like the pews of a church. As Keene looked around to see where
he should pick up his tray, his eyes suddenly locked on a pudgy little
con sitting in the corner. It was Larry Hall.

"I thought, 'Damn, there's the dude already,'" Keene says. "After all
the months of looking at his picture, to see him there was too much."
He had put on a few pounds and was clean-shaven—without the muttonchop sideburns from his mug shot—but he still had that faraway
gaze. Despite the chaos swirling around him, he seemed locked into his
own world.

Jimmy knew he was supposed to stay cool and detached, but even
after he sat down at the opposite end of the cafeteria, he still couldn't
take his eyes off Hall. He felt his heart pound and his clothes tighten
with sweat. His whole future was now wrapped up in this one man.
He had hardly eaten a bite before the buzzer sounded and he was back
on his feet. Now the tide of prisoners was sweeping him out of the
dining room, and Hall was directly in his path, just a few yards away.
As he stumbled closer, Keene's mind raced with the possibilities. "I
was thinking, 'Maybe I should talk to him, but what should I say?
Should I even say anything? They told me not to say anything to him.
But maybe I can talk this guy into helping me. But why is he going to
help me? He doesn't give a shit about me. He just wants to help himself. But then maybe I can beat it out of him.'"

Despite all his inner turmoil, Keene still felt himself drawn to Hall
like a magnet; closer and closer until—thump—he bumped flush into
his shoulder. Startled, Hall spun around, his eyes swimming, confused,
then fearful.

"Shit," Jimmy thought, "what have I done?"

4.

Life in the Cemetery

THINGS NEVER WENT BETTER FOR ROBERT HALL and his family than when he worked as a sexton in the Falls Cemetery on the southwest side of Wabash, Indiana. He dug graves along its winding paths and tended to hilly grounds no bigger than a pocket park. For manual labor, the job paid well—as good as factory work—and better yet gave him the right to live in the sexton's house, a big shambles of a place with white clapboard shingles. It sat on a ridge, in the corner of the cemetery, overlooking gravestones and mausoleums, but with a backyard that included a babbling brook and more green space than anyone else had in that part of Wabash. The spooky backdrop aside, it was pretty fancy digs for the son of a housepainter, and the perfect place to raise a family.

The Falls is one of the oldest independent cemeteries in Indiana, but in the twenty-five years Hall worked there, the surrounding neighborhood changed as much as at any time in its history. Just blocks away, on either side, huge factories opened, which then recruited out-of-state workers to man the shop floors. The newcomers moved into ranch houses that cropped up across empty fields and ash pits, right to the edge of the cemetery. Since many of them came from Kentucky, locals from elsewhere in Wabash disparaged the enclave as Wal-Tucky, or worse, Wal-Trash. To accommodate the mushrooming population, a secondary school complex was built in the valley down the hill behind the Falls equipment shed, and the once-quiet streets around the cemetery rang with the shouts of children.

For most of those who grew up in the neighborhood, the sexton and his wife could be strange and intimidating figures—like trolls in a fairy tale. Robert had a broad, florid face and a burly body made that much more powerful by his work. Some felt threatened by his gruff manner and the ever-present smell of beer on his breath, but he loved impressing little boys by ripping catalogs and Bell phone books in half as easily as most people tore up envelopes. His wife, who was known by her middle name, Berniece (her first name was Aera), did not go out of her way to impress anyone. Instead, she is remembered as a grossly overweight woman with a pinched face and sharp tongue, especially sharp in defense of her rambunctious twin sons, Larry and Gary.

When the boys were born on December 11, 1962, the Halls were considered, in that era, fairly old to have babies. Robert was then forty and Berniece thirty-three. She already had a sixteen-year-old from her first marriage. This birth would be difficult; the doctor told her that Larry emerged from the womb looking blue—or deprived of oxygen—and nearly died. A more recent diagnosis of his condition would be "twin-to-twin" or "fetofetal" transfusion syndrome, which is unique to identical twins. According to multiple-birth researcher Elizabeth Bryan, "The phenomenon arises when blood from one baby crosses to the other baby and the recipient doesn't give as much back." Ironically, as they mature, the identical twins that survive the syndrome look more different than fraternal twins. Because of Larry's complications, the babies and their mother stayed in the maternity ward for another week before they went home.

Their parasitic relationship in the womb—where Gary thrived at the expense of Larry—would become inverted during the rest of the twins' childhood. Gary emerged taller, slimmer, and more outgoing, while Larry was pudgy and painfully shy. Gary was always the one to make friends and initiate any activities. Larry tagged along like a soft and silent shadow.

Despite their modest means, Robert and Berniece doted on their sons. Ross Davis, who became one of the boys' best friends, remembers that he was attracted more to the toys than the twins. "They always had something," he says, "like a minibike or a go-cart or a dirt bike; things my parents couldn't afford to give me. You could always go up to their house and ride and hang out with them and have a fun time."

But the spacious yard outside the Halls' home contrasted sharply with the squalor inside. "The house was a big place, but it was a dump," Davis says. "It was like a path to walk through. Stuff was piled everywhere. Mrs. Hall was always having a rummage sale, and we used to joke that they lived inside a rummage sale. All the years I knew that family, I never once saw her do any cleaning. They would eat out every day because she was too lazy to cook. That's why they never saved a penny. She was just a big fat lady who sat around the house all day and did nothing but yell and stir up a lot of trouble."

Once, when the twins played with Davis at his home, they all got into a fight and Ross went inside. To get him to come back out, the brothers threw stones at the house until Mr. Davis chased them away. When he called to tell Berniece what her sons had done, Ross says, "She laid it all on me. She told my dad, 'That little son of a bitch Ross was up here throwing shit at our house yesterday, and they're just getting back at him.' That's the way it was with her. Her kids could do no wrong."

But according to Davis, as the boys got older, they increasingly did do wrong. They started out with fairly harmless pranks, such as leaving a wallet stuffed with money in the middle of the street and then using fishing line to jerk it back through the hedges when drivers got out of their cars to investigate. "We'd be watching and laughing behind the curtains of their windows as those people tried to find that wallet." They next directed their hoaxes at the police, dressing up dummies and placing them in the gutter as though they had just been hit by a car or passed out. "They'd wait and listen on the police scanner. When somebody called in and reported it, then they'd run back outside, grab the dummy, and throw it behind the hedges. The police would look all over the place for it and give up. But after they left, the Halls would throw the dummy back out there again and keep the cops running all night long. Those boys really did have a thing for fooling the cops."

At the age of fifteen, the Hall brothers graduated from practical jokes to property damage and were arrested for breaking downtown storefront windows. Some friends believe they were led into the mischief by another neighbor who also had relatively elderly parents and limited supervision.

Wabash detective Ron Smith and his partner were assigned to the case, and they questioned each boy individually. Usually, teenagers crumbled quickly under those conditions, but Smith says, "It took a long time before we could crack the Hall brothers. They were just kids, but they held up better than hardened criminals, even over something as petty as broken windows."

Larry was the first to crack and later explained that he confessed only to get the cops off his back and that most of the damage was really done by Ross Davis's older brother. Whatever the truth, the Halls were the ones who had to cough up $500 for the damage, which was then a hefty sum, and Larry had to earn it back by mowing the lawn for his father. Smith believes the boys were "terrified" of Robert, which is why they were reluctant to confess and face the consequences from him. "The mother," Smith says, "was another story. As far as she was concerned, it was always someone else's fault. Never her boys'."

Growing up, the twins were inseparable. As teens they bonded even further with a shared passion for hobbies that followed them into adulthood. It began with collecting old beer cans, a craze that swept blue-collar communities in the seventies. Ross Davis remembers, "If me and my brother had one hundred beer cans, we thought we was doing good, but the Halls would have a thousand. And their dad would just take them anywhere they wanted to go. He knew where all the old dumps were, and they would run around all weekend just so they would have a better collection than everybody else did."

While searching the woods and fields around Wabash, the twins began to keep an eye out for Indian arrowheads, too, and this would come to mean more to them than beer cans. Their father always spoke about having Miami Indian blood, and although he could not point to any specific ancestor, the twins themselves had the jet-black hair and eyes that many in the area identified as Native American. The Halls were not alone in claiming Indian heritage: for many in central Indiana, romance and royalty are both associated with Miami blood—probably because so few certifiable members of the tribe remain.

Besides the name of Wabash itself, the area where the Halls grew up was studded with landmarks associated with the Miami Indians and the various skirmishes that ultimately decimated them—no place more so than the Mississinewa 1812 battlefield, just ten miles south of their home.

The Miami only reluctantly and belatedly followed the other tribes of the Northwest Territory in allying with the British in the War of 1812. But the Miami were the best fighters of the bunch, routing the Americans from several forts. Once the states regained the upper hand, the U.S. military returned to the area with a vengeance. They tried to massacre the Miami as they slept in their villages along the Mississinewa River and killed dozens, but were bloodied and rebuffed by the fierce warriors yet again. Each year, reenactments of there skirmishes are conducted in a designated battlefield area, just north of Marion, that locals refer to as "1812."

The government ultimately prevailed over the Miami, first taking their land and then, in the 1840s, physically removing them first to Kansas and then to Oklahoma—all despite the tribe's best efforts to assimilate. It is both poignant and telling that one of the best known Miami is Frances Slocum, a white woman kidnapped by Indians as a child. She chose to remain with the Indians even after her blood relatives had tracked her down. Remnants of the Miami who stayed in Indiana or straggled back at the end of the nineteenth century were given property as individuals, but no reservation or recognition as a tribe. In the 1960s, as if to further obliterate their memory, the Army Corps of Engineers dammed the Mississinewa River for flood control, creating an expansive lake and reservoir system that swallowed up the ancient Miami village sites.

The twins avidly read stories about Slocum and the Miami's greatest warrior chief, Little Turtle. Imagining themselves to be Indian braves, they hiked and fished the reservoir area, always keeping an eye out for arrowheads. Often their searches covered the untilled fringes of nearby farm fields, although they were careful to ask the farmers' permission before they picked across their property.

Little of the twins' curiosity about their Native American roots translated over to schoolwork. They were C and D students at best. When they hit high school, one teacher remembers, their indifferent study habits were coupled with an "ornery" attitude. They wore their hair down to the shoulders and hung out with serious troublemakers from the neighborhood, impatiently biding their time until graduation. There is no record that they participated in extracurricular activities or even submitted photos for the junior and senior yearbooks.

"We used to say our high school was divided between jocks and grits," Ross Davis says. "The Halls and people like me were the grits." Grits worried more about cruising in the right car than going to college. The focus of the twins' social life became their "street rods" (souped-up production cars as opposed to customized "hot rods"). From the time he was a little boy, Larry had an interest in cars, and he would watch as Robert and his equally gruff neighbor, a dwarf named Bobby Allen, worked under the hoods of their old vehicles. Allen has only fond memories of Larry—maybe because his own son was so unruly. "That was a good kid," he says. "Never obnoxious, never drank or swore. I will never say a bad word against him." As a foreman at the factory, Allen was well-off compared with Robert Hall. He had the money to spend on used cars and took Larry under his wing to show him how to fix them.

The experience with Allen encouraged Larry to devote his senior year to taking vocational courses in auto repair. Although the classes never led to a lasting job, they did give him the ability to bring some decrepit junkers back to life. While other teens may have been attracted to hot cars like Gary's flashy 1957 Chevy Bel Air, Larry developed a lifelong affection for the more plebeian Chryslers and their Mopar parts. His car was a 1967 Dodge Dart.

But for all of Larry's expertise in auto mechanics, he and Gary were still at a disadvantage compared with their friends. "They were just poor boys," says Ron Osborne, who was part of the Wabash street-rod scene. "They could only fix their cars up a little at a time with whatever money was available to them." At times, he suspects, they couldn't even afford the gas to run them.

Not that there were all that many places for them to go in Wabash during the early eighties—the most popular stretch for cruising was just a couple of blocks long, and it ran only from a fast-food stand to an auto-parts store and back again. This was the scene for showing off your macho swagger and, if you were so fortunate, your girl—two aspects of the street-rod culture that Larry was not ready to deal with. His twin was another story.

"Gary had a mouth on him," Ross Davis says. "That was Gary's problem. He didn't care who it was that he'd run his mouth to, and it got him beat up a couple of different times."

Silent, awkward Larry was more the target of loudmouths and, at five feet four inches, was far from a threatening presence. But Davis remembers one night when Larry decided not to take any more taunting from one of the toughest boys in school. "Larry and this guy slugged it out; they slugged it out pretty good, actually. You didn't want to push Larry into a corner because he would fight, and he wasn't really bad at it for a little short guy."

If Larry had an edge over Gary as a fighter, there was absolutely no competition between the two when it came to girls. Throughout his teens, Larry had serious acne, which compounded the insecurity and shyness he already felt. None of his friends remember him having a girlfriend—ever. But with his long hair and more chiseled features, Gary had several, especially after they graduated high school in 1981.

While Gary's dates might have been an expected part of teen life in most families, they were loathsome interlopers for Larry. The twins could not share this experience like their hobbies. Instead, the girls took Gary out of the house and away from Larry for extended periods.

It would get even worse in 1984, when Robert was abruptly fired from Falls. The cemetery association's board had always been uneasy about his heavy drinking, but when they discovered that he'd been putting bodies in the wrong gravesites, they had to let him go, which meant he had to vacate the sexton's house as well. At sixty-two, Robert was not about to find comparable employment, so his family took up residence in a dilapidated wood-frame shack with just one bedroom. Larry's bed was crammed into the tiny living room in the front of the house.

No matter how shabby the old place was, their new home—at the end of a bleak side street—was a stark comedown for the Halls. Gary further disrupted the tight-knit clan when he refused to make the move and chose to shack up with his girlfriend instead. She was Gary's height, with shoulder-length, brown hair and a pear-shaped figure that only got plumper after she became pregnant with a daughter in 1985, the only child they had together. They eventually married in 1987. Although she was five years younger, she tended to call the shots for the couple—much as Berniece did with Robert.

Despite the upheavals in the twins' relationship, they did manage one last bonding adventure before married life took a firm hold on Gary: a car trip out to the West Coast along with another male friend. To save money, they pitched tents on campgrounds instead of stopping at motels. The three also once picked up a woman. Years later, Gary confessed to a police detective that they took advantage of her in some fashion. It may have been his way of initiating Larry into sex. Whatever they did, Gary would feel increasingly guilty about the incident as he got older, especially about the impact it may have had on his twin.

Back home, the Hall brothers left rebelliousness behind with their teens and attempted to become industrious, law-abiding citizens. Gary bounced among several different jobs, including factory work and a stint as a bag boy. He was also employed by a janitorial service, which then hired the other twin. Although Gary soon left that job, Larry found a lasting career there and saw the company's owner, Robert Heath, as both a mentor and friend.

Larry worked the night shift, sweeping and cleaning businesses that ranged from banks and variety stores to factories. If necessary, he dragged the plastic bags of trash back to his two-tone '84 Dodge van for later disposal. When Heath suddenly died, his major account, the Farm Bureau Credit Union, rushed to make Hall an employee. He was so trusted that he had no supervisor and no requirement to punch in or out. If he had to report to anyone, it was directly to the general manager.

Despite the confidence he inspired in his employer, his few friends thought he could not have led a bleaker existence. His days were spent in suffocating, squalid close quarters with aged, cranky parents, and his nights were devoted to menial labor in the eerie solitude of empty offices. Although his pay significantly improved with the credit union, his work became even more tedious and confined to three squat brick branch buildings where he was unlikely to see a soul. He may have been shy, but he also hated to be by himself.

No wonder then, friends thought, that he poured himself so completely into his hobbies. He pursued his passion for vintage "Mopar" Chryslers and drove the countryside looking for deals. "Larry could find old cars and old car parts like nobody I ever knew," says Ross Davis. "I used to have a body shop in Wabash, and when I would think that all my sources were dried up, Larry would come and tell me, 'I was going down this old country road, and the car you're looking for is sitting back there behind a barn.' He just burnt the roads up looking for that stuff."

By the late eighties, another diversion became even more important to Larry—Civil War reenactment. A 1986 TV program first drew him to it, then, in 1988, he got up the nerve to join a local group that portrayed the Nineteenth Indiana Volunteer Infantry Regiment, the Union Army's "Iron Brigade." Known for their distinctive high "Hardee" hats with the folded brims and bugle emblems, the Nineteenth were a valiant if luckless crew who probably lost more men per capita than any other blue company in the war.

Most of the Iron Brigade reenactments were "fought" in county parks around the Midwest. They would set up camp on Friday, often sleeping in tents on the grounds, then spend the rest of the weekend in uniform, conducting drills and mock battles for the local residents and schoolchildren who stopped by to observe. For Larry, the events were a welcome break from his solitary lifestyle, offering both camaraderie and a ready-made antidote for his limited social skills. Since reenactors were supposed to behave like Civil War soldiers, they could create elaborate alter egos with jobs and families appropriate to an infantryman from Indiana in the 1860s. To hold up his end of the conversation, Larry bought used books on regional Civil War history and studied harder than he ever did in school.

Reenactment would be the one shared interest of the Hall twins in which Larry boldly led the way. Initially, Gary balked at the expense of the vintage regalia, but once he saw Larry's rifle and uniform, he was hooked. True to form, Gary made himself so popular among his fellow soldiers from the Nineteenth that he was voted a promotion to be their corporal. By all rights, the much more knowledgeable Larry should have won this distinction, but he never let on that it bothered him.

The Nineteenth Indiana looked so authentic that they were invited to become extras for two Civil War movies: *Glory,* filmed outside Atlanta in 1989, and *Gettysburg,* which was shot near the historic battlefield in 1992. (In the latter, Gary is briefly visible scrambling down a hill, the only glimpse of either twin in either picture.) *Glory,* though not nearly as lavish a production, became the more rewarding experience for Larry. Fellow infantryman Micheal Thompson hitched along with the Halls for the ride to Georgia. He had grown up in Wabash, but didn't meet the twins until they all joined the Nineteenth Indiana. He remembers "laid-back Larry" driving as frenetic Gary gabbed on and on in the passenger seat. If the brothers bickered, it was over directions, with Larry usually winning out. Still, Thompson says, "I thought Larry liked the trip we took to get there as much as he liked being there."

The moviemaking turned out to be more exciting than Larry expected. "It was actually my first reenactment combat," he later told a reporter for the Marion, Indiana, *Chronicle-Tribune.* "I learned a lot, but it was also dangerous." Usually, reenactment bayonets were dull, brittle pieces of metal intended for show. But those wielded by soldiers in the film were sharpened steel, and one nearly stabbed Larry as he backed up into it. He found the pyrotechnics for cannon blasts even more frightening. "They had a stuntman in front of me during one scene. He was blown six feet into the air by an explosion. It was planned, but even that seemed dangerous."

No one was more quoted for the article than Larry, his enthusiasm for reenactment evidently bubbling through his typical reserve. "It's really just a neat hobby," he said, adding, "I've learned a lot historically about the war, too." But when asked the major reason why he enjoyed reenactments, he replied, "It's like traveling to the past. That's why I do it: to travel back in time."

This wistful sentiment was further illuminated by the photograph of Larry, Gary, Thompson, and a friend that ran alongside the article. All stand at ease with their hands clasped around the barrels of their rifles. While his comrades, in character, look at the camera with grim determination, Larry is turned slightly at an angle and gazes off in the distance with a contented, tight-lipped smile.

The filming for *Gettysburg,* a little more than two years later in July of 1992, would bring higher per diem pay and generous buffet meals for all three days that the extras were on set. But the trip would also expose the increasing divergence in the twins' personal lives and their commitment to the Nineteenth Indiana.

Micheal Thompson was unable to get as much time off as the Halls, so he took a bus out to Pennsylvania to meet them. A tense family scene awaited him. Gary had broken the all-male sanctity of their Civil War pilgrimage by bringing a woman along. Although he had divorced his first wife a little more than a year after he had married her, he had got hitched again, this time to a slim, athletic redhead named Deaitra. A few nights before Thompson arrived, the Halls had decided to splurge on a motel. Larry was both shocked and offended when he learned that he couldn't share a room with his brother and Deaitra. He stormed off in Gary's car, which they used for the trip, and didn't return until the next morning.

Although Thompson didn't know about the incident when he

arrived, he couldn't help but detect some frostiness from Deaitra. "She was another control person like his first wife," Thompson says, "but a bit more on the wild side, and she made it clear she wasn't all that interested in reenactment."

It would be the twins' last extended road trip together, for a reenactment or anything else. Instead, they went to Midwest events that were just a few hours from Wabash. Looking at photographs from this period, it's clear that Gary's family obligations were starting to intrude. In one sepia-tone period portrait, seven members of the Nineteenth Indiana pose at a campsite, with Gary's blond infant daughter, in a white pinafore, perched incongruously on his knee. Her uncle Larry kneels next to them in a rifle-ready position, seemingly oblivious to her presence.

If Gary was getting tugged back to reality by his personal affairs, other photos show Larry immersing himself that much more deeply into his fantasy life. By October of 1990, he appears with full muttonchop sideburns, his bid—as he later explained to a reporter—to get promoted from foot soldier to commanding officer in local reenactments. He wanted to portray General Ambrose Burnside, an Indiana native, whose distinctive facial hair made him the namesake for both the hybrid half-beard mustache as well as the more ordinary "sideburns" (his name inverted). Hall would not get the part because, as he later discovered, the general was six feet tall. His height was unusual for the era and as much a distinct part of his identity as his facial hair. Larry still kept the "burnsides," believing they helped him look more authentic—even if he had to remain in the infantry.

Of course, Hall's desire to blend in with the nineteenth century made him stick out that much more in real life. It was surprisingly flamboyant behavior for a man who had been so painfully shy. His neighbors, says his high school friend Ron Osborne, thought the whiskers were "a little weird." But Larry did not mind the stares or snickers. He had finally found a community he could embrace—and more important, one that would embrace him back. He continued to attend reenactments into the early nineties, often on his own. He even went to Revolutionary War events such as the one in Georgetown the weekend before Jessica Roach's disappearance, but still wore his Civil War uniform. Gary Miller, the Vermilion County chief investigator, soon discovered that other attendees were quick to place Larry on the scene. As one would later testify, "He had an exquisite set of burnsides."

After listening to Hall blurt out his dreams and "out-of-body" experiences in the Wabash city council chambers, Miller says, "I felt he was capable of killing Jessica Roach, and I felt he was certainly a suspect in the true sense of the term *suspect*. But I still didn't think he was absolutely the guy." In all of his years as an investigator, Gary Miller had learned to never get too excited by one interview.

Tempering his enthusiasm was the reaction of the other detectives in the City Hall conference room. Although they were clearly disturbed by Hall's "dreams," they dismissed him as a "wannabe"—a police term for geeks who become obsessed with a crime and imagine themselves a part of it, often because of a fixation on the victim.

Hall, they insisted, was harmless, but they divulged further information that only reinforced Miller's suspicions. In just the past month, he had been arrested for stalking a jogger. There had been previous complaints about stalking as well, but Detective Amones had referred Larry to a local counseling service in response to those. Then there was the Tricia Reitler abduction. Even though the Marion police were adamant that someone else was responsible, in his gut Miller knew that there were too many similarities with the Jessica Roach case for this to be a coincidence.

As Miller drove back home from his first interview with Hall, he mulled over all that had transpired during his few hours in Wabash. If anything, the trip reinforced his concerns about the Indiana police, and he faced the real possibility that they might take the case away from him. Although Roach was probably abducted from her home in Illinois, that was not certain. But her body was unquestionably found on the other side of the state line. If he so desired, the local Indiana state's attorney could claim jurisdiction, despite the fact that an Illinois detective had tracked down the defendant.

Miller would then make the single most fateful decision of the entire investigation—he would bring in the Feds. Immediately upon his return, after receiving permission from the sheriff, he called Frances Hulin, the U.S. attorney for the Central District of Illinois. Larry Hall, he told her, had crossed state lines to abduct and kill Jessica, making it a federal case.

Usually, the police don't take homicides to U.S. attorneys. Murder—unless it's committed during an act of terrorism—is not a federal crime. Hall could still be convicted of kidnapping, which brings a life sentence, but the assistant U.S. attorneys who would try the case would not necessarily have as much experience with a murder trial as an assistant state's attorney would. Worse yet, after an indictment, the investigation would be turned over to the FBI, the Bigfoot nemesis of all local detectives.

Still, for Miller, none of the potential problems with the Feds outweighed the danger of letting the Roach case go "to the other side." Besides, he had a close working relationship with Ken Temples, the FBI agent for his region. Going to the Feds looked even better when Hulin assigned Larry Beaumont as the lead prosecutor. Before he had joined the U.S. attorney's office, Beaumont had been an assistant state's attorney, which gave him plenty of experience with capital cases.

The next step for Miller was to return to Wabash as soon as possible to give Larry Hall a polygraph (or, as it's commonly known, a lie detector test). Miller explains, "For me, a polygraph is simply an investigative tool. It's not something that will tell you absolutely that a guy is guilty or innocent. But if someone is willing to take it and a good polygraph examiner tells you he passes, then you can pretty much eliminate him from the investigation."

Miller had a favorite polygraph examiner who worked for the state of Illinois, but even at this early stage in the investigation, Miller would be overruled by the Feds. They insisted that he use an FBI agent for the examination, and one would not be available for two weeks. Miller had to impatiently cool his heels, wondering if Hall would ever return to the Wabash police station of his own volition.

On Tuesday, November 15, 1994, Wabash detective Jeff Whitmer fetched Hall from the tiny front room of his parents' house. He told him that Miller was back, this time with an FBI agent, but once again Larry did not seem unduly alarmed and agreed to drive himself downtown. He never contacted a lawyer or even informed his family of where he was going. Whitmer took him to the old station house and a tiny interrogation room barely big enough for the two desks inside it. On one end was a tiny window, propped open above a hissing steam radiator; on the other, a darkened two-way mirror. Miller sat waiting with Mike Randolph, a short, balding man in suit and tie. He had a mild, Bob Newhart–like manner that for Hall must have been a welcome contrast to the burly brusqueness of the Vermilion County investigator. When they all chatted a bit, Hall made some eye contact with Randolph in a way that he never did with Miller.

Randolph matter-of-factly explained that he would be hooking Hall up to the polygraph to ask some questions about Jessica Roach. He presented Hall a series of forms to complete. The first was his waiver of rights, which Randolph had him read out loud before he signed it. Next came the consent form for taking the polygraph, but after reading it over a few times, Hall put the pen down.

"I can't do this," he told Randolph, "because I don't believe I will pass it."

Miller practically jumped out of his seat. It was pretty much what he had expected, but a big break nevertheless. By refusing the polygraph, Hall had now incriminated himself more than if he had failed. They couldn't use it in court, but in essence he was telling the investigators that he knew something he didn't want to tell the truth about.

But Randolph was going for more than a refusal. He gently probed to see why Larry thought he wouldn't pass. Suspecting that the FBI agent might get more from Larry on his own, Miller stood up and left the room, but he continued to watch them through the two-way mirror from next door.

Once again, Hall went on about his dreams to Randolph. This time he called them nightmares and confided to the FBI agent that they were interfering with his sleep and making him depressed.

Both men spoke softly, and Miller could barely hear what they were saying through the glass. All around them, the station house was in chaos as the department prepared to move that day to new quarters. Miller would pop back into the observation room a few times, but then he got some coffee and tracked down Whitmer to see what more he could learn about Hall. As they talked, an excited Randolph rushed over to interrupt them.

"He's going to make a statement," Randolph told Miller. "I need you to witness it."

FBI agent Randolph would later testify extensively about how he had gotten Larry to open up during that hour after Miller had left them. First, Randolph told Hall that he needed treatment to stop his nightmares and depression. Larry replied that he had been referred to a mental health center by Detective Amones, but that the young counselor who had been assigned to him could not deal with his issues. At times, Larry told Randolph, he was lonely and felt an "urge" to be with women. Randolph asked if that urge was irresistible, and Larry had said yes, the urge was something he had to satisfy to "feel better."

Randolph then pulled out a photo of Jessica Roach, as he had been prompted to do by Miller. Again, Hall looked away, but this time a tear rolled down his cheek. For the next few moments, they sat in silence. Then Randolph asked, "Why don't we start talking about that weekend?"

In his flat, quiet voice, with his head down, Hall started to talk. He spoke in detail about Jessica Roach: where he had abducted her, what he had done with her in his van, and how he had killed her. "I just do things," he said. "I am not in control. This was one of those times when I was not in control." He had almost as much to say about Tricia Reitler and then made vague comments about killing other "girls"—at least two in Indiana and one in Wisconsin near a reenactment. "All of the girls looked alike. I cannot remember all of them," he told Randolph. Later, in a similar vein, he added, "I picked up several girls in other areas, but I can't remember which ones I hurt." There were no more tears, but as Larry spoke, Randolph noted, his face twitched and he compulsively wrung his hands.

Hurrying back to the interview room with Randolph, Miller suggested that they tape Larry as well as get his statement. That way, a jury would know that the confession was not coerced. But to Miller's surprise, Randolph refused. FBI policy prevented him from tape-recording a confession. Instead, from what he recalled of Larry's confession, Randolph wrote down a statement in his own scrawling hand on two blank sheets of paper and then asked Hall to sign each one. Miller countersigned as a witness. Neither lawman noticed that the document began, "I, Larry DeWayne Daniels." In his haste to get everything down, Randolph had copied the format from another statement and forgot to change the last name from Daniels to Hall. Also, neither he nor Miller balked when Hall block-printed his name instead of signing it in script.

What Hall told Randolph was still not enough for Miller. He wanted more details about the Jessica Roach abduction that could only be known by her killer. Since Miller wanted to record his conversation with Larry, the FBI agent got up and left the room. But now that they were alone, when Miller pulled out the tape recorder, Larry objected. He explained that he did not want to ever hear his own voice repeating the horrible things he was about to describe. Miller had to be content with notes.

Throughout the day, as Larry talked to Randolph and Miller, the Wabash cops hovered outside the interrogation room in anticipation. During a break, Jeff Whitmer walked in and handed Hall a can of pop. "He was sitting there all slumped over and all upset," Whitmer remembers. "I put my hand on his shoulder and I said, 'Larry, it will be all right.' He looked up at me and he said, 'No, it's not all right and it's never going to be all right.'"

5

Breakfast with Baby Killers

BY BUMPING INTO LARRY IN THE DINING HALL so soon after his arrival in Springfield, Jimmy Keene had violated every admonition that had been laid down by the FBI agents and U.S. marshals. As Hall backed away from him, Keene thought about pushing past, as though it had been an accidental bump and nothing more, but he spoke to Hall instead: "Hey, excuse me, man," he said. Then, "Hey, you look cool. Do you know where I can find the prison library?"

Hall was again startled. "It's in this building," he said in a drawl that sounded slurred by medication. He pointed down the hall. "I go there to read the paper every day. Do you want me to show you where?"

Keene said he did, but Larry stayed rooted and asked, "You think *I'm* cool?"

"Hell, yeah. Look at the other guys around you."

Hall laughed. As they walked down the corridor, Jimmy tried to size him up out of the corner of his eye. It was bad enough that he had practically knocked Hall over. How could he have also called him "cool"? This was the last person in the world that anyone would

call cool. But if Larry was suspicious, he didn't show it. He just am-
bled forward with no expression on his face.

When they reached the library, he turned and went inside. It was
tiny compared to Keene's old workplace in Milan. Bookshelves lined
the walls from floor to ceiling, but there were only two metal tables
for reading. Hall flipped through a rack that kept newspapers on
long sticks. He fished one out and sat down. Keene did likewise—
barely noticing what he pulled—and sat opposite Hall. When Jimmy
snuck a peek, he was surprised to see Larry reading the *Wabash Plain
Dealer,* but he learned later that the prison would, upon request, sub-
scribe to any inmate's hometown paper.

Hall methodically turned each page and scanned it from top to
bottom before he went on to the next. When he finished, he got up,
returned the paper to the rack, and left without any further acknowl-
edgment of Keene. But Jimmy had acted as if he were paying no attention to Hall, either.

Later that morning, Keene had his first doctor's appointment with
the Medical Center's chief psychiatrist. According to Beaumont, the
doctor would be Keene's only contact in Springfield who knew his
real reason for being there, but when the doctor came out to the waiting room to greet Jimmy, he gave him a quick, officious handshake.
He was in his fifties, tall and thin with glasses and a professorial air. As
with the other medical staff at Springfield, he always wore a tie and
was either in shirtsleeves or a suit. Without saying a word, he glanced
at Jimmy's file as he led him into his closetlike office. But once the
door closed, Keene says, "The masks came off." The doctor tossed the
file aside and perched on the edge of his desk.

"I know what the whole plan is," he said, "and I'm completely
behind it. If anything happens, I'll be the guy to get you out. If you
have any problems with the guards, tell them you need to see me and
I'll be right there to help."

He had placed Keene in a cell directly across from Hall. He'd also helped concoct a new rap sheet for Jimmy that had him smuggling arms across state lines—a crime that was more likely to put him in Springfield than drug dealing. The official diagnosis for Keene would be severe depression—Jimmy had already been diagnosed with mild depression in Milan—and they would use complications from Jimmy's allergies as an excuse to keep him under the direct care of the chief psychiatrist.

Before Keene left his office, his contact wanted to give him one last warning. "Be careful of these prisoners. Most of them are under medication, but they can be very unpredictable. We can't have you getting in any fights." The doctor wasn't just worried about blowing Jimmy's cover. He was also concerned that his own participation in Beaumont's scheme would become known. "Long after you're gone, I still have to deal with the patients here," he told Keene. "I've spent many years developing a reputation as someone they can trust. That will all be lost if they think I'm working with the government against one of them."

To some extent, his concern came as no surprise to Keene. "Nobody in prison likes a narc," he says. Even the guards who try to get prisoners to snitch on each other have contempt for the ones who do. But Jimmy was starting to learn that the issue of privacy rose to a whole new level at Springfield: the medical staff really did see the inmates as patients first and prisoners second. If word of Keene's mission got out, the doctor's colleagues would condemn it as much as any inmate.

That night, after dinner, when everyone else had returned to his cell, Jimmy was surprised to see that Hall's cell was empty. For some reason, Larry had the run of the place along with privileges that most of the other prisoners did not have. Only later, when Keene's door was locked down along with the others on the floor, did he see that Hall had returned. The upper wicket in his cell door had been left open and light from the inside shone out. As his head went by, the narrow beam would blink on and off. With their meeting that morning and Hall now so close, Keene's mission no longer seemed so impossible. Perhaps it could be over in weeks instead of months. Jimmy kept peeking out at Hall's cell until the light went out. It was like watching money in the bank.

If the bizarre and mostly hidden challenges of Springfield could be summed up in one prisoner, he would be Clayton Fountain. Trained to kill by the Marines, he first put those skills to use on his staff sergeant in 1974. Once in the civilian correctional system, he joined the Aryan Brotherhood and rose in their ranks as an enforcer with at least two murders to his credit, in both cases plunging barely sharpened metal into the vital organs of his victims. When the U.S. Bureau of Prisons (BOP) built the Administrative Maximum facility—or Super Max—in Marion, Illinois, it was expressly designed to be the end of the line for lethal federal inmates like Fountain, with systems and structures to provide an unprecedented level of security. Still, once inside, Fountain managed to get at a rival gang leader, stabbing him sixty-seven times, while screaming, "Die, bitch, die." He then dragged the bloody corpse the length of the tier before returning to his cell. The next year, in 1983, he found a way to slip his handcuffs and repeatedly stab three of Marion's correctional officers, killing one and crippling another.

The media dubbed Fountain "America's Most Dangerous Inmate," but his Super Max rampage against the guards did more than embarrass the BOP. It also posed a difficult question: since Fountain could no longer stay in Marion, then where was the end of the line *after* the end of the line?

The answer, oddly enough, was not another Super Max, but somewhere that sounds much more bucolic: the U.S. Medical Center for Federal Prisoners (MCFP), in Springfield, Missouri. Far from state-of-the-art, Springfield is a relic, with buildings dating back to 1933, when it was the first medical facility in the federal prison system. If it is known for anything, it's as the place where old Mafia dons go to die, since it holds one of the few hospitals where the BOP can treat critically ill prisoners in a secure setting (even in the operating room, handcuffs are not removed until the patient is unconscious). But in addition to medical patients, Springfield also houses nearly three hundred men with chronic psychiatric disorders. Some can erupt in savage and unpredictable ways. As a result, the MCFP has developed a wide array of strategies for dealing with violent behavior. Some go back to the days of Alcatraz, which shipped its own hard cases to Springfield when they went crazy or fell ill. Fountain's MCFP treatment plan could have come from that bygone era. For the next decade after his arrival, he lived in a cage inside a cage—a contraption that cost $40,000 to build. He was prohibited from touching any person, including his mother, and ate only with a plastic spoon. On those rare occasions when he was taken out of his twofold containment, the *Springfield News-Leader* reported in 1989, "His legs [are] locked with irons, his wrists frozen with two sets of handcuffs. With every movement, a sea of guards surrounds him like an armada."*

Over its many decades, Springfield has not just held the nation's most violent prisoners, such as Fountain, but also the most passive— the terminally ill, hunger strikers, and conscientious objectors—who presented their own challenges. Indeed, much about the institution's history is as bipolar as any inmate it's ever had to treat. Although no household name like Leavenworth or Alacatraz, Springfield has still incarcerated, if only briefly, some of the most famous inmates in the

---

*Eventually Fountain converted to Catholicism and educated himself to the extent where he studied for a master's degree and provided college professors with critical analysis on research about prison life and solitary confinement. Although some of his restrictions, including the cage, were lifted, he was kept in solitary until he died of a heart attack in 2004 at the age of forty-nine.

history of the Bureau of Prisons, including Robert "Birdman" Stroud, who made his name at the two more famous penitentiaries but spent his last years at the MCFP. Although no prisoner has ever escaped Springfield for more than a few hours, within its walls there can be remarkable freedom for a favored few, and even a measure of protection against the federal prosecutors who put them there. Meanwhile, the treatment of other inmates has fluctuated wildly from progressive experimentation to old-fashioned repression.

The Medical Center's split personality is rooted in the 1930 congressional act that created it, giving oversight of the facility to both the U.S. Public Health Service and what was then the embryonic Bureau of Prisons. Although the designated inmates were indelicately defined as "Defective Delinquents," the law held forth an ambitious mandate: to both treat their illness *and* cure their criminal conduct through "study, classification and rehabilitation," in essence making the MCFP a penitentiary petri dish for behavior modification. With such faith in the potential of science, Congress gave medical staff the upper hand in running the place with the convoluted requirement that the superintendant be a physician—but still appointed by the attorney general with the approval of the surgeon general.

The doctors clearly called the shots in designing the MCFP's compound and architecture. As opposed to the cement-block fortresses of Leavenworth and Alcatraz, Springfield has the institutional brick exterior more common to the big psychiatric hospitals that were then springing up in the Northeast. A total of ten buildings were planned, none taller than five stories. At the center of the complex, four of the largest structures are connected by low walls, creating a quadrangle to surround the massive prison yard. In the final architectural drawing for the site, the ring of rust-hued buildings, swaddled by lush green grass and trees, looks more like a Tuscan village than a penitentiary.

In reality, the Springfield compound was flatter and much more barren than the one depicted in the architect's drawing. What made it most attractive to prison authorities was not the landscape but the location. It sat, like a bull's-eye, at the center of the continental United States—equidistant from penitentiaries on either coast—which would reduce the overall costs of transportation for the prisoners who needed immediate care in the hospital.

Nothing is more surprising about the MCFP's early history than the eagerness of Springfield, Missouri, to embrace it. Today, few public projects would be less welcome in our backyards than a prison or a psychiatric hospital, let alone a combination of the two. But in 1931, at the depths of the Depression, Springfield's civic leaders saw the murderers and madmen as manna from heaven. They would rain down on the local economy with $3 million in construction funds to house them, hundreds of jobs to care for them, and countless contracts from local vendors to keep them fed and clothed. As earnest money to secure a deal with the government, Springfield's Chamber of Commerce raised $142,000 in notes to purchase the 445-acre site (previously considered for a golf course), which it then handed over gratis to the U.S. attorney general. The fund-raising campaign took only six weeks, bringing in contributions from businesses and individuals across the region, and was trumpeted by a *Springfield Daily News* headline as the "Greatest Triumph in History of City." The accompanying article also touts the complex as "the largest hospitalization project ever attempted by the federal government" and explains, with modern-sounding "stimulus" spin, "The program is in line with President Hoover's plan to relieve unemployment over the country by stepping up federal building projects."

In this and other newspaper reporting from those early, boosterish days, there is little mention of "Defective Delinquents" or the Medical Center's dual mission to treat psychiatric as well as physical illness. Stories focused instead on the bonanza for local building contractors and the pace of construction.

Neighbors did not get their first look behind the brick walls until July 1935—two years after the Medical Center first received inmates—when the *Springfield Leader and Press* ran a four-day series written by columnist Docia Karell. Her reverent and breathless tone is summed up in the headline for the kickoff piece: "Government's Battle to Reclaim 'Lost Men' at Medical Center Here Holds Interest of Entire Nation." Although billed as the "inside story," the introduction explains that it is also the "official story," vetted by the hospital administration.

No doubt the series was partly intended—by both the editors and prison officials—to dispel rumors that were frightening the community. Karell repeats some of the "Strange Tales Told," but she is so ambiguous that it's hard to know exactly which tale is really false. She writes:

> Stories get abroad, of course. Some of them perhaps are not true at all. Others undoubtedly were born of truth, though they may have outgrown it. Some are stories of odd characters or one-time prominent persons living there. Others are stories of violence within the walls, of rioting and fighting, when prisoners get out of bounds and tear down even the fire extinguishers to hurl as weapons. There is belief in Springfield that at times like these officials send in haste for the Catholic chaplain to come and quiet the turbulent men—that this quiet clergyman has "some strange power" over them. . . . It is related that some of the most famous and dangerous criminals in the country are in the hospital here, entered even with aliases on the prison records.

Although Karell calls some of the stories "absurd," she also adds, "Undoubtedly it is true that even those which have a basis in fact are often much exaggerated. Partly, of course, these tales and their exaggerations grow out of the very secrecy which shrouds the place."

But some readers could have found Karell's facts even more disturbing than the rumors. She reports that the Medical Center had just 44 guards to watch over 475 prisoners. Of these, 285 had DD or DEFECTIVE DELINQUENT stamped on their denim shirts, and the rest were "trusties" (trusted inmates), who helped operate the facility and were known as PCs, because they could stay in a low-security prison camp. No matter how well behaved the trusties were, the ratio of prisoners to correctional officers was ridiculously high (by today's standards for a high-security federal prison it should be no more than four to one). Staffing aside, Karell describes MCFP security as state-of-the-art. "Stout locks and armed guards help to keep it impregnable," she gushes. "At night, powerful lights can play upon the whole place [as needed], bringing every wall and corner to a bright, shadowless visibility so that there is no place for one to lurk in successful hiding, or to move unseen. At any hour, the screaming steam sirens are waiting to broadcast the warning that a man has escaped."

But despite these "impregnable" defenses, within weeks of the MCFP's opening, at least two prisoners had escaped. They were caught soon after, but a few more guards were immediately hired, and security was stepped up another notch. So it would go for much of the MCFP's early history as the medical administrators' best intentions for treatment would be slapped back by the conduct of their prisoner patients.

Karell may have best summed up the divided soul of the Medical Center with her introduction of its first superintendent, Dr. Marion King, for whom "the inmates are men as well as patients, and patients as well as prisoners." The life in the complex that she goes on to describe sounds more like a summer camp than a prison, where days start with nourishing breakfasts in the cafeteria, followed by hearty work in the Medical Center's feedlots and fields (more than one hundred acres were under cultivation), afternoon games of baseball in the prison yard, and evenings spent painting in the crafts shop or learning foreign languages in classrooms. Sunday mornings are devoted to church, and evenings to watching movies in the auditorium. Karell gets so swept up in the wholesome bustle that she wonders why these prisoners were sentenced in the first place. "Mostly they are a good-natured gang. . . . Some of them are unusually handsome. They look like kids that started out to do a little general hell-raising out of sheer exuberance, meaning no harm, and got into trouble by accident."

These are not your typical dangerous prisoners or unsavory mental patients. Instead, in Karell's eyes, their disabilities make them almost childlike, a sentiment that was probably mirrored by Dr. King and his staff. In this early period, they lived on what they called "the reservation" inside the compound's fences and barbed wire, some even with wives and young children. Mary Virginia Moore Johnson, daughter of Springfield's first chief surgeon, remembers, "We never locked our doors, which was very normal."

But just three years later in 1938, when work started on the last major structure in the complex, the doctors turned the project over to the same engineer who had supervised the construction of Alcatraz. Clearly, security concerns had come to the fore. From then on 10 Building was known as Springfield's "Little Alcatraz," a testament to both its higher security level and the limits of high-minded treatment for the MCFP's patients. With three hundred beds, 10 Building more than doubled the Medical Center's psychiatric population. Even with the added capacity, Springfield could not begin to house all of the supposedly psychotic inmates that other federal prisons wanted to dump on it. Most of these transfers had more management issues than certifiable psychiatric disorders. To cope with the demand, the Medical Center instituted a rigorous evaluation process, only keeping the very worst of the bunch for long-term residence.

During this era, even other public and private psychiatric hospitals had a difficult time dealing with severe psychoses such as schizophrenia. But the degree of difficulty increased exponentially with men who had a history of violence and symptoms exacerbated by the beatings or solitary confinement that they had received in other facilities. To hold the sheer number of them at Springfield, medicine was forced to make way for correction. Special wards in 10 Building were reserved for the most "assaultive," with status charts posted next to their cells. A "4 Man Order" required the presence of four guards when the door was open. Especially uncontrollable prisoners were tied to their beds with metal cuffs and "soft restraints"—leather or canvas straps—until they calmed down.

As Springfield's prisoner population passed one thousand, it left much of the "innocence" of the Medical Center's first decade behind. In 1941, 10 Building prisoners rioted for several hours, nearly killing a corrections officer and wreaking extensive damage on a cellblock. But the incident received no coverage in the press. In fact, the Springfield newspapers gave no hint of the rising tensions inside the MCFP until a sudden cloudburst of negative publicity in early 1944. It was precipitated by a band of Socialist conscientious objectors who were sent to Springfield for forced feeding after they had conducted hunger strikes in other prisons. While upset with their own rough handling by guards, they claimed to be horrified by the treatment that other inmates were receiving, especially blacks and those with visible psychiatric issues. Charging that the guards tortured prisoners, they filed a complaint with the U.S. attorney general, who promptly opened an inquiry and sent James Bennett, the director of prisons, to Springfield for hearings.

An undercurrent of clashing cultures rippled beneath the controversy. From the Springfield perspective, the Medical Center was a proud Ozarks institution that was being smeared by draft-dodging, left-wing Yankees. The Socialists saw the prison as a callous Southern backwater under the dominion of redneck guards. Bennett arrived with much fanfare on a Sunday, and the conscientious objectors, in another show of defiance, staged a sit-down strike after the evening movie, refusing to leave until Bennett made an appearance in the auditorium. They got up only after the superintendent, Dr. Michael Pescor, promised that they would be represented at the hearings.

The guards, now on the defensive, went to the local press with their own grievances, venting for the first time in the MCFP's history. They were not only battling violent prisoners, they complained to a reporter, but they were also fighting with "temporizing" medical administrators who would not let them use the force necessary to subdue "unruly" or insane prisoners. Within days after the guards talked to reporters, almost on cue, two prisoners escaped, and just a few weeks after that, 10 Building erupted again. Although no one was hurt, the prisoners caused more than $5,000 in damage, and this time the riot made the front page of the *Springfield Leader and Press*. A large photo of the trashed unit carried the caption "After the storm." Dr. Pescor blamed a hard core of thirty-seven "tough guys" for all the trouble, some of it dating back to the previous riot. Charging that they only faked mental illness to enjoy the comforts of Springfield, he dispersed them to other penitentiaries across the country. Upon their departure, a headline read, "Tough Inmates Scattered to Other Prisons." It was one of the first tacit admissions by the local media that their "U.S. Medical Center" was indeed just another prison.

The 1944 riot did serve one institutional purpose: it muzzled the conscientious objectors and quickly hamstrung Bennett's hearings. They ended with a whimper, and no charges were filed against Springfield's staff. (As one newspaper put it, "Medical Center Charges Called Hallucinations.") Despite the expulsion of the "tough guys," sporadic violence continued over the years, culminating in another riot in 1959. This was the worst yet, again confined to 10 Building, but with 5 guards held hostage for fifteen hours before 125 guards rushed in—most of them through a window that they had torn out of the TV room. Using clubs—in a haze of tear gas—they fought prisoners supposedly armed with their own clubs and homemade knives. Fifty-three prisoners were injured, and one of them later died from his head wounds. Just one of the attacking guards and one hostage were hurt.

After the 1959 riot, there was no more "temporizing." Springfield operated much more like other federal prisons in terms of security and lost some of the softer features that had made it unique. The farming, once seen as so therapeutic, was shut down, and the excess acreage was returned to the city. The hospital staff's families moved off the reservation. But the MCFP still remained the only psychiatric hospital for prisoners in the federal system. While the patient population swelled beyond capacity, the psychiatric staff shrank as the government had more trouble competing with the private sector for doctors. Other more imaginative treatments had to be developed for the "highly aggressive inmate."

In the early seventies, lawsuits revealed that Springfield was experimenting with a behavior modification program known as START (Special Treatment and Rehabilitative Training). The MCFP director, Dr. Pasquale Ciccone, summed up the system as "granting rewards for correct behavior," but it left some stubborn prisoners naked and hungry and sounded like something out of the recently released movie A Clockwork Orange. Citing budget concerns, the director of the BOP shut it down. But by then Springfield, like the psychiatric hospitals on the outside, was relying on the most effective management tool yet—the needle. Narcoleptic drugs such as Thorazine and Haldol could tame any inmate. Springfield guards administered the injections themselves, often while prisoners thrashed in soft restraints— another queasy cocktail of medicine and correction, this time reminiscent of the Soviet Union. In 1978, lawsuits forced the MCFP to use nurses to dispense all drugs, but ironically, in that same year, supervision at the top of the facility went in the other direction: Dr. Ciccone retired and became the Medical Center's last MD superintendent. He was replaced by a BOP warden.

Since that time, if Springfield has been noted in the national press, it's for the celebrated criminals who touched down there briefly to be treated for physical illness. Almost all of them wanted out as soon as possible. Mobsters from Mickey Cohen to John Gotti have complained about the quality of health care; so, too, did deposed Panamanian dictator Manuel Noriega and Larry Flynt, who needed special treatment for his paralysis. During the porn magnate's stay, the town played host to his flamboyant entourage, which had Springfield society talking for years—even though he was at the MCFP for just five weeks. Blind sheikh Omar Abdel Rahman, mastermind of the first World Trade Tower bombing, stayed three years to receive care for his diabetes and high blood pressure, but complained most about the guards, who he said humiliated him with frequent strip searches and showed contempt for Islam by repeatedly interrupting his prayer sessions.

Throughout the federal prison system, Springfield guards had the reputation for being a tough and insular crew, but their hardened attitude toward prisoners was forged by the bizarre demands of the facility. Despite the prison's overcrowding, it remained the dumping ground for BOP odds and ends who didn't quite fit anywhere else—men such as Clayton Fountain, but also an enormously ungainly eight-hundred-pound cocaine dealer,* various crackpot con men, putative presidential assassins, and 116 psychotic Cubans from the Mariel boatlift who had literally burned down their previous prison.

In his book *Echoes of Mercy,* Randy Greer provides readers with the perspective of a longtime Springfield corrections officer. While he tries to put the MCFP in the best light, he does not hide the eerie atmosphere, describing wards with constant "banging and kicking on

---

*It took a special plane to haul the cocaine dealer to Springfield in 1989, but he died soon after and presented other challenges in getting his corpse back out of his cell.

the doors" and "screaming obscenities [that] eventual[ly] break down into loud, tearful sobs." As a routine part of his job, he deals with prisoners who throw body waste through the slots or do disgusting things to themselves (he was called to one cell where an inmate had torn out his own eyes). Although Greer confronted violent prisoners in a previous job as a guard in a state prison, he finds Springfield more threatening because it is so unpredictable. As proof, he describes an incident with a dwarfish Cuban in the Medical Center who suddenly jumps on his chest, screaming that Greer is the devil. He writes, "He hit me quicker and more times than I have ever been hit. I had survived being a police officer and a correctional officer at two state institutions without any serious type of injury, but now found myself momentarily helpless at the hands of this crazed convict." By the time the prisoner is pulled off him, Greer's nose is broken and his eyes are swollen shut. Although the Cuban was segregated for sixty days, after his mental condition was stabilized, he was eventually released back into the general population.

Meanwhile, from the prisoner's perspective, Springfield was far from the most popular stop on the BOP carousel by the time Jimmy Keene arrived in 1998. The aged buildings were run-down, and the distressed condition of the psychiatric patients was depressing. It was "gloomy," according to one directory of federal prisons. But even that word was too kind for inmate Jonathan Jay Pollard, who described Springfield as "an environment of total bedlam." An American naval intelligence analyst convicted of spying for Israel, Pollard believed, like Sheikh Rahman, that he was sent to Springfield more for punishment than treatment, although the BOP claimed the MCFP was the only facility that could handle his psychosomatic illness. "The inhuman screams of the patients around me sounded like something straight out of Dante's *Inferno*," he wrote his sister in a letter from prison. "And then there were the attempted suicides. Witnessing a man cut his own throat from ear to ear was something I could have done without."

After eleven months in Springfield, Pollard gladly accepted a transfer to solitary in the Marion Super Max.

During Keene's second morning in Springfield, he saw Larry in the dining hall but didn't want to approach him again so soon. Besides, Hall sat in a corner with what looked like a regular group of friends, and it would have been pushy to butt in without an invitation. "In every prison, you have to be careful where you sit down," Keene explains. "You have to earn your place by knowing the people around you. Nothing starts more fights than taking someone else's spot."

Jimmy sat alone, picking at his greasy eggs and still wincing at the din in the cavernous room. "I was a lost puppy," Keene remembers. "I missed Milan. It had been like home to me. I had developed a lot of relationships there in a short time and I had a group of people I was really tight with."

As he scanned the dining hall, Keene wondered whom he could ever become tight with here. It wasn't just the visibly ill inmates who repelled him, but also seemingly healthy ones, who had a different sort of blank stare. "When some guys end up at a place like Springfield," he says, "they're done, and they know they're done. They got sentences of life one or two times over. You can see it in their faces. There's no soul left inside them."

After the buzzer sounded, Keene went to the laundry in the adjoining building to exchange his clothes. He wanted to turn in his camouflage pants for a pair with deep pockets just like in the army, and he needed a better fit. How he looked in prison mattered as much to him as how he looked on the outside. "I've got to have the right shit on me. It was like that when I was on a football team," he says. "My uniform always had to fit just right, with nothing baggy. It made me feel more powerful."

He returned to his cell to find two guards waiting for him inside.

"Keene, you gotta get a job here," one told him. When Jimmy protested that he had a medical condition, they laughed. "What are you talking about? Everyone here is sick."

But then he showed them the letter about his allergies. "They got all pissed about that," he says, "but there wasn't anything they could do about it." Unlike at Milan, no jobs were available in places such as the prison library that would be hypoallergenic.

Although Jimmy got out of work, he quickly realized that a monotonous routine awaited him instead. Down the hall was a little cinder-block room with a tiny TV bolted to a stand blaring *Jerry Springer.* A couple of inmates sat in scattered plastic, stackable chairs, watching listlessly, their jaws slack. "If you didn't have a job in that place," Keene says, "then you had to be a real wacko."

There was a weight room, but nothing like the elaborate setup in Milan. It had only one pathetic Universal cable machine. Keene used every station, but a full workout on it took less than an hour. After a few hours, he was so bored, he couldn't wait to be called for his next meal—no matter how inedible it turned out to be.

He needed something else to occupy him, so after lunch, on his second day in Springfield, he says, "I decided to start my spying missions." He went first to Hall's cell, trying to see as much as he could from outside the open door. Family pictures were on the shelf, one with his brother in a Civil War uniform. Larry was also allowed to attach a paper cross to the wall, another privilege given only to the best-behaved prisoners.

After checking out Hall's room, Keene fanned out in wider circles from their building, through the tunnels and into the rest of the complex where he had access. "I wanted to see where he checked in for work, where he worked, and where he took a break. I even cased the office where he went to see his counselor." As Keene soon discovered, Larry did not have the same schedule as other prisoners. "When the buzzer went off each morning," Keene says, "he was already out of his cell. He was like a member of the staff. Because he had been a maintenance dude on the outside, they could use him on the inside to swab their floors and fix their boilers." While many buildings were restricted to Keene, Hall appeared to go almost everywhere, not just for cleaning, but for recreation as well. From what Jimmy could tell, Hall spent many evenings in the wood-shop section of the Arts & Crafts center behind the dining hall. Keene would have to be in Springfield six months before he could even walk through the shop door, then would have to get on a waiting list to use the equipment.

After a few days, Jimmy determined a place and a time in the tunnels where he could pretend to accidentally cross paths with Hall. So shortly before lunch and just after Larry got released from work, as they passed each other, Keene stopped, as though surprised to see him, and said, "Hey."

Hall rocked backward, his head doing the slow-motion roll until he seemed to recognize Keene and smiled.

"You know that paper I saw you reading in the library the other day?" Jimmy said. "Was that your hometown paper?"

Hall nodded. "I'm from Indiana."

"Really. Well, I'm from Kankakee. I don't know if you ever heard of it, but it's on the border right next to Indiana."

Hall just nodded again.

"Do you want to meet me down in the library?" Jimmy asked.

"No. I don't go there now. I go later. At two thirty."

Keene made sure to be there a few minutes early, and as promised, Hall appeared. But just as before, he took out his paper and sat down to methodically read each page. "I was right across the table from him for at least fifteen minutes," Keene remembers, "and he never said a word; never so much as made eye contact. When he was done, all he said was 'I'll see you later, James,' and just walked out."

The same thing happened the next day and then the next. "And now I'm getting frustrated," Keene says, "and as I look at him reading his paper, I'm thinking, 'Man, are you a fucking reject. Are you a waste of human life.' And then, when I had totally given up on him, he looked up from the paper and said, 'Do you want to have breakfast with us in the morning?'"

It was another breakthrough, and Keene had barely been in Springfield a week. Once again, his hopes soared and he could barely sleep that night. But the next morning, when he arrived at Hall's corner of the mess with his tray, he realized that their meals together would be a little more complicated than he thought. First of all, he could see heads turn at the other tables around them. There was a reason why Hall and his friends ate with a buffer of empty chairs around them. As Keene would later learn, the men at this table were collectively known as the "baby killers" and were outcasts—even among the lifers and lunatics of Springfield. Merely by sitting with them, Keene was making himself the object of the more common criminals' scorn.

As Jimmy introduced himself to Larry's breakfast companions, he could understand their lack of popularity. One was in his twenties, tall and skinny, with a mullet haircut and big bug eyes. He sat erect, and his head swiveled like an owl's, staring out at the room around them. Supposedly he had taken a chain saw and, for no reason, murdered the family in the house next door. Another tablemate was in his thirties with a froglike face and reading glasses always perched at the edge of his nose. He had killed little girls—or so Keene was told by other inmates. The third was big and fat with a bad case of acne. Jimmy never learned his crime.

For most of the meal, Keene was the only one who talked. He cracked jokes; he complained about the food and asked what they liked to eat. Only Hall seemed to tune in to him and even brightened a bit when Keene spoke. Out of the corner of his eye, Keene could see that Larry was squinting at him with increasing interest, almost as if he recognized a long-lost friend.

The next time they saw each other at the library, Hall was a little more animated, saying hello as well as good-bye and making a brief comment about the news. For some reason, he liked the formality of calling Keene, "James." Keene found him most chatty at 7:00 p.m. when they stood together in the pill line outside the nurse's station down the hall from their cells.

"What are they giving you?" Hall asked. It was the first question he ever asked Keene.

"Trazodone," Jimmy said, "for depression."

"I haven't heard of that one before." Hall then asked him a series of questions about the drug regarding "classes" and "compounds" and technical terms Keene had never heard before.

"Larry found it fascinating to compare medicine," Keene says, "and he knew a tremendous amount about the pills people took in there: how they were made, what they were supposed to do for you, the side effects. Just when you thought the guy was a waste case, he'd come up with information like that and you realized he was a lot smarter than you thought."

The nurse doled out a fistful of pills for Hall and he dutifully swallowed them. Keene kept his one pill under his tongue. When he returned to his cell, he ground it up and washed it down the drain. He had stopped taking his medication back in Milan because he hated the side effects, but he learned that he had to dispose of it immediately. If guards ever found the pills in his cell, they could accuse him of hoarding them to sell on the prison's black market.

Despite all the progress with Hall, Keene was careful to keep these developments to himself. Everything had moved much more quickly than the Feds had anticipated or desired, and Jimmy didn't want to take the chance that they would shut him down. Contact with his FBI handlers was only to be in person during visiting hours. Still, Keene was caught totally by surprise when he was summoned to the administration building on his first Sunday in Springfield. Told he had a visitor, he expected to see Big Jim. Waiting instead was an attractive blonde, who was nearly his height when she rose to greet him. She had short-cropped hair and wore a conservative blazer and skirt. When Jimmy extended his hand, she grabbed him by both shoulders and pulled him into a kiss. "Don't ever shake my hand," she whispered into his ear. "I'm supposed to be your girlfriend."

Her real name was Janice Butkus, and she was a niece of the iconic Chicago Bears linebacker Dick Butkus, but she was also a career FBI agent, working out of an Illinois office, and had signed in at the visitors' desk with an assumed name. She had gone to some length to develop the alias, in case anyone at Springfield checked up on her. This need for secrecy seemed odd to Jimmy. "You would think the FBI and the Bureau of Prisons would be one happy family," he says, "but I could see that they really didn't trust each other."

As they talked, to keep up the pretense of being her boyfriend, Keene held her hand—above the table as required by BOP visiting-room regulations. She gave him a phone number he could call to reach her in an emergency and again stressed that he not be too quick in approaching Hall. Keene assured her he was still keeping his distance.

In fact, he was eating breakfast with Hall every morning. But even as Jimmy continued to show up at their table, it did not make the other Baby Killers any more cordial. "They'd just sit there all spaced-out," Keene says. "Some of that was due to their medicine, but I don't think these guys were ever all that interesting. If they had anything to say, it would be 'Hey, you gonna drink that milk?' or maybe 'All right, guys, I'm getting ready to go.' And their voices were so dull and slow. At least I was quick with my speech, awake, and alive; not drugged out like everyone else. When I talked to Larry, it was about normal stuff, and I could get him to feel like he was free again and remembering what life was all about on the outside. It would bring out the kid in him. Sometimes he even looked a little happy."

Bit by bit, Larry opened up a little more about his hometown of Wabash and his family. Often he compared Keene with his brother,

Gary. Jimmy had seen Gary's picture in Hall's room when he looked inside from the corridor, so he was surprised to hear that they were identical twins. But everything Keene learned came in quick snatches. Their time to talk was limited to the thirty minutes they had for breakfast. Keene still didn't know where Hall spent his afternoons other than the library, and they couldn't have a conversation in there.

Jimmy had come so far in only a few weeks, he figured he could wait out Hall a little longer before he invited him to his cell or some other place where they could talk. But then a conflict arose that neither he nor the Feds ever anticipated. It started one afternoon while Keene was walking down a lonely tunnel corridor before lunch. When he turned a corner, three white weight-lifter types with slicked-back hair surrounded him. He had seen them in the dining room and assumed that they were Mafia. Usually, they hovered around a stooped, elderly prisoner whom Keene figured to be a mob boss. "I pulled back," Keene says, "because it looked like they were ready to jump me, but instead they said, 'The old man wants to talk to you.'"

The old man was Vincent Gigante. Then seventy years old, he had been the leader of the Genovese crime family in New York City. For most of the nineties, he had frustrated federal efforts to prosecute him by pretending to have dementia. He wandered the streets of Greenwich Village in a robe and slippers with a vacant stare. Newspapers dubbed him the Oddfather. In fact, he was among the most sophisticated bosses in recent New York Mafia history, overseeing an extensive syndicate for illegal sports-betting rackets and using his control of trade unions to shake down construction sites.

Keene knew nothing about Gigante's background, but he had got along just fine with the mob guys in Cicero and Milan prison. He figured he should hit it off with them in Springfield, too. Gigante's men hustled Jimmy into a corner where the old man was waiting. Up close, he had a passing resemblance to the actor Jason Robards, with wavy gray hair, dark eyebrows, full lips, and a lantern jaw that had

earned him his nickname, the Chin. According to mob lore, his under-
lings were forbidden to ever mention his name, in case their conversation was picked up on a bug or a wire. When referring to him, they
pointed to their chin instead.

Gigante gave Keene the once-over and then started poking him in
the chest. "Lemme ask you a question," he said in a high-pitched,
nasal voice. "Why you hangin' around with them Baby Killers?"

Keene rocked back on his heels, totally shocked by the question.
He stammered and then said, "I didn't even know what they did."

Gigante swatted the air with his hand in disgust. "Oh, c'mon! Are
you crazy or something? Everybody in the prison knows what them
guys are here for. You want somebody should put a knife in your
back?"

Keene shook his head no.

"All right then," Gigante said with a royal wave. "From now on,
you eat breakfast with us guys."

6.

"I can't see the faces, but I can hear the screams"

AFTER LARRY HALL SIGNED HIS STATEMENT CONFESSING
to the murders of Jessica Roach and Tricia Reitler—among others—
Vermilion County deputy sheriff Gary Miller was not going home
without him. "I really felt that if I left him in Wabash," he says, "we
would lose all control of the case." Time was of the essence. It was
Tuesday afternoon, and there was no telling what the local police in
Wabash or Marion might do in the week ahead of them.

First of all, Miller needed a car. Because he had never expected a
confession, he'd hitched a ride to Wabash with Ken Temples, his local
FBI agent. After the deputy sheriff left Hall, one of the first calls he
made was to his office. "Whoever that investigator was who picked
up the phone," Miller remembers, "I told him, 'Get in your car and
get over here, and I mean as fast as you can.'"

Miller also needed a warrant for Hall's arrest. Even though he expected the case to end up with the U.S. attorney in central Illinois, he
first called his local state's attorney so that charges could be filed the
next day. Some Indiana jurisdiction might also seek Hall's arrest, but

Miller was confident that he had the most developed case, at least for the attempted abduction of the girls in Georgetown.

Finally, Miller needed Hall's cooperation so he could take him across state lines. To his surprise, Larry instantly waived the extradition proceedings (Indiana was one of the few states where he could do so without a hearing before a judge). In return, Hall had a request of his own. He did not want strangers disturbing his parents and poking around his things. Miller readily agreed to let Wabash detectives Phil Amones and Jeff Whitmer lead the first police visit to Hall's house. Miller knew that in time the FBI would seek a search warrant and return to do a more thorough job.

To book and hold Hall, the Wabash police transferred him to the Grant County jail in nearby Marion. Miller stayed the night in a Wabash motel, but he hardly slept. "I had to get my thoughts together of what to do next," he says. Since the jail was only a few miles from where Reitler was abducted, Miller believed Hall might be ready to show him where he buried her or any other victims. "I had a full day planned for what we could do in that area."

But his plans abruptly changed the next morning when he arrived at the jail. "It was like an alien spaceship had just landed," he recalls. A cordon of TV-station vans surrounded the building, all sprouting satellite antenna poles. As Miller pushed past the reporters and video cameras, he realized that he couldn't take Hall anywhere in Marion without attracting a crowd. Instead, he had to concentrate on getting him out of town as quickly as possible.

The media onslaught had been touched off by the chief of the Wabash City Police Department, who had held an impromptu press conference the day before. When asked about the extent of Hall's crimes, he replied, "We're not talking about [just] one or two cases— [but] at least possibly four. We're not exactly sure at this point."

The mere suggestion of multiple murders and a possible serial killer sounded an irresistible siren call to news outlets across the state and country. It was not just the potential number of victims that drew them, but also the connection with Tricia Reitler's disappearance, which was a much bigger story than Miller had ever realized.

When Jessica Roach first disappeared, Miller had been anxious for all of the publicity that he could get. But now the deluge of attention was no more welcome to his investigation than a rainstorm after a flood. Up to that time, the Wabash and Marion police departments had been content to watch from the sidelines. Now they were suddenly swept into the fray, determined to show the locals that they were on the ball. Meanwhile, back home in Danville, Illinois, the phone lines were jammed—not with tips, but requests for media interviews. After a few months, the surge of interest would subside, but it would wreak more havoc than bring anything of use to the deputy sheriff or the prosecution. Miller understood that there was no avoiding publicity for a putative serial killer, but he adds, "It was the premature news releases in Indiana that were so detrimental to the investigation."

The blowback began with Hall himself. As Miller bundled him into the car for the trip to Illinois, Larry said he had talked earlier that day with his twin, Gary, who had been reading the morning paper. "My brother told me I better shut my mouth and get a lawyer because I'm in a lot of trouble."

During the long ride to Danville, Miller had hoped to spend time going over details of Hall's statement, but now, as he corkscrewed in the front passenger seat to talk to Hall, he could see that Larry was in no mood for further confession. "He wasn't showing a lot of emotion but he was clearly upset," Miller recalls. "I made a determination that it was more important for him to relax than feel any more pressure from me. So we talked instead about the Civil War, the Revolutionary War, and some of the historic sites we were passing."

What Hall told him surprised Miller as much as anything Larry had said in his confession. "I can assure you he did most of the talking because my knowledge of those subjects goes no further than what I learned in the fifth grade, but he was *very* knowledgeable about that stuff—and about Indians, too. He told me the places in northern Indiana where he would search for their artifacts and what he found there. You just listened to him for a while and you realized that he wasn't as simple as you first thought when you saw him."

However chatty Hall seemed in the car, he would not have much more to say about his crimes. If anything, he wanted to retract what he had already said. Almost as soon as he was settled in the Vermilion County jail in Danville, Miller started calling FBI agent Mike Randolph to ask for another interview. When Randolph did meet with Larry, just three days after his initial confession, Hall told the agent that he did not remember exactly what he had previously told him in Wabash, but that he had done no more than disclose his dreams. Nothing that he mentioned in the statement had actually happened. Randolph replied that both he and Deputy Sheriff Miller believed Hall was confessing to real murders, which is why they had him arrested. According to Randolph, Larry then changed course yet again and confirmed that the statement had been truthful. But over the next two weeks, Hall kept calling Randolph, more adamant each time when they talked that he had confessed to dreams and nothing more. Finally, he requested a polygraph, something the FBI agent could not do until a federal court appointed Larry counsel.

No matter how much Hall dismissed his confession as fantasy, it always had the ring of truth to Gary Miller. When he returned to Illinois and drove around Jessica Roach's home, he discovered that the statement was consistent with many distinctive features of the local landscape. Working with another deputy sheriff who grew up near Georgetown, Miller was able to weave those elements into a plausible route for Larry's peregrinations after the abduction of Jessica Roach. For example, Hall had spoken to Miller of a steel bridge. The escape route that Larry described to Miller did lead to a steel bridge—a truss bridge—the only steel bridge in the area at the time (it has since been replaced by a cement structure). Hall talked about heading east to get into Indiana and then crossing over a highway. That was Highway 63—the only major thoroughfare in the area—and it runs parallel to the state line. Once he was in Indiana, he described his frenzied attempts to go farther east along deserted dirt roads. Each one came to a dead end on the Wabash River. This, too, conformed with actual geography. At last, he said, he took a paved road, which appeared to lead to a bridge crossing, but instead veered south into another dirt road that wound only deeper into the woods. With no one in sight and the sun setting, he decided to stop near a pond to rape and then murder his passenger, who was bound in the van's cargo bay but starting to cry out. Again, Miller was able to pinpoint two adjoining roads in the buggy-whip shape Hall had described just two miles from the cornfield where the remains of Jessica Roach were finally found.

This was not the route that a cold, calculating killer would take. Instead, it was the panic-stricken, haphazard trail of a stranger who had no familiarity with the local terrain, which gave it all the more credence to Miller. As Hall freely admitted, he had been in George-town after the reenactment to scout out an old Dodge Charger listed in an *Auto Trader* classified ad. He stumbled on Jessica Roach by chance and had attacked her because she appeared so vulnerable while walking her bike down a lonely country road.

But to build a strong case against Hall, the government needed more evidence than his confession. To his chagrin, Miller now had to rely on others to pursue the investigation, starting with Wabash City Police Department detectives Phil Amones and Jeff Whitmer. They were the first to search Larry's room, just hours after his confession.

As Whitmer drove over to the Hall house with Amones, he says, "I was thinking, 'Oh, shit, is this really happening?' Larry was never someone I worried about." He could see that his partner, Amones, who had referred Hall to counseling after the stalking incidents, looked even more upset. It was one thing to be embarrassed because their instincts about Larry had been wrong. It was another thing if young women had died as a result.

Their stomachs took a second turn when a stunned Robert Hall let them into his home. Instantly they understood why Larry was so sensitive about the intrusion of strangers. "It was just a real mess," Whitmer says. "Stuff piled everywhere." Larry's room was no better than the rest of the house. As the detectives waded calf deep into the clutter, Whitmer remembers, "All we could do was move things around. At one point, Phil picked up a pile of stuff in the closet, and all of a sudden he jumped back and the eyes about popped out of his head. He's one of those flatliners who usually don't show much emotion, so I had to see what this was about, and there, on the closet floor, was a human skull. But when we looked closer, it was plastic. Some kind of gag gift. We both got a kick out of that. I don't remember finding anything else."

But Wabash police officers were still driven by the fear that a mass murderer had been operating under their noses. For those who knew Larry's family, their first thoughts went to the ghoulish backdrop of his upbringing—Falls Cemetery. After receiving permission from the cemetery association board, the police chief dispatched Whitmer on another grisly mission—this time to search the cemetery mausoleums for any sign that Hall had hidden his victims there. He remembers, "It was an eerie feeling to open up those crypts, and to be honest, it was kind of shocking to see how the people inside decomposed. But as far as we could tell, there was no double occupancy."

Although it seemed as if the nation's attention was on them, the Wabash City police didn't even have an official case against Hall other than for stalking. It was up to the FBI to lead the way, and it took three weeks after Hall's arrest before the Evidence Response Team from Washington, D.C., arrived in force. They were assisted by the Marion police, who were still contemplating charges in the Tricia Reitler case.

Together, they removed the piles of paper and clothes from Larry's room for off-site sifting. Earlier they had seized his two vans: the 1984 Dodge Ram and a more dilapidated 1980 Plymouth Voyager, which no longer ran, but was used for storage. It had been planted in the front yard for years before the police hauled it off to a local garage.

Since he drove the Dodge to work, Larry kept its front bucket seats and rear bench relatively clean, but the cargo bay was filled with boxes, old license plates, and piles of clothing. Trash rose to the windows of the Plymouth like water in a tub: car parts, two-by-fours, buckets of tools and bolts, plywood. On the surface, none of it appeared to incriminate Hall for more than slovenly pack-rat ways. There were no obvious weapons, bloodstains, or implements of restraint.

But upon further examination, chilling evidence did emerge— none of it forensic, as the crime-show cops would say, but some of it truly graphic: photographs of young women torn from pornographic magazines had been marked to show mutilation, strangulation, and stabbing. Teeth were blacked out and blood was drawn dripping from the mouth. On the bottom of one page, in pen, was written, "Jessica," with blood drawn dripping from the letters. Her name was also found in a 1993 U.S. Postal Service book of Christmas stamps. Less sensational but even more compelling were Indiana maps marked with dots, including one that indicated the spot where Jessica Roach's body was found and another where Gary Miller believed him to have murdered her. (Hall confirmed that the maps and marks were his when Randolph went to visit him in the Vermilion County jail.)

Other writing was found, too, notes tucked under the carpeting of the Dodge van and pulled from Larry's room. At first, the notes appeared to be no more than lists, but on closer inspection, they also contained fevered commands and obsessions that broke out like welts on the white scraps of paper. Pieced together, they comprised an instruction guide to serial rape and murder in central Indiana. If there was any question as to whether the notes were some sick charade or the modus operandi of a real killer, one of the few complete sentences among all the writing appears to give the answer: "I can't see the faces, but I can hear the screams."

While Larry sat in his Danville jail cell, back home the local newspapers reported on his community's stunned response to the charges against him. A neighbor who described herself as "in total shock" explained to one reporter, "He always struck me as being very quiet, kind of backward. . . . He always appeared shy, willing to help. . . . I feel sad for his parents."

It took those parents a day to respond to the press, but when they did, the Halls were vociferous in their son's defense. The headline for the interview blared, "Hall's parents talk of 'kind' son." His mother, Berniece, told reporters, "Any women he ever meets he treats with kindness. You can talk to any of his friends here in Wabash, and they'll all tell you he treats women with respect." She added that he had several girlfriends who would concur, although she did not name any. His father, Robert, chimed in, "We think he's an awful nice boy and he's not capable of this. We brought him up the way he was supposed to be brought up, and he turned out right."

To further prove her point, Berniece volunteered that Larry was an identical twin, as if to argue that he could not have committed such crimes without involving his brother. She added, "All Larry and Gary want to do is hunt arrowheads, collect coins, and do Civil War reenactments. Murder isn't in their book."

Those sentiments were echoed by the friends who knew them best, starting with next-door neighbor Bobby Allen, who had watched the twins grow from children to men. "They're not no violent people," he told a reporter. "I never seen Larry with a rifle, a BB gun, or even a slingshot. If he went hunting, it was for old beer cans."

Micheal Thompson, the fellow foot soldier in the Iron Brigade, had probably spent as much time with the brothers as any outsider during the many hours they traveled to Civil War reenactments. "To be honest," he remembers, "I thought if either one was guilty, it would be Gary. I couldn't imagine that Larry could be that aggressive with anyone."

Still, even in the first newspaper articles about his arrest, other information about Larry emerged that was at odds with the portrait of the gentle soul painted by friends and family. A reporter for the *Wabash Plain Dealer* found one woman who claimed that he had stalked her and a friend as they jogged in the early-morning hours a few months earlier. When she complained to the police, they told her that Hall had already been arrested for stalking on several occasions and one time needed a "letter of credibility" from his boss at the Credit Union to get released from jail.

But for most Wabash readers, more eye-opening than the stalking charges were the connections Hall had with the Tricia Reitler case in Marion. They would come to light in the same article that included the parents' defense of their son. (It also appeared on the day that Larry met with FBI agent Randolph to recant his confession.) As the newspaper reported, eight months earlier, a policeman from Gas City stopped him just two miles from where Tricia Reitler was last seen the year before—almost to the day. He was stalking teen girls just as he had in Georgetown on the anniversary of Jessica Roach's murder. But this time, the police caught him before he drove away from the area with "items" that supposedly implicated him in Reitler's abduction.

Hall's parents angrily dismissed the story. "If Gas City police don't retract what they said, someone's going to get a lawsuit," Robert Hall told a reporter. His son's van had been impounded after the traffic stop, Hall explained, but it was then returned. "I was with Larry when he went to get his van and nothing like that was in it."

As she did when Larry was younger, Berniece turned any charges against her son back on his accusers. "Gas City just did this for publicity," she said. "Gas City has picked on that kid."

But Gas City police were not about to retract anything. The chief replied, "I will verify everything in the report. I was at the scene where the van was stopped and saw the items. Marion police also were called to the scene and photographed the items."

For people in Wabash and Gas City, one question loomed over all of these revelations was, why had the Marion police done nothing further after the stop in Gas City? But in Marion itself the question had long since been answered. "Privately, [Marion] police say they don't believe Hall did it," *Marion Chronicle-Tribune* executive editor Alan Miller wrote shortly after Hall's extradition to Illinois. As summed up by the column headline, Miller was more concerned that the news would bring another "Agonizing day for the Reitlers," meaning Tricia's parents, Garry and Donna. In fact, the Marion police were immediately in touch with the Reitlers to downplay Larry's confession to Randolph and Miller. The *Chronicle-Tribune* quoted Donna saying, "[Hall] gave no more information than he could have gleaned from your newspaper. If he had given us something a little more concrete, then that would have been a possibility. I think it was a man seeking attention."

The Marion police felt they had a much more likely suspect in Tricia's abduction than Hall. Neither Larry's confession nor the developments in the Roach case could convince them that Hall was anything more than a "wannabe" serial killer.

But how would a *real* serial killer have behaved? Surprisingly, the Indiana detectives did not know, and most other police departments don't either.

Next to the mobster, if any type of criminal has won celebrity status in America's popular culture, it is the serial killer. *Psycho* and *Silence of the Lambs* are respectively the twenty-third and twenty-fourth most searched films in the Internet Movie Database, and since the silent era, more than one thousand movies have been devoted to the subject. A serial killer has been featured in hundreds of television shows, dozens of documentaries, and even has the starring role in one recent series. Amazon has more than twenty-two thousand books for sale that deal with serial killers, as well as two hundred comic books and graphic novels, including one series called *Psycho Killers,* which devotes each issue to an actual serial killer. In the words of criminologist Steven Egger, who has studied the phenomenon, serial murder has become "a growth industry."

Despite all the fascination with serial killers and the extensive coverage of their crimes and trials, Egger writes, "Law enforcement agencies today are simply not adept at identifying or apprehending the murderer who kills strangers and moves from jurisdiction to jurisdiction." As opposed to fictional villains such as Hannibal Lecter, Egger argues, the men who actually commit multiple homicides are not all that proficient at killing—the cops are just not very good at catching them.

The failings of local police aside, the general public is still confident that a higher authority in law enforcement, the FBI, will protect them against serial killers. Thanks to TV crime shows and such movies as *Silence of the Lambs,* this faith is buttressed by the belief that the Bureau has access to comprehensive databases of information and that oracular special agents—known as profilers—can sift through this data to predict the identity of potential predators with uncanny precision.

But in truth, there is no real clearinghouse for information about unsolved homicides or missing persons—with the FBI or any other federal agency. Although crime writers often refer to the FBI's Violent Criminal Apprehension Program (VICAP), it is limited to information voluntarily submitted by local police departments. HOLMES, the

United Kingdom's counterpart system, has proven much more effective because all levels of British law enforcement are forced to participate and provide uniform data. HOLMES also includes missing-person reports, which can be essential in identifying a serial-murder spree when the bodies of only a few victims have been found. In the United States, the friends and relatives of the missing must file notices with a hodgepodge of authorities to get their loved ones on lists that can vary by state, county, city, and, in the case of Pennsylvania, even by State Police troop.

As for the vaunted FBI profiles, these, too, have come under fire. In a *New Yorker* article titled "Dangerous Minds," Malcolm Gladwell quotes forensic scientists who have analyzed FBI profiles after the perpetrators had been caught and found them to be either wrong or too vague to be of any real use to investigators. According to criminologist Egger, any proactive role played by the FBI—in either the detection or prevention of serial murder—is a "myth" that is "carefully manipulated [by the FBI] through the media." Instead, he writes, "The identification of a serial murderer frequently occurs through happenstance or a fluke," as a result of "routine police work in response to a seemingly unrelated criminal event."

Larry Hall's arrest would certainly qualify as one of Egger's flukes. Had he not been tracked down by Gary Miller for stalking in Georgetown, there is no telling how much longer he would have been on the loose. But he had already been caught stalking—in another fluke—by the Gas City police and the Wabash City police before that. Egger writes that typically "police do not exchange investigative information on unsolved murders to police in different jurisdictions," a failing he labels as "linkage blindness." But in Hall's case, Gas City police immediately contacted Marion detectives, who then followed up with their colleagues on the Wabash City force. Although the Gas City police were convinced that they had caught Tricia Reitler's killer, both Marion and Wabash were just as convinced that Larry was "harmless."

Ironically, one of the items seized from Hall's van by Gas City police was a 1984 *Newsweek* article on serial killers. In it, a forensic psychiatrist comments on the nonthreatening appearance of most multiple murderers: "These aren't the people who are camped under freeways talking to themselves. Their overt sickness is a momentary thing—very episodic, very impulsive."

This clinical description of the serial killer's startling duality—so serene one moment, so savage the next—sounds much like the legend of the werewolf. Werewolves held a particular fascination for Larry Hall, who was known to draw them or cut out clips about them in prison. Stories of men who switch back and forth into wolves date back to Greek mythology, but according to *The Book of Were-Wolves* by the nineteenth-century folklorist Sabine Baring-Gould, werewolf tales became more prevalent in Europe during the Middle Ages after several notorious incidents of actual serial murder by deranged noblemen.

Like werewolf hunters in fairy tales, real-life detectives searching for serial killers must see through the hypernormal veneer that a serial killer displays to the outer world—what psychologist Joel Norris calls the "mask of sanity." Although it may be difficult to predict exactly who is committing a string of similar unsolved homicides, once a suspect is in hand, investigators can look at both his personal history and alleged criminal behavior to see how he compares with men previously convicted of serial murder.

Giving Hall that sort of evaluation in 1993 would have been like running uranium past a Geiger counter. Of the twenty-one psychosocial "patterns" identified by Norris in what he calls the "serial killer syndrome," Hall shares as many as *fourteen*. These include repeated efforts to confess and seek help, sleep disorders, issues with memory, placid "no-affect" appearance, low self-esteem, an alcoholic father, problems at birth, and the probable difficulties his older mother had during pregnancy.

Hall's out-of-body experiences and inability to distinguish dreams from reality, which the Marion police found so interesting—but not incriminating—are conditions common to serial killers. Norris describes these as "periods of blackout or gray-out in which the person experiences long periods of floating sensations." Citing the research of neuropsychologists, he attributes these episodes to "deep brain dysfunction," which may correlate with birth trauma or early childhood head injuries. During the acts of violence, he writes, "The person seems to meander in a semi-dream state, experiencing hallucinations or delusions as if he were a healthy person on the very edge of sleep."

For those who rape and murder, there is also a high incidence of a "smothering" overprotective mother, much like Berniece Hall. In many cases the son's intense feelings for her are complex. If he's a victim of maternal abuse, he may be obsessed with either killing his mother or women who remind him of her. But with men like Hall (who would call Berniece "darling" and "sweetie" when he talked with her on the phone each week from prison), the sentiments for their mothers are remarkably tender—especially considering the brutality they inflict on their female victims. If nothing else, the mother's dominance leads to "inadequate socialization," which may have contributed to Larry's extreme shyness and his failure to consummate a normal romantic relationship with a woman, yet another trait of serial rapist killers.

Even Hall's involvement with Civil War reenactment—what seemed like his healthiest outlet—would make criminologists suspicious. To assume Norris's "mask of sanity," serial killers often draw attention to themselves with a high-profile disguise. The most famous example is John Wayne Gacy, who killed thirty-three young men in Chicago while he won awards for his charitable activities performing as Pogo the Clown. When Ted Bundy went on a rape and murder spree that claimed more than thirty-five college coeds in the Pacific Northwest and Florida, he simultaneously volunteered to work on suicide hotlines, campaigned for local politicians, and even wrote a handbook on rape prevention. Creating a convincing alter ego is not a stretch for serial killers, Norris argues, because "they have spent a lifetime repressing the cancerous rage at the core of their personalities."

According to Norris, these extracurricular activities also serve as "camouflage" to help the killer find new victims—rootless young men for Gacy, and for Bundy, attractive young women who were also volunteers. With Hall, reenactments and the search for classic-car parts gave him a ready excuse to travel widely. "Many killers have extraordinarily high mileage on their cars," Norris writes, "and this can lead to their identification and arrest."

The proximity of victims to their killer is an essential part of the typical serial killer profile. The "megamobile" killer, such as Bundy, has victims spread across wide stretches of geography. The "megastat," such as Gacy, primarily kills close to home. But if Hall's confessions were to be believed and the actions preceding his arrest taken seriously, then he appears to have been an especially lethal mega-combination, with victims close to home and across the country. Whether a serial killer is "stat" or "mobile" may depend on his circumstances more than his desire.

With the far-flung destinations of Larry's leisure activities—and the virtually unsupervised nature of his job—he had the opportunity to be a menace both near and far. He also had the personal freedom necessary for the all-consuming double life of a serial killer. As Norris writes, because the serial killer's homicidal behavior "is a compelling urge that has been growing within him sometimes for years, he has completely amalgamated this practice into his lifestyle. It is as though he lives to kill, surviving from one murder to the next, stringing out his existence by connecting the deaths of his victims."

This compulsion to kill brings with it other telltale obsessive and compulsive activity—most tellingly for Hall, his need to return to the scene of his abductions and to collect or create items associated with them. Norris compares serial killers to "wild animals" because "they are fascinated with the remains of their crime. They visit the graves of their victims and attend their funerals." Even after the burial, he explains, the serial killer "likes to keep the crime alive in his memory by reading about the dead victim in the newspapers and even visiting the site where he first found his victim. When many murders have been committed at the same site, it is likely that the killer periodically returns there even when he has no victim to kill."

Hall's return to the scene of the crime one year after Jessica Roach's abduction was his ultimate undoing. As Gary Miller's investigation revealed, he did not just troll for girls near Georgetown, where he abducted Jessica Roach. On that same day he also pursued a young woman rollerblading alone in Indiana—one hundred yards from the cornfield where Jessica's body was found.

But when Hall was picked up in Gas City, it was not only his proximity to Tricia Reitler's college that made him so suspicious to the patrolman, or even what the police later described as "an abduction kit" in his van. It was all the paraphernalia he had collected that was connected to her disappearance. Again, this is in line with Norris's research, which shows that "serial killers are also compulsive record keepers. They maintain scrapbooks and organized memorabilia concerning the killings. . . . Among the items of memorabilia catalogued by the serial killers in our study were scrapbooks with press clippings of the murders [and] press clippings of other or similar serial killings." It is like a ballplayer who collects trading cards of other players, and this habit would explain why Hall hung on to the old issue of *Newsweek* with the long article about serial killers. Clearly his knowledge of them was as extensive as his knowledge of Civil War generals. On the bottom of one defaced magazine pinup, Hall had scrawled a name that mystified the FBI investigator, who read it as "Sam Hain." In fact, Hall meant "Samhain," the Celtic god of the dead misconstrued as a devil figure by serial killer David Berkowitz, who referred to himself as Son of Sam.*

While much identifies Hall as a serial killer to a savvy investigator, several aspects to both his personal history and criminal behavior are unique. Most obviously, no other documented serial killer has an identical twin. Second, he defies easy classification into the categories that criminologists use to distinguish different types of offenders who commit sexual violence. Beyond his tendencies to be both megastat and megamobile, he is also what FBI profilers would call both "disorganized" and "organized" in the way he commits his crimes. His impulsive decision to abduct Jessica Roach, his frantic efforts to take her across state lines, and finally his slipshod disposal of her body all suggest the profile of a *disorganized* offender.

But the notes on the scraps pulled from his car and room indicate something quite the opposite: a predator that stalks, pounces, and kills with the utmost care—the essence of *organized* behavior. Indeed, most of the women he confessed to killing have never been found, and for those that have, no physical evidence—no DNA, hair, fibers, or mud—has linked him to their rape or murder. If credit is due for this forensic feat, it goes to the author of these notes—no doubt Hall, but clearly a side of him that no one has heard before: an insistent, calculating inner voice that prods soft Larry into action. Properly assembled, the notes provide chilling insight into the young women he pursued and the methods he used to abduct them during the early nineties.†

Get one . . . Find one . . . Find one now . . .

The notes refer to his quarry in terms that don't define sex or even humanity. They are his "prospects," "joggers and bikers," "singles,"

---

*Although *Newsweek* briefly profiles Berkowitz in "The Random Killers," it does not mention Samhain, so Larry must have read about Son of Sam in other sources.
†Although these notes were entered into evidence, the FBI apparently made little effort to fully decipher them or arrange them in chronological order as is done here.

or "walkers." But sometimes he slips. "Seen many nice girls," he says of one location; in another note he reminds himself, "Take a lot of clothes, blankets—to keep her out of sight."

Get one around the southeast Grant.

He has his own shorthand, but it can be deciphered with only a passing knowledge of local geography. By "Grant," he means Grant County, just south of Wabash in the northeast quadrant of Indiana.

Maybe check Taylor areas, or Marsh at Hartford City.

Taylor University is a small Christian college in southeast Grant County, and the Marsh supermarket, in nearby Hartford City, is frequented by Taylor students.

Place to find one. Anderson College or Mounds Mall.

Anderson is another Christian college farther south, and the mall is another local student destination. Neither Taylor nor Anderson is a major university insulated by expansive campus grounds. Instead, they are small schools closely hemmed in by residential streets, industrial strips, and farmland. Students walking to class or dormitories are easily observed by outsiders who drive past on local roads and highways.

It's apparent from these notes that Larry Hall continually drove down from Wabash to circle in and around the Christian-college campuses, over and over. "Trolling or cruising activity associated with a search for a victim," Norris writes, is another part of the serial killer's compulsive behavior. "Like the relentless animal hunt for food."

Seen several singles walking, teen-age, few older, close to country . . . Seen joggers and bikers, many alone . . .

He is looking for "singles," or those who are alone and in areas that are sparsely populated—empty side streets, parks, and countryside. These are his "spots." The notes remind him to "check spots," and if he finds a prospect, to make sure that "zero people" are "closer."

Seen many police cars around Taylor [University]. Very risky.

If he is worried about the police, he is not just looking for "nice girls" to chat up or ask for a date. The Larry we hear in these notes may be aggressive, but he is exceedingly cautious, too. He checks for the presence of law enforcement and, just in case, plans for a quick getaway. So as not to raise suspicions and to cover his tracks, he replaces his own license plate with abandoned ones. The notes instruct him to find a plate for each of the counties he frequents. He must always remember "to look over E Plans. Three possible." These could be his "*Escape* Plans," because he charts routes away from his "spots" along country roads known by their scenic landmarks or just numbers.

Take 300 to 500 [Bradford Pike] *east into Jay Line to the old house* [where he and his parents used to live]. *Take out east wilderness to Jay. Most likely to safety.*

His directions repeatedly refer to the "Jay Line," his own name, perhaps, for the county's meridian road—as wide as a highway—that slices down south from Wabash, alongside the old Jonesboro train line, through two Christian-college towns and just a slight jog from a third. It is his pulsing glide path to action and then back home again to "safety."

Things to have done for trips . . .

On the surface some of those "things" don't seem necessarily harmful. For example, he writes, "Buy two more cans of SF." He probably means "starter fluid," an ether compound that can be sprayed into carburetors to turn over old engines, but it can also produce light-headedness or unconsciousness if sprayed into a rag that's placed over the mouth and nose. Other items on his lists proceed similarly from the quotidian to the queasy: "Buy new tarp to cover the whole rear, no exposed carpet, no remnants, no body contact, buy condoms, buy two more leather belts, take Buck knife, gloves, mask." Buck is a popular brand of hunting knife and creates a jarring juxtaposition to the condoms, gloves, and mask. It also makes you wonder what he intended to do with those belts. Elsewhere, he reminds himself to bring rope.

A theme throughout the notes is avoiding "contact": body-to-body contact and contact of a body with any surface in his van. He includes the following on one list of chores: "Buy two more plastic tarps, clean out van rear, put curtains back up in windows, furnace tape tarp [to] van, ready to haul, zero contact equal safe, silk sock to cover it, underwear, head cover, rear door plastic, bleach rear of his van." What does he intend to cover with the sock—a used condom? The silk, as opposed to some other fabric, would keep it from leaking. What is a "head cover"—something to cover a prospect's head? There is no question what he means by "zero contact equal safe." Next to another reminder about covering the rear of the van he adds, "No evidence. No forensic residues."

If his old friends had looked through all of Larry Hall's notes, none of the writing would have amazed them more than a poem found on a discarded piece of paper in his room. He was a poor student in school, even considered developmentally disabled by some teachers and acquaintances. But the voice in this piece is a sophisticated companion, who can be as wistful as he is calculating. He writes:

Now, I know it's hard, so hard sometimes
To leave the ones you love behind.
But I feel a calling from deep inside,
Sometimes so strong it's hard to hide.

I can feel the winds of change, my friend.
I feel them blowing through my mind.

And I know it's time for me, my friend,
To be moving on down the line.

In early 1993, weeks before the abduction of Tricia Reitler, the "winds of change" were blowing Larry to the streets surrounding Indiana Wesleyan University in Marion. Like Anderson and Taylor, IWU is another small Christian college shoehorned in among local residents and commercial strips. A large factory assembly plant is just a block away from the campus in one direction, farm fields a block away in the other. Here, too, a Marsh supermarket is a few blocks from the dormitories, and this is where Larry reminds himself in the notes that he has "seen many nice girls."

He loops in and out of the nearby streets, around and around, over and over, monitoring the movement of students in the afternoon and evening. One long stretch of the road leading to the supermarket is deserted by the end of the day. The early-evening walkers are especially important to him because he has decided that this is when he should strike: "to let the time [be] near dark," he writes, with enough light to still give his prospects a false sense of security while the curtain of darkness relentlessly falls.

Ready end of February? Plan and plan. Check over again.

For anyone familiar with the research, these notes are very much in keeping with the behavior of serial killers. But for anyone familiar with Larry, they are strangely at odds with virtually everything friends knew about his personality. The commands are as blunt and bold as those from a drill sergeant. They have a confidence and even a cockiness that the shy individual had never shown in any other pursuit.

This curious contradiction in character was of no concern to the

FBI evidence technicians. Even on the surface, the material pulled from his vans contained incriminating information about Hall's involvement with Roach and Reitler as well as several other unsolved crimes, including young women still listed as missing. Some of the evidence was as explicit as a bottle of birth control pills with the victim's name on it found in the piles of clothes. Within days after Hall's extradition to Illinois, an FBI spokesman told the press that a "multijurisdictional group of detectives" were investigating Hall for his connection to the Roach case. Two weeks later, the same group was now looking at other cases "across the country." By the end of December, a federal grand jury in Illinois indicted Hall for the abduction of Jessica Roach, but word kept leaking out about his association with yet more victims, which finally reached a crescendo with the January 21, 1995, headline from the Associated Press: "Report: Hall linked to 20 murders."

Although that list has never been completely released to the public, it was known to include at least three areas where there were clusters of women suspected killed or reported missing. Two clusters were in Indiana. By the state line with Illinois, besides Jessica Roach, a year earlier Holly Ann Anderson had been found three miles away, stabbed to death in a drainage ditch. Two miles from where Tricia Reitler was last seen on campus, Wendy Felton had disappeared from her family's farmhouse in 1987. The third cluster was in central Wisconsin, near a historic mansion that hosted a Civil War reenactment each summer. In July 1990, Berit Beck was abducted in Appleton and then found strangled to death in a drainage ditch six weeks later. In August 1992, Laurie Depies was seized from a parking lot in Menasha, leaving behind a cup of soda on the roof of her car. Her body was never found. They were pretty young women under the age of twenty with striking physical similarities—almost all had brown, shoulder-length hair and short, athletic builds.

Looking back on those heady days, Deputy Sheriff Gary Miller is still amazed at how he took a minor stalking report out of little Georgetown and touched off such a massive nationwide investigation. He is even more amazed at where it all led. "A lot of people ended up believing I was the crazy one," he says, "and they still believe that to this day."

7

America's Most Wanted

JIMMY KEENE MAY TECHNICALLY HAVE BEEN in the Spring-field MCFP, but after meeting the Oddfather, he was also confined to Vincent Gigante's jail, and the mob boss enforced a strict regime. The next day, he expected Keene to join him almost as soon as the dining hall opened. "The mob had their own table," Keene remembers, "and Gigante would be there first thing with his guys." These breakfast companions seemed fairly normal compared to the Baby Killers, if a little bulked up. As Jimmy learned later, they had not been assigned to Springfield because of medical or mental issues but to staff the kitchen, laundry, and maintenance crews. They were all still deeply involved with the Mafia. From what Keene could hear, the old man used snatches of code words to issue commands that were relayed back home.

As he ate breakfast, Jimmy couldn't help but sneak a glance at Larry's table. "He kept looking over at me. I think he had liked having breakfast with me, and it really hurt him to see that I was now with Gigante. That really pissed me off."

For his part, the old mob boss wolfed down his food. "Hey, kid," he said between mouthfuls. "You good at boccie?"

Keene shook his head. He had never even heard of it.

Once again, Jimmy had amazed Gigante. "You *gotta* be kidding me," he sputtered. "C'mon and I'll teach you to play."

After breakfast, they went outside to the prison yard, where a long rectangular court stretched out by the baseball diamond's left-field line. It had gravel squares on each side with grass in between that was manicured like a putting green. Keene had seen similar layouts at other prisons, but never knew their purpose. As he watched Gigante expertly bowl the hard, colored wooden balls toward a smaller target ball on the green, he instantly understood why the game was so popular with aging mafiosi. It took minimal physical effort, but required cunning and ruthlessness as you knocked your opponents' balls off the court.

"It didn't matter how cold it was," Jimmy says. "Gigante was always out there playing. Although he was old and hunched over, he was still exceptionally good. It took a while before I could beat him." Since Keene's allergies exempted him from a prison day job and the Oddfather had his own medical pass for a heart condition, Gigante expected Jimmy to be his morning boccie buddy until the others got out of work. On those rare occasions when it rained or snowed, they would sit together and watch *Jerry Springer* instead.

Whatever they did, Gigante did most of the talking. He was practically a generation older than Calabrese Sr., but also a more genteel breed of mob boss. While Calabrese still seemed obsessed by his brutal business, Gigante dwelled instead on his huge extended family: kids, nephews, grandchildren, his brother the priest—the life they had in Manhattan and especially the food they ate. Sometimes Jimmy didn't know what Italian delicacy Gigante was talking about—this was not the cuisine served by his grandmother or the mobsters in Cicero— and the old man would give him another exasperated "Ya gotta be kidding me. You never had *prosciutto*?" He always punctuated his culinary memories by adding, "And look at the slop we got to eat in this place."

One freezing morning in October while they were alone outside on the boccie court, Gigante cocked his head up at a wing of a building where hospital patients stayed. "You know they brought Johnny Gotti in here today. He's right up there in that window."

Gotti—the Dapper Don—was the one New York mobster Jimmy knew about and, in those days, was probably the most famous mafioso of them all. Keene couldn't help but look skeptical, which infuriated the old man. He sidled closer to the window, made some quick whistles with two fingers, and yelled, "Hey, Johnny! Johnny!"

Keene peered up at the window, he says, "And all of a sudden there he was—John Gotti; standing right there on the second floor, wearing the same khaki shirt as the rest of us, but thinner and paler than he looked in the newspapers. They started talking to each other using some kind of code language with their hands. Then they waved good-bye."

Gigante turned and punched Jimmy in the arm. "See?" he said triumphantly. "And you didn't believe me, did you? I knew he was here the moment he arrived. They're doing that thing on his throat."

As Keene later learned, "that thing" was surgery for cancer, which would eventually kill Gotti. What Jimmy never knew was that the Dapper Don and the Oddfather were blood rivals back in New York (the government even charged Gigante with plotting to kill Gotti). To look at the old man on the boccie court, Keene would have thought that they were once the best of friends. Gigante's eyes misted up and he gave another nod toward the window. "Look at how they've crushed us," he said, referring to the hated Feds. "Now we're all in here together. Even a guy like you! You're no crazy psycho killer. But you could be here another fifty years if they had their way."

Keene nodded sympathetically, but inside he was thinking, "Not if I can help it." He had now been in Springfield for nearly two months, and his freedom was as close as Larry Hall, but mornings with the Oddfather were not helping him get out any sooner. Keene was desperate to find time alone with Hall. For a while, all he could do was lag behind in the dining hall after breakfast as the old man made his way to the boccie court with his crew. Once the mobsters were out of sight, Jimmy grabbed a tray and joined Hall at his table, but Larry was clearly bent out of shape by the new seating arrangements. Besides, they never had more than five or ten minutes together before Hall had to get up and leave.

When Keene could break away from Gigante, he tried to shadow Hall during the day to find any other opportunities to meet him outside of the library. But if Larry had any spare time, he tended to spend it in the wood shop, where Jimmy was not yet allowed. Keene was mystified by what attracted him there. Watching Hall from the doorway, it appeared that he was always working on the same project—a small wooden bird that looked like a falcon.

Finally, Larry again provided an unexpected opening. One day as Jimmy was jumping up from his second breakfast with Hall to join Gigante outside, he said, "Larry, I'll see you later at the library."

"You know, James," Hall replied, "if you want, you can start meeting me and my friends in the little TV room on Saturday nights where we watch *America's Most Wanted*."

Keene nodded and tried not to look too enthusiastic, but he was bubbling inside. "As crazy as it sounds," he says, "that show was the luckiest thing that ever happened to me."

If Hall had not invited him first, Keene would never have thought to look for him in that room. It was hardly bigger than a cell with just a few dozen chairs crammed inside. A TV with a screen the size of an old-fashioned portable's was bolted to a metal cart by the door. Although it blared during the day, Keene did not think that anyone bothered to watch it at night since two much larger areas had bigger-screen TVs—one was controlled by the black inmates and the other by the whites. But none of the "programmers" for those rooms liked to watch *America's Most Wanted*. Larry and his friends had to make do with this tiny TV.

Hall and the three other "Baby Killers" usually sat in the middle of the room a few rows from the front. A smattering of other inmates were scattered around the remaining chairs. The first night he joined them, Keene sat right next to Larry, but if he thought there would be any time to chat, he was mistaken. "Once the show came on," he says, "it was like Larry was in his own little world. That screen was all he could see. When he got up to leave, I don't think we said any more to each other than we did at the library."

Keene still forced himself to show up the next week. He nearly fell out of his chair after the credits rolled and he saw the topic of the week—serial killers. It was the first in a series of four hour-long shows. Hall had never talked about why he was in prison to Jimmy, and Keene could not act as though he knew. For the first part of the show, Jimmy stared straight ahead at the screen and looked at Hall out of the corner of his eye. "Larry was absolutely mesmerized," he says. "And all the time I'm thinking, 'How can I use this stuff to get him to open up without scaring him?'"

That moment seemed to come near the end of the episode when the parents of a missing victim—like the Reitlers—pleaded for the killer to tell them where he'd buried their daughter. At the next commercial break Jimmy decided to make his move. "You know, if I was the guy that killed them girls," he said, "I'd just tell everybody where l left them."

Hall, his eyes wide, turned from the TV screen to Jimmy. "You would?"

"Why not give the families some kind of closure?" Keene replied. "Let the parents give their daughter a proper burial and ease their

pain. It's not like I'm ever getting out of prison." Jimmy then remembered the cross on Hall's wall and that he went to church most Sunday mornings. "At least this way I'd find some kind of peace with
God and try and redeem myself."

Hall nodded, but turned his head back to the screen.

Keene figured he would not push too hard. They had three more
shows to watch, which were sure to give them opportunities for
more discussion. When Keene arrived the next Saturday, he found
the same sparse audience—the Baby Killers and a handful of other
inmates. But just ten minutes into the program, a muscular black
prisoner barreled into the room. Keene instantly recognized him.
"He was the kind of belligerent guy who was always getting into
fights over stupid things. They probably threw him out of the black
TV room. When he came in and took a look at us, he decided we
weren't going to watch our show either."

Without a word of explanation he clicked the television off, then,
in a huff, sat down in the chair directly in front of it. Keene heard
Hall mumble under his breath, "That ain't cool. We were watching
that show," but he and the others remained motionless, staring at the
blank screen. Keene says, "I realized that this was my opportunity to
show Larry I could be his buddy and even his protector in that place."

Jimmy jumped up, pushed through the chairs to the television, and
turned it back on. Then the black inmate was on his feet and clicked it
off again, saying, "White boy, you better not touch it or you'll have
a problem."

Keene looked him straight in the eye, reached over to the set, and
clicked it on. As soon as the intruder pulled back to swing, Jimmy
nailed him with four quick punches to the face. When he sprawled
back over the chairs, Keene jumped on top of him, stomping his head
and chest. He still hadn't finished when the alarm sounded and a
squad of guards bull-rushed into the room, sending stackable chairs

flying in all directions. They threw Keene up against one wall and his opponent against another. After they shook Keene down for weapons, they put him in cuffs and shoved him out of the room.

They marched him down into the tunnel, past the stairs he would take to the dining hall, then much farther than he had ever been allowed to go on his own, until they reached the double gates of the infamous 10 Building—where they kept the most unmanageable psychiatric prisoners—and, in the farthest wing, the hole. The guards opened a metal door, removed his cuffs, and shoved him inside. "Their hole," Keene says, "is a dark, nasty cement box with no window and just a toilet and a metal slab for a bed. In Springfield, they actually had moisture seeping out of the walls, like a dungeon in the old movies."

He stayed up pacing through the night, wondering if he had overplayed his hand by getting into a fight. The FBI agents and chief psychiatrist had specifically warned him against doing that. In this case, it would be hard to prove he acted in self-defense. The other man in the fight didn't land a punch, but still got hammered pretty badly by Keene.

Shortly after dawn, the flap on the lower opening of his door was lifted up and his breakfast tray shoved through. On the other side of the door he heard a guard bark, "James, the hearing on your assault is at nine. We'll come by and get you, so be ready."

Keene was happy that it came so quickly, but then, he says, "I started to get real paranoid. If an assault went on my jacket [or file folder], and if I didn't get anywhere with Hall, they could send me back to Milan having to do more time and not less."

For the hearing, Jimmy was outfitted with shackles and a harness belt to go with his cuffs, then seated in front of a panel of six men and women in business attire. Before the panel asked Keene for his side of the story, a correctional officer presented them with the results of his investigation. "Lucky for me," Jimmy says, "all of them serial killers stuck up for me and said the other guy started the whole thing." The panel released Keene from the hole the following day with no further mention about the incident on his record.

The next time Keene saw the chief psychiatrist, he told Jimmy that he was aware of the fight. "I won't let anything negative get put in your jacket," he said, "but if this happens again, they'll look at you like any other inmate who keeps getting in fights, and they're going to be totally against you. I don't know how long they'll keep you in the hole before they let you out."

But despite the potential long-term risk, Keene found that the battle for *America's Most Wanted* won him major gratitude from Larry and his friends. Absolutely no one had ever stood up for them before. The dividends paid out the following Saturday night when, for the first time, Hall invited Jimmy back to his cell after the TV show was over.

For any visitor from outside the prison, Larry's living space would not have seemed like much, but in those tiny confines, Jimmy saw trappings that only came with longevity and privilege. He was most impressed by Hall's atmospheric lighting. "One of the most depressing things about prison is how bright they make it in your cell—like you're a piece of meat in a display case. But Hall had a dimmer bulb for one light and had the other one turned off completely. That really made things much more comfortable; very homey and lived-in." To complement the soft lighting, Larry muffled the legs of his chair with tennis balls that had been sliced in half, so he could push back and forth while seated without the same screech everyone else experienced.

Hall also had more displayed on his walls than the typical prisoner, most notably the cross. Such displays of spiritual devotion were only allowed by the chaplain if they were backed up by active churchgoing. On closer inspection, Keene could see the cross was made of hand-decorated construction paper—probably because a real crucifix of that size could have been used as a weapon. The pictures on display were mostly of family members: the identical twin, Gary, who looked nothing like Larry, and a hunched-over elderly couple, who Jimmy was surprised to learn were his parents. They appeared old enough to be his grandparents. If Hall spoke of anyone in his family, it was his twin. "My brother would do anything for me and I would do anything for him," Larry told Keene. "If he could, he would switch places with me."

Keene also noticed the piles of magazines and stacks of books on Hall's shelves, more reading material than he had ever before seen in one man's cell. The goggles and gloves Hall needed for his various janitorial jobs hung from special hooks, and his closet was filled from one side to the other with neatly hung clothes. In comparison, Keene says, "My place looked pretty barren."

More than anything, Hall's cell permitted them to have the sort of discussion they couldn't have anywhere else in the prison. Usually Keene sat in the chair while Larry leaned back on his bunk. Conversation came easier for Hall if it dealt with any of his passions, such as the Civil War, Indian lore, or vintage cars. "I know his lawyer made him out to be a borderline retard," Keene says, "but he was not dumb. Not at all. There were things he discussed in history that I really didn't have a clue about. But there were more things where he was totally ignorant. He just wasn't what you would call a well-rounded person."

Despite the breakthrough he had made, Keene would not report it to Butkus or the chief psychiatrist—afraid that they would think he was moving too fast. He could only confide in Big Jim, and that had its own drawbacks. Despite some lingering shakiness from the stroke, his father could not stay away from his son for long. Although everyone back home tried to talk him out of it, he drove eight hours to Springfield so he could make at least one personal visit with Jimmy and see the Medical Center for himself. Meanwhile, they continued to talk every day, but just once and usually at night. Knowing their calls could be monitored, Jimmy tried to say just enough to let Big Jim know he was making progress. "I'm finally gaining grounds on this situation," he told him one night.

But his worried father quickly scolded him, "I hope you're not talking to this guy yet. Remember what Beaumont said. Son, you're not supposed to be talking to this guy yet."

Keene shot back, "I'm not supposed to be talking to you about this either. I just want you to know things are moving in the right direction."

After a pause, Big Jim asked, "So are you really talking to this guy?"

"Dad, please. We can't talk about it."

"Well, I'm not the one talking about it," Big Jim shot back. "You're the one talking about it."

Although Jimmy had moved faster than anyone thought he could in gaining Hall's trust, he was not going to blow it now. He would take as much time as necessary for Larry to confide in him. Mostly Keene talked about normal life on the outside the way he did at the breakfast table. If he was to bring up anything about Hall's crimes, it would have to be prompted by something Larry said first. "Since he was the one who asked me to watch *America's Most Wanted* with him, I felt I could talk to him about the serial killers and not make him suspicious." As they sat under the cross in Hall's cell, Keene says, "I tried to play the religion card. I'd say, 'That guy on the show's done what he's done, but he can still be redeemed.' And then Larry would ask, 'Do you believe that somebody could be redeemed for that?' And then I'd quote him something that I remembered from Scripture, like, 'Let the wicked man forsake his ways, and return unto the Lord, and He will have mercy upon him.'"

But Hall would just nod in response and the conversations would go no further. If anything, the Bible talk would shut him down more than it opened him up, and Keene wondered whether religion had become another hiding place for Hall instead of a way to cleanse his soul.

Besides, the biggest problem in Hall's life was not the spirit, but the flesh. "Larry had so many mixed and conflicting emotions about women, it wasn't even funny," Keene says. The mere suggestion that his magazines were porn sent him into paroxysms of head-spinning giggles. "If I said anything about naked women, he would go all weird—like a kid who just hit puberty. This was obviously a guy who had never had consensual sex with a girl in his life."

In trying to get inside Larry's head, Keene thought back to a friend in high school. "He was a little outcast guy himself and every-body used to mess with him, until I took him under my wing and forbid anybody from touching him. It's not that he was a screwup. In fact, he was pretty smart, and he could be very funny. And he wasn't really that much of a nerd either. Instead, all of his problems revolved around girls and how awkward he was with them. Like we used to say, he was one of those guys who couldn't get laid if he had a hun-dred dollars in a whorehouse. There was truly nothing he could do to make girls like him or even talk to him. Some would go out of their way to mistreat him, and I could understand how he came to hate them. So I started to think it was the same way with Larry. I tried to feel his pain."

With this in mind, Keene began what he called his "girl bash-ing." If in a conversation he mentioned an old girlfriend, he would add how badly things turned out with her. "You know," he told Hall, "I can understand where a guy could be pushed to the edge with a girl." A few days later he added, "There are girls out there who use you for money, shit all over you, and then run off with your best friend."

Each time he said these things, he could see lights go off in Hall's eyes. "It was like pushing buttons on a robot." Finally, one night Larry did some bashing of his own: "Ever since I've been a young boy, girls have rejected me. I'd try to be nice to them, James. I really would. But they always treated me like shit."

None of these slights ever rolled off his back. He would go on and on about a girl who would not respond after he said hello, another he thought had laughed at him, or a cousin who had complained to her parents that he looked at her the wrong way.

Even as Hall felt free to reveal his inner misogyny to Keene, he came nowhere close to discussing what he had done to women in return or even admitting why he was in prison. "He would just out and out lie to me," Keene says. "He tried to tell me that he was a weapons runner—just like I was supposed to be. And you only had to talk to him for a minute before you realized that he didn't know anything about guns. He didn't even admit that he had a life sentence. He would tell me that he was in for forty years, which doesn't seem like a big difference on the outside but is night and day from a life sentence for a convict."

Keene now spent his mornings with Gigante stamping out the damp autumn cold on the boccie court. He had hoped to be home for Christmas with Big Jim, but as he got deeper into October, that seemed impossible. If anything, Jimmy says, "I could feel the walls were closing in on me."

While the Feds had preached patience, two incidents convinced him that the longer he stayed in Springfield, the more he would be in danger. The first was a fight. Like the one he had had with the alphabet gang in Milan, this scrap was totally senseless and as unexpected as a flash of lightning. Once again, it all started innocently enough. In the never-ending bazaar of prison barter, Keene had gotten a pair of wraparound Koss headphones from a six-foot-eight-inch biker. Supposedly, he had killed several people in Iowa while high on crystal meth. He had the same lanky, muscular build that Clint Eastwood had in his prime, with funky spiderweb tattoos around both elbows. His pockmarked, beet-red face looked as if it had been dragged over concrete. "The headphones were cool," Jimmy says, "but like everything else that you get in prison, they were a piece of shit." In exchange, Keene only had to buy the biker $10 of requested merchandise from the commissary.

No matter their cost, the headphones still brought admiring looks from other inmates—especially a long-haired hippie who fancied himself the prison's go-to guy for "imported" paraphernalia, like Morgan Freeman's character in *Shawshank Redemption*. Jimmy readily told him where he had gotten the headphones since the hippie appeared to be friendly with the biker.

But later that day, when Keene returned to his cell, the biker was waiting for him inside, practically blocking out one of the lights with his towering height. He poked Jimmy's chest with fingers that felt like lead pipes. "Why's my name coming out of your mouth?" he screamed, eyes blazing and flecks of spit flying from his lips.

Keene was shocked. "What are you talking about, man?"

The biker poked him again. "You told somebody about my business, about them headphones, and I want to know, why's my name coming out of your mouth?"

"Look, dude, you're getting way overirate about this. That guy's your friend." But this time, when the biker went to poke him, Keene slapped his hand away.

"My name never comes out of your mouth or I'll fucking rip your fucking head off."

There was no calming the biker down. "His face scrunched up and kept getting redder," Jimmy remembers. "Maybe it was the drugs he was on, but I figured that he was going to beat me up to make me an example."

When the biker next went to poke him, Keene caught his hand, twisted it, and shoved him across the cell. When the biker threw himself back at Jimmy, swinging wildly, Keene's wrestling instincts kicked in. He shot down for the biker's spindly legs and lifted him up.

"All of his power was above his waist, so once I had him in the air, he was like a rag doll." Keene then slammed him down hard on his back and kept pounding him with both fists until the guards came crashing into the cell. "This time," Jimmy says, "the guards were really rough on me. First they maced me and then they pushed me in the corner and hit me all over with their sticks. They knew about my other fight, even though it wasn't on my jacket." Keene was clearly becoming a problem for the correctional officers, and they were going to inflict their own punishment irrespective of the hearing panel's decision.

Keene spent another night pacing in the hole, wondering if he had blown everything by participating in such a senseless fight. When he was brought to the hearing, he was surprised to see the chief psychiatrist sitting on the panel, but he never said a word during the entire session. Although the circumstances were certainly in Jimmy's favor—"The clown was waiting for me in my cell," he testified—Keene did not like the weary looks of those who had been in his other hearing. He was quickly developing the "assaultive" reputation that the chief psychiatrist had warned him about.

Ironically, the biker came to his rescue. "When they brought him in," Jimmy says, "he was totally hard-core and wouldn't answer a single question they asked. Because of that, they had to find him at fault. For punishment they threw him in the hole for a good long time." When he got out, the biker confronted Keene in the TV room, but this time he stuck out his gargantuan fingers to shake hands and not poke him. "We ain't got no problems anymore, do we?"

Jimmy shook his hand, but neither had any intention of being friends. "The only reason he shook my hand," Keene explains, "is because he was the only one who knew how bad I beat his ass. If I did it again, his big-bad-biker rep would go downhill really fast." Even though the biker wouldn't again be a threat, Jimmy realized that the clock was ticking before some other nutcase touched off a fight.

But then someone appeared who would scare Keene far more than a six-foot-eight biker. He was eating breakfast with Gigante when he heard a shout from across the dining room: "Hey, Jimmy. Jimmy Keene."

It was Malcolm Shade, the pudgy, little identity thief who had been Keene's cellmate at the Chicago MCC lockup. He rushed over to Keene's table, clapped him on the shoulder, pumped his hand, and said, "How's it going, man? This is the last place I expected to see you." The only reason the BOP had sent Shade to Springfield was to stabilize a kidney disease.

"At first," Keene recalls, "I was happy to see him, too. He could be a fun guy to hang out with, but immediately, right in front of the mob guys, he asked, 'So how is that big drug conspiracy case of yours going?'

"He said it loud enough for everyone to hear. I turned my head and could see Chin and all of his guys looking at me. As far as they knew, I was in prison on weapons charges, so what the fuck is this guy talking about?"

Keene jumped to his feet, grabbed Shade by the arm, and pulled him to the side. "What are you doing?" he hissed. "You can't just walk up and talk about my case in front of a bunch of strangers."

Shade threw his head back as if he'd been slapped. "Whoa, whoa, whoa, Jimmy. I didn't mean any harm. I just wondered what was going on with you."

Keene then returned to the table and laughed Shade off to the mob guys, but they stared at him with quizzical looks. If they knew he was lying about his case, they would immediately suspect he was there to inform on them—another reason for him to get Gigante's knife in the back.

No matter how often Jimmy scolded him, Shade couldn't shut up about Keene's drug case. They used to talk about it so much when they were in the MCC, he wanted to know how Jimmy made it go away, and usually he'd ask when a mob guy was within earshot. Because he was black, Shade would not be embraced by the Italians the way Jimmy was, but Malcolm had more in common with the mobsters than he did with the gangbangers who made up the bulk of Springfield's African-American population. Keene feared that in time Malcolm would become friendly with someone in the crew and spill everything he knew about Keene's life as a drug dealer.

Between Shade and the unpredictable nature of the other inmates, Keene felt he could no longer sit around and let Larry decide when he would confess to his crimes. Jimmy needed some other way to force the issue. He thought he found it one night in Hall's cell when he pointed to a big manila envelope. "It's from my lawyer, Mr. DeArmond," Hall said. "It's about my appeal."

This was the perfect opportunity to start asking about his case, even to discuss the basis for his appeal. Among other things, Keene remembered from Beaumont's briefing it regarded expert testimony as to whether Hall's confession had been coerced by the police. But Larry would not go into details. Instead, he kept looking at the envelope and his eyes welled up. Then he said, "You know, he won my last appeal."

Keene did know that to be true. He also knew how much the appellate court's decision annoyed Beaumont. Hall continued, "And he'll win this appeal, too."

Jimmy had heard that one before. It seemed as if everyone in prison with a pending appeal believed he would win it—even Frank Cihak, Keene's library coworker in Milan, and Gigante, hardened old-timers who should have known better. "That appeal was their last hope," Keene explains. "And once they had finally lost all their appeals, it was like their lives were over."

But seeing how Hall had gotten all teary at the mention of his appeal and his lawyer, Keene suddenly realized that Larry truly believed he *would* win it. And he believed with a fervor that was different from that of all the other convicts.

"If Larry had religion," Jimmy says, "it had nothing to do with the cross on his wall. His lawyer, Mr. DeArmond, was his God. Larry believed he was going to save him. And if he really did believe that he was getting out, why would he ever admit to me what he had done?"

8.

Innocence

THROUGH MOST OF GARY MILLER'S CAREER as a deputy sheriff
in Vermilion County, Craig DeArmond had been a familiar presence
behind the prosecutor's table, first as an assistant state's attorney and
then, for eight years, as the state's attorney. Tall and distinguished
looking, he had a Lincolnesque profile and a deep, deliberate voice.
As a frequent witness for the prosecution in criminal cases, Miller had
watched him in action many times. "I'd say DeArmond was a hell of
a lawyer," the deputy sheriff says. "Probably one of the best trial lawyers in the area."

Over the years of working together, the two became friendly, if
not necessarily close friends—even after DeArmond opened a private
practice and, as Miller puts it, "went to work for the other side." Still,
the deputy sheriff never expected, by any stretch of the imagination,
that he would be facing off against the former state's attorney in the
most important case of their respective careers. But this was to be
one more consequence of bringing federal charges against Larry Hall.
Since the Central District of Illinois then had no federal defender's

office, U.S. judge Harold Baker had to tap a local private attorney to represent the indigent Hall, and given the considerable challenges of the high-profile case, he chose the most qualified candidate.

If anyone on the government's side expected DeArmond to go through the motions with Hall, they were sadly mistaken. Instead, he mounted a ferocious defense, enthusiastically joined by the defendant, his family, and their friends back in Wabash. Emboldened by his attorney, Larry reached out to the press from his Danville jail cell in February 1995. "Hall: FBI framing me" was the headline for one article, which quoted Larry saying, "I did not kill or kidnap Jessica Roach or any other girl. Unfortunately the truth will come out as another helpless girl comes out missing. And the real killer is still free to choose among the innocent people of this whole area."

Hall also complained that the extensive press coverage—with FBI spokesmen citing steadily increasing numbers of his putative victims— would discourage any future jury from believing him. "It's come to the point where I'm completely snowed under by the FBI's reports and stuff," he said. "And I feel I'm not going to have a chance." Later he added, "I'm just basically a helpless individual. I've just been totally taken advantage of by the FBI."

Between Hall's remarks to reporters and motions filed by DeArmond, the contours of Hall's defense strategy had already come into shape. First was to discredit—or ideally discard—Hall's confession statement because, as DeArmond argued to the court, it was "improperly coerced." Second was to establish an alibi. Hall claimed to reporters that "many witnesses," principally his twin brother, Gary, would testify to seeing him at an Indiana reenactment far from Georgetown on the day of Jessica Roach's abduction.

Miller had no doubt who really orchestrated the interviews. "DeArmond," he says, "uses the media perfectly." But despite his respect for Hall's counsel, Miller had no regrets about his role in making

Jessica Roach's abduction a federal case. "I still say that it was the best decision I could have possibly made, because we got Larry Beaumont as our prosecutor, and he was exactly what we needed."

Miller first got to know Beaumont after the new federal court was built near Miller's office in the sheriff's department. "He kept locking his keys in the car and calling over to see if we had a slim-jim to get the door open," Miller says, laughing. As he would later learn, the forgotten keys were not the sign of an absent mind, but one working overtime. "He was the sort of prosecutor who left no stone unturned," Miller says. "And I mean not one stone."

Such would be the case with all the evidence submitted by the defense. For example, to help bolster Hall's alibi, DeArmond turned up a receipt for a transaction on the day Jessica Roach disappeared. It came from Helfin's Sheet Metals, the auto supply store in Wabash that Larry and his friends would cruise their street rods around. Besides displaying Larry's full name as the recipient of the service and the date of the transaction, the slip also provided the time of the transaction—5:30 p.m. That would have made it impossible for Larry to abduct Jessica Roach during the afternoon in Illinois and then drive 150 miles in time to pay Helfin that evening. "When Larry [Beaumont] showed me that receipt," Miller says, "I told him that there's got to be something wrong here, and he said, 'You bet there's something wrong with this.' The typical prosecutor would have told me to look into it, but Larry Beaumont went to Wabash with me, and we both met with Mr. Helfin. Beaumont let him know that we'd have to examine that receipt closely and ask him to testify under oath about it. After a while, he said, 'Okay, wait a minute. I did a guy a favor. [Larry Hall's father, Robert] came in here and asked me to make this receipt and then an hour later came back and had me add the time, too.'" As a result, the time was on the slip that Robert Hall took with him, but not on Helfin's carbon copy.

Beaumont was now able to flip the defense evidence into powerful ammunition for the government's case. On rebuttal he could call in

Helfin to testify about Robert's request for him to create the receipt. That sort of testimony usually had a big impact on a jury—innocent men should not have to rely on such concoctions. Of course, Beaumont could also have brought charges against old man Hall for fabricating the evidence and tampering with a witness, but Miller says that they never had any intention of doing so. "We figured he was just desperate to help his son. There are probably a lot of fathers out there who would do that."

As the Hall family went around town enlisting witnesses to support Larry's alibi, they contacted Ross Davis, the twins' friend from childhood. He had rented some space in his barn for Larry to store two vintage cars. On occasion, after Larry was done working on them, Ross and his wife would invite him to drop by for something to eat. Now Larry was telling his lawyer that one of those dinners occurred on the night he was accused of abducting Jessica Roach. Ross did have him over that week, but a few nights later. He could pinpoint the exact date because they had looked at some car parts that had just arrived and Davis still had the delivery slip.

Of course, this was not the corroboration that Larry's family and lawyer wanted. Gary Hall asked if he could visit Davis's home with DeArmond. "He was pretty impressive," Ross says of the defense lawyer. "He told me how he had been a prosecutor himself, and then he started talking about the investigators on Larry's case, and he said, 'I know these guys and they put several people in prison for crimes they didn't commit. Now they're on a head hunt for Larry to blame him for a lot of unsolved cases. They're going to put him away if you don't help.'

"I don't think he wanted me to change my testimony or anything," Davis says of DeArmond. "I think he was just trying to feel me out. But I told him, 'You better tell Larry not to talk about having dinner with me, because I'll have to testify against him if he does, and that will be a sad thing for all of us.'"

Davis had another reason to doubt Hall's veracity besides his dinner story. A few months before Larry was arrested, Ross was listening to the police scanner with his wife when they heard a call about a man driving a two-tone van stalking a teen girl. Immediately his wife suggested that the van might be Larry's, and Davis reached for a pad to take down the license plate number that the girl's family reported. A day or two later, when Hall dropped by to work on his cars, Ross checked Larry's plate and then confronted him. "I said, 'Larry, I want to know what the hell is going on here. What's all this shit I heard on the scanner?'"

After Ross told Hall what he had heard, Larry replied without hesitation, "Oh, that's not true at all, Ross. Here's what happened: I'm going down the street—and there's cars parked on both sides with just enough room for me to get through—when I see these people working on a car. They've got it jacked up, and this big fat-ass bitch is bent over the fender, and there's no way to get by. I honk the horn for her to move, but then they all start to holler at me, and we about get in a fight. Next thing I know, the police are pulling me over.'"

Hall was so sure of himself that Davis backed off. "But I then said, 'Larry, I don't know what you're into, but if there's anything you need to get off your chest, go ahead and tell me. I'm your friend and I'm not going to tell anybody about anything you say.' But he didn't have anything to say, except to go on about that big fat-ass bitch. You know, the story sounded real and I almost believed him. In fact, I wanted to believe him. Who wants to think his friend is trying to abduct young girls?

"I didn't hear about his arrest [for murder] until a day or two after it happened. As soon as I did, I thought back to us standing in my barn and how quickly he dreamed up that story about the lady with the fat ass and how completely he lied—right to my face. About a half hour after that the FBI pulled up to my house wanting to search the place."

When Garry Reitler thinks about his daughter Tricia, he often remembers when he took her back to Indiana Wesleyan University for the last time. The four-hour drive from their home outside Cleveland was usually a good chance for the two of them to share a few long conversations. A homebody, Tricia had trouble adjusting to life at school away from her close-knit family, not just the parents she considered her best friends, but her two younger sisters and brother. She stood out on the conservative Christian campus with her taste for denim cutoffs and colorful leggings. A bubbly free spirit, she could take two aerobics classes in a day, call her mother to check that she, too, had done her exercise, then go running in the evening. According to a journal entry from an IWU writing class, she did much the same back in Ohio, on occasion running through the streets of her neighborhood while the rest of the family slept.

Her freshman year at IWU had been tough on Garry, too, mostly because he missed Tricia so much. Growing up, she had been as much a buddy as a daughter, able to talk sports or even debate like an adult. Meanwhile, Garry was going through a rough patch of his own, trying to build a furniture-manufacturing company from a woodworking trade, but Tricia was so mature, he could even confide in her about his own struggles.

During the trip, they picked up a young couple who were hitchhiking across the country, and Garry took them a few hundred miles to their next destination. The travelers were living something of a hippie lifestyle—one distinctly different from that of the Reitlers, who were just as openly straitlaced and ardently religious. The Christian character of IWU was what most attracted Tricia to the school. Garry listened as the three young people had a spirited debate about spirituality. "The thing with Tricia," Garry says, "is that she never judged them. She really wanted to understand why they thought the way they did. She was just such a unique person in that way. After we dropped them off, the two of us talked about religion on a deeper level than we ever did before."

Tricia had entered IWU as a psychology major and had started to consider a career in family counseling. She returned to memories of her family in an essay for a Bible-study class. "While I watched other 'Christian' families fall apart and give into the world, mine never did. . . . My prayer is that I can take a stand when I raise a family and do half as good a job as my parents."

Two weeks after she submitted her essay, at 12:22 a.m., a phone rang in the Reitler household and life was never the same for them again. A Marion policewoman was calling. The previous evening, Tuesday, March 30, 1993, Tricia's roommate reported that their daughter had not returned to the dorm in more than twenty-four hours. "Could she be in Ohio?" the policewoman asked.

Something was terribly wrong, and both the school and Marion police soon shared the Reitlers' distress. By the time Donna and Garry reached IWU on Wednesday, the college was locked down in full vigil mode. Police were posted around the campus, and some with dogs combed the grounds. The deafening whir of a National Guard helicopter split the air. Students, whom newspapers described as "stunned," moved in cautious clusters around the campus. Wary of the press, they chatted in hushed tones among themselves. A few sobbed uncontrollably.

The IWU president brought Donna and Garry into his office and introduced them to the police chief, who grimly told them about the first major development in their investigation. Earlier that morning, they had discovered the clothes Tricia was last seen wearing—a shirt, jeans, and tennis shoes—piled under a tree in a secluded park on the edge of the campus. Although it was not initially reported, a few drops of blood were found on the pants leg, on a nearby sidewalk, and on an earring that had evidently been torn from her ear.

In all the horror of this information, none of it seemed more senseless for Garry than that pile of clothes. As he later told a reporter, "For her clothes to be taken off, she would've had to fight. I know Tricia's personality. She would have fought for all she was worth."

If there was any comfort in the midst of the Reitlers' nightmare, it was in the sincere concern for them that radiated from the entire Marion community: the faculty and administration; the students who jammed the chapels in prayer and posted signs of support in their dorm windows; the anguished police officers, firemen, and even volunteers from the community who searched for Tricia as though she were their daughter or sister. A literally iconic poster was created with Tricia's smiling face and full, curly hair inside a cross. At the top it read, "Missing as of March 29, 1993. Tricia Reitler"; and at the bottom, "Please Pray." As much as the town focused on the missing girl, they were also drawn to her parents, so youthful that they looked as if they could have been in college themselves: restless Garry with his sandy brown hair and neatly trimmed beard; and tight-lipped Donna, her face framed by her straight brunette hair. Seeing their picture in the newspaper, one law officer said of the Reitlers, "And knowing they are deprived of the right to know where [Tricia] is. That is enough to drive a policeman, to make [him] spend hours working."

But the first night in Marion, Donna and Garry also remember sitting in the apartment of a psychology professor. In yet another of the kindnesses bestowed on them by strangers, the professor had let them have the place to themselves as long as they needed it. She had even left a pot of potato soup boiling on the stove. But looking at each other in the stillness of that apartment, they felt so alone and helpless. Some of that aching loneliness has never left them. They would try to sleep, but they would keep waking up, "in a panic," Garry says—as though the phone would ring the way it had the night before.

The rest of the week unfolded as though they were at the bottom of a tidal basin—during the day they were inundated by well-meaning searchers and the swirl of the media; and then, during the interminable nights, all the activity rushed out and they were beached again, alone with their panic.

They did the best they could to be helpful, organizing friends and family who came from their hometown and across the nation to help in the search. They were joined by more police and fire departments and additional units of the National Guard. More than 150 people—including local residents—spent the weekend combing the countryside around the campus. The Reitlers tried to rally the search parties, but despite their numbers they could only nibble at the edges of the wilderness that surrounds the nearby Mississinewa River and reservoir. Even the usually upbeat Garry felt overwhelmed. "It's just so vast," he says.

A week after they arrived in Marion, the Reitlers gave what a newspaper described as "an emotion-filled speech" to the IWU student body, then went back to Ohio to celebrate their son's eleventh birthday. They had left him and his two older sisters at home with friends, and there, they, too, had been besieged by well-wishers. The house was filled with gifts of food and fruit baskets, and the streets outside were lined with TV and newspaper crews.

The Reitlers would return to Marion in a few days and there would be more massive search parties of hundreds, but no amount of work or good intentions would turn up Tricia or any more clues of what had happened to her. Two weeks after her disappearance, Donna spoke the unspeakable, telling reporters, "We have a good picture that she won't be coming back home."

Still, for the Reitlers, the mission could never be complete until they found "closure." This meant not only finding out what had happened to Tricia, but also recovering her remains. As Donna explains, "I want some place to bring flowers." A few weeks later they even took to the national airwaves as guests on *Jerry Springer*—in the earlier, less manic version of his show. They talked about Tricia and issued a plea for anyone who knew anything about her abduction to come forward.

For some time to come, almost reflexively, when any bones or skeletal remains were found, the press in Indiana and Ohio connected them to Tricia Reitler. It would start eight months after her disappearance when a woman's body was found in a cornfield near the Illinois state line. A few tantalizing days would pass before the remains were identified as those of Jessica Roach. The next year, more heartbreak followed after a skull was found in the Mississinewa River. Each time a call came, Garry Reitler says, "It felt like someone had torn off a scab."

In retrospect, the most important development in Tricia Reitler's case came just weeks after her disappearance when the body of another missing young woman was fished from a pond in La Porte, an Indiana city two and a half hours north of Marion. Sixteen-year-old Rayna Rison was last seen leaving her job at a veterinary hospital a month earlier—three days before Tricia's disappearance. As noted in the *Marion Chronicle-Tribune,* Reitler and Rison bore striking similarities. Both victims were short with long, curly hair and blue eyes. As with Tricia, it appears that the abduction took place in an isolated setting. Rison was found just a few miles from a secluded lane where her car had apparently broken down. Her cause of death was strangulation, common to many victims of serial murder.

The local newspapers were quick to see a possible connection, but the local police departments were just as quick to dismiss it. In April the *Marion Chronicle-Tribune* carried an article with the headline "Police won't connect Reitler with La Porte case," and quoted Marion police detective lieutenant Jay Kay saying, "As of now there is nothing that links the two [cases]."

From the start, no one became more closely associated with the Tricia Reitler investigation than Kay, the detective supervisor for the Marion police, a diligent officer with hawklike features and brushed-back blond hair. He would be as obsessed with solving this case as Gary Miller was with finding Jessica Roach's killer. In an interview with the *Chronicle-Tribune,* he admitted that Reitler was "constantly on his mind and that he even wakes up in the middle of the night thinking about [her case]." Over time, he became especially friendly with Garry and Donna and won their absolute trust in return. "I can't even tell you my feelings for Jay," Donna Reitler once said to an Associated Press reporter who asked whether police on Tricia's case were getting discouraged. "I know he's still looking. And he probably will look until the day he dies. I can't even tell you what a comfort that is." Posters of Tricia, aerial photographs of the campus, and diagrams of the suspected crime scene stared down at Kay from a bulletin board above his desk, "a constant reminder to police officers [that they are] still working to resolve the case," as the paper put it.

Unlike most local detectives, Kay reached out to other police departments for assistance, and although he dismissed a connection between the Reitler and Rison cases, he also told the *Chronicle-Tribune* that he had been in touch with the La Porte police department when Rison had first been reported missing.

However, Kay did not divulge the real reason why each police department lost interest in the other's case—they both were hot on the trail of local suspects. In Rison's case, the most obvious target for investigation was her brother-in-law, who had, in 1989, been convicted of molesting her. It was not as easy to bring charges against him as it was initially thought, but local prosecutors still tried—four years after a bottle of birth control pills with Rison's name on it was found in Larry Hall's van. The charges against the brother-in-law were finally dropped in 1998 for lack of evidence.

In Marion, detectives were convinced that they already had the culprit in Reitler's abduction behind bars—Tony Searcy. He was twenty-eight at the time Tricia disappeared. A former IWU student, Searcy still came on campus to visit with a woman who worked in the school cafeteria where Reitler had a student job. In the early-morning hours after she was reported missing, Searcy made a 911 call to the Marion police reporting the theft of copper wire. Searcy himself had already been arrested three times for stealing copper from train depots. He later admitted that he called to get a rival thief in trouble, but in the minds of the Marion police he was really trying to throw them off the trail of Reitler's abductor. They traced the call and picked him up soon after Tricia's clothes were found. When asked about his activities on the night she'd disappeared, Searcy failed a lie detector test. Police became even more suspicious when search dogs sniffing the trunk of Searcy's car appeared to pick up the scent of a cadaver (although the presence of copper has been known to fool cadaver dogs because of copper secretions in the liver of a corpse).

But for Marion police, nothing about Searcy may have been more incriminating than his antagonistic personality. He had no qualms about admitting to his previous crimes—although none involved assault or anything of a sexual nature—but he still railed against the unfairness of the American justice system. He was also outspoken on the state of Christianity, and IWU faculty claimed that he had developed frightening "apocalyptic" views during his four semesters at the school. When he was arrested on April 22, 1993, four weeks after Tricia Reitler's disappearance, the charges against him were only related to copper theft, but prosecutors continued to hold him in jail and delayed proceedings through the summer. In an August letter to the *Marion Chronicle-Tribune,* Searcy wrote that his trial "will be continuously postponed until Miss Reitler is found." He continued, "As God is my witness [and] may he take my life if I'm lying, I've had nothing to do with the disappearance of Miss Reitler, neither do I know who has."

When Searcy ultimately did go to trial in October, he claimed that the charges against him were trumped up by the police because they suspected him of Reitler's abduction. Upon his conviction for theft, he felt the judge gave him an especially harsh ten-year sentence for similar reasons.

On the one-year anniversary of Tricia's disappearance, the *Chronicle-Tribune* devoted a full spread titled "A Test of Faith," to an update on the investigation and a visit with the Reitler family. Although charges had yet to be brought against him in the case, Tony Searcy was still cited by Detective Kay as the "prime suspect."

But on the very next day after this article was published, a new development, like a bolt from the blue, would test the faith that Kay and the Marion police department had in their investigation. Another suspect in Tricia's abduction, complete with incriminating evidence, would be delivered to them on a silver platter. His name was Larry Hall.

That afternoon, in the neighboring town of Gas City, Hall had reportedly been circling a yard where two girls—fourteen and seventeen—were playing basketball. Before he drove away, their father wrote down his license plate number and reported it along with a description of the two-tone van to the Gas City police. Minutes later, Patrolman Neil Pence spotted a van matching that description parked in an empty Kmart lot. As he drove closer to check the plate, Hall tore out of the parking lot, but when the patrolman pursued him with his lights flashing, Larry pulled to the side of the road. Evening had fallen and Pence approached the van with his flashlight trained on the driver's face. He asked Hall for his license and registration. As Larry rummaged through his glove compartment, Pence peered through the van's side windows into the cargo bay. The beam of his flashlight first glinted off the blade of a big hunting knife, then fell on coils of rope, a ski mask, a can of starter fluid, a pair of gloves, and a wad of cotton. But nothing in the bay would startle the patrolman more than the "Please Pray" missing poster for Tricia Reitler.

Patrolman Pence, like everyone else in the region, was intensely aware of Reitler's disappearance and the as-yet-inconclusive investigation. Now, it appeared, he had stumbled on the perpetrator of the most notorious crime in the recent history of central Indiana. He immediately called his superior officer, who just as quickly called the Marion police. Detective Bruce Bender took the call. He had been assigned to the Reitler case from the start under the supervision of Jay Kay. Bender called Kay at home and both rushed in separate cars to Gas City.

They found Hall at the side of the road in the same spot where Pence had pulled him over. Hall would later charge that Pence's commanding officer, James McNutt, had at first threatened him for stalking girls on a street where policemen lived and then shoved him against the car. While a few Gas City officers guarded Larry, others swarmed around the van. McNutt had already gone through the vehicle and was displaying items in the cargo bay that he thought to be suspicious. In addition to what Pence had initially spotted, there were several articles about Reitler's disappearance; a page torn from an Avon lingerie catalog with "IWU" written on the panties of a model; and mock Indiana Wesleyan University stationery with Tricia Reitler's name pasted on it. Just as alarming was a newspaper story from the previous November titled "Marion police interested in body," about the remains found in the Perrysville cornfield that were later identified as belonging to Jessica Roach. At first, a ten-year-old issue of *Newsweek* seemed at odds with the other paraphernalia until the police flipped inside and found a lengthy story on serial killers titled "The Random Killers."

By this time, Gas City police headquarters had completed a check on the plate and discovered that the registration on file did not match the description of the vehicle or Hall's name. At the very least, the police could impound the van, but they could only charge Larry with "false and fictitious registration" for displaying the wrong plates— a misdemeanor.* After Patrolman Pence issued the ticket, Bender

---

*As a result of the ticket, Hall then kept the proper registration plates on his van. Otherwise, Gary Miller would have never been able to track him from Georgetown to Wabash.

asked Hall if he would go with him to Marion police headquarters and he agreed. Kay stayed behind to sort through the items pulled from the van.

Larry Hall remained in the custody of the Marion police detectives until three thirty that morning. He spent much of the time with Bender by the wall of photos and diagrams relating to the Reitler case, while Kay paced the corridor outside and occasionally popped in to listen to the informal interview. At one point, Larry volunteered that he had had a "nightmare" about killing Tricia Reitler. He even agreed to show Bender and Kay where he buried her in his dream. But when the three drove to an area around the historic Mississinewa battlefield, he claimed to lose his bearings. Instead of booking Hall or even holding him for further questioning, the Marion detectives returned him to his home.

Marion PD's quick dismissal of Hall's confession left Patrolman Pence and the rest of the Gas City police dumbfounded. But for Kay, the confession was literally too good to be true. In his eyes the memorabilia about Reitler did not expose Hall as a serial killer, but confirmed instead that he had a morbid fascination with the case. As far as the Marion detectives were concerned, he did not disclose anything new about the abduction. Instead, he simply parroted back to them information contained in the articles he'd collected. No doubt they were also unimpressed by his nonthreatening appearance. Compared to the muscular and confrontational Tony Searcy, Hall was a little doughboy—timid and overly polite.

"Marion PD was never going to let Hall become the suspect," one policeman from another town says, "because they already had Tony Searcy as their suspect. No matter what they said about keeping an open mind, they had total tunnel vision on him."

Deputy Sheriff Gary Miller admits that serial killers are the UFOs of homicide investigations. With the Jessica Roach case, he didn't even consider the idea of a serial killer until he had exhausted all other possibilities. "You just can't conceive that a guy has appeared out of nowhere to kill someone in your community for absolutely no reason. It's so out of your control, you prefer to believe it didn't happen."*

In their defense, the Marion detectives were not the only ones who considered Larry Hall harmless. Their initial impression was reinforced the day after he confessed to them when Kay called Wabash City police. Phil Amones agreed with Kay that Hall had trouble separating reality from fantasy and assured him that Larry was getting treatment at a Wabash mental health center. Amones offered to stay in touch if anything emerged from the counseling that might implicate Larry in a violent crime, but at that stage his counselor agreed as well that Hall was no more than a wannabe.

But the next time Marion detectives heard from Amones, it was to inform them that an investigator was coming to interview Hall about an abduction and murder in Illinois. Kay and Bender paid yet another call on the turf of a nearby police department, then looked on anxiously as Gary Miller grilled Hall in the Wabash City Hall conference room. Amones called them again two weeks later when Hall confessed to Miller and FBI agent Randolph. That night, unbeknownst to Miller, the Marion detectives picked up Hall from the Wabash police station, ostensibly to transport him to the county jail. But along the way, they stopped to buy him a hamburger and then, once again, took him to the Mississinewa wilderness area. Once again he had them drive in circles and claimed that he could not remember exactly where

---

*Besides the Rayna Rison case, in several other instances local individuals were charged for crimes committed by outside serial killers. Most notably, in 1985, two men, Rolando Cruz and Alejandro Hernandez, were sentenced to death for the rape and murder of ten-year-old Jeanine Nicarico in Naperville, Illinois. Their convictions were thrown out, but the local prosecutors tried them again even though Brian Dugan, an imprisoned serial killer, confessed to the crime and DNA evidence bore him out. Finally, in 1995, Cruz was acquitted and charges were dropped against Hernandez. In 2000, then Illinois governor George Ryan gave both men a full pardon and cited their cases when he declared a moratorium on the state's death penalty.

he had buried Tricia Reitler. When they deposited him at the Grant County jail in Marion, they were more convinced than ever that he was not the real killer of Tricia Reitler—just a wannabe.

The whirlwind of publicity that followed Hall's arrest and indictment did little to sway the Marion detectives' opinions about Larry or Tony Searcy. Although Lieutenant Kay continued to call Searcy the "prime suspect" in the Reitler case, he was always careful to leave the door open for Hall should there be more convincing evidence of his guilt. Other Marion officers working on the investigation were not so nuanced. "Tony [Searcy is] the guy. There's no question in my mind," Sergeant Darrell Himelick, chief investigator for the Grant County sheriff, told the *Chronicle-Tribune*. In the same article those feelings were echoed by Kay's boss, Marion chief of police Dave Homer. "Personally I believe [Searcy is the top suspect]," he was quoted as saying. "I felt that way from the beginning."

But from the perspective of Beaumont and Miller in Illinois, nearly as much incriminated Hall in the Reitler abduction as in the Roach case. Beyond just the physical similarity between the victims (same height, build, and brown, shoulder-length hair), Hall also made specific references in his notes consistent with what is known about Tricia's last hours on the campus.

For example, he refers to the Marsh supermarket on the edge of the IWU campus as a place where he has "seen many nice girls." He writes, "Lots of walkers at 7:15, walking to apartments on Nebraska [Street] and 44–43 [streets]. Must be housing for the university." Tricia was last seen shortly after 8:30 p.m. at the drugstore next to Marsh in the same strip center. The most direct route from the stores to the dorms is Forty-fifth Street, bounded by athletic fields on one side and a park and pool house on the other, which is where her clothes with drops of blood were found.

But most telling is an entry Hall makes on "April 5, '93." Reitler had been abducted the week before. If she had indeed bled inside his van, then the following actions that he itemizes are especially ominous: "Replaced rear grass carpet in van, cut out stained carpet, vacuumed van thoroughly, sprayed down chemical, wiped with Armorall, burn paint tarps, buy new hacksaw blades, clean all tools with denatured alcohol." It's not clear why he must clean those tools, especially the hacksaw, but the stains he is cutting out and the residue he is vacuuming or wiping away very much appear to be the "forensic evidence" he constantly reminds himself to destroy in other notes.

Just as intriguing are the final lines in his April 5 entry: "Take tires off and clean mud from under fenders. 700 West Frances Slocum Trail." By that address, Hall could have meant one of several locations. Frances Slocum was the white woman abducted by Indians as a child who spent the rest of her life with the Miami tribe. Many different roads in the area bear variations of her name, but all are located in or around the Mississinewa reservoir, where Larry fished and searched for Indian artifacts with his brother. If mud went into the wheel wells and under the fenders, Hall evidently took his van off the road and it sank deeper than he expected. Given the sequence of activities in his notes, he may have gone off road to bury Tricia Reitler. Elsewhere in the notes he reminds himself to "put a bag of lime at the spot and spade under the bridge."* The lime would have helped speed decomposition if he had indeed buried a victim there. He would have made note of a nearby address so he could return to it, as he did the cornfield where he left Jessica Roach's body.

Evidence of Hall's fixation with the IWU campus went beyond his notes. After the extensive publicity surrounding his arrest—including copies of his mug shot with the distinctive muttonchop sideburns—two young women recognized Hall and came forward to

---

*FBI agent Ken Ivan read "spade" as "spode" when he testified on the notes during Hall's first trial. Given Larry's experience at Falls Cemetery with his father's job, it can safely be assumed that he knew that lime is chopped into the earth by a "spade."

testify about something that happened when they were roommates at the school. It occurred one evening just a week after Tricia Reitler had disappeared. They had gone shopping at the Marsh supermarket, and on the way back to campus, as they walked along the same street where Tricia's clothes had been found, they noticed a van slowly following behind them. The driver leaned out of his window to yell something, so they had a better look at his face. The students didn't wait to find out what he wanted. They rushed back to their dorm to immediately report the incident to campus security, and a guard soon spotted the van as well. When he had the driver pull the van over, Hall told the guard that he had been looking for a friend's house in the area and had gotten lost.

For Beaumont and his investigators, all of the Tricia Reitler evidence, complete with eyewitnesses, was too valuable to pass up. He could not charge Hall with her murder without complicating the Roach case—especially since Tricia's body had never been found—but he could still use the Marion case to show the jury a pattern of behavior that would be duplicated in Georgetown: the stalking, the collection of memorabilia about the victim, the returning obsessively to the scene of the crime.

But from a media perspective, any evidence about Tricia Reitler was sure to upstage the Jessica Roach case. Reitler's disappearance had been much more publicized both regionally and nationally. As far as the Marion investigators were concerned, Beaumont was unnecessarily dragging their case into his, either to make a point about their dereliction or just to poke a finger in their eye. When looking back at how the law enforcement agencies in Illinois and Indiana viewed each other, Gary Miller says, "It did get kind of personal."

In the rivalry, Craig DeArmond saw an opening for his client. When he produced a list of the defendant's witnesses, it included several members of the Wabash and Marion police departments.

On May 23, 1995, when the curtain lifted on Larry Hall's trial, the jurors could not have asked for a more dramatic opening—Assistant U.S. Attorney Lawrence Beaumont played the segment about Jessica Roach from *America's Most Wanted.* John O'Brien, then a seasoned court reporter at the *Danville News-Gazette,* had eagerly awaited the proceedings, and they didn't disappoint. "Any homicide trial in Vermilion County was considered big news, especially where you have a stranger abduction of a young girl," he says. "But the added element for me was watching Beaumont and DeArmond. You really didn't have two better lawyers in the area, and every day they just slugged away at each other like two heavyweights."

But aside from the initial glitz of *America's Most Wanted,* Beaumont spent four days methodically laying out his evidence. First he established how Jessica suddenly disappeared with testimony from the sister who saw her off on the bike, the bus driver who first saw that bike abandoned in the middle of the road, and the parents, who then reported her missing. Beaumont next presented eleven witnesses who had either been targets of Hall's stalking or witnessed it, including the IWU students, the two young Georgetown girls whom Hall followed as they rode their bikes, and the father who then drove around town looking for Hall's two-tone van to get the license plate number.

For the government, the voices of all the young victims of Hall's stalking joined into a compelling chorus of the ones-who-got-away. They would be a counterpoint for Jessica Roach—the one who didn't. Her body was discovered, jurors learned, when a farmer, Rusty Smith, spotted "something that just looked out of place; something dark." He was followed to the stand by a parade of forensic experts, who established that the grisly remains that he found were those of Jessica Roach.

To place Hall in the area at the time of Jessica's disappearance, the government called four witnesses who had seen him observing the nearby Revolutionary War reenactment—he stood out like a sore thumb in his Civil War Hardee hat and muttonchop sideburns. Also, approximately six hours after the abduction, Monte Cox, a gas station attendant returning from a late shift, saw a "stocky" man emerge from the cornfield where Rusty Smith would find Jessica a few weeks later. Cox thought the man was some out-of-towner cut short by Mother Nature who had pulled over to relieve himself. But, he testified, "I thought that was strange, too, since it was so far from the highway." He would be the only witness to place Hall directly at the crime scene, but he waited two months before he called Crime Stoppers, and his vague memories of both Hall and his van, parked across the road from the cornfield, were the easiest to shake under cross-examination.

The two government witnesses who spent the most time on the stand were Mike Randolph and Gary Miller. Beaumont took them step by step through their sessions with Hall and how his confession had unfolded. Beaumont's case culminated with the pictures, notes, and paraphernalia discovered in Hall's rooms and vans—especially the map on which Larry had marked in the spots corresponding to the cornfield where Jessica Roach's body was found and the woods by the pond where Miller believed she was killed.

Right from the start, in his opening remarks, DeArmond indicated the tightrope he had to walk with his client. "You may not like Larry Hall," he told the jurors. "But he is not here for a popularity contest." The lawyer admitted that Larry acted in suspicious ways—but only to get attention. As he explained, "[My client] suffers from a number of mental and emotional problems that led him to engage in a series of very serious and self-destructive behaviors that included planting false evidence in his van, behaving in a manner intending to arouse suspicion, and, eventually, making incriminating statements which were not true."

As DeArmond admitted, it was hard to understand Hall's "self-destructive behaviors," but he assured the jury "that police quite often confront people who, for one reason or another, make false admissions or confessions about crimes. They even have a term for it. It's called wannabes."

To the astonishment of both Beaumont and Miller, the excuse that the Wabash and Marion police departments had used for not taking Hall seriously had now become the central tenet of his defense. Beyond the wannabe explanation for Hall's actions, DeArmond still needed testimony to refute the government's evidence, but his most persuasive argument pointed out what the prosecution lacked—namely, despite the best efforts of the FBI and all of its celebrated crime laboratories, "not one tiny speck" of physical evidence linked Larry to any crime he "supposedly confessed to."

The rest of the defense case proved much more difficult to sustain during Beaumont's cross-examination and rebuttal. DeArmond started with the alibi, lining up friends and family to testify that Larry was elsewhere on the day that Roach was abducted. Leading off these witnesses was a stooped Robert Hall, who looked and acted older than his seventy-two years. He apologized for his hearing, caused an early recess so he could walk back to the car to get his reading glasses, and, when challenged on the auto parts receipt, admitted, "I am getting feebleminded." He was followed by Larry's twin, Gary Hall, who testified that on the day of Roach's abduction, Larry attended a Native American reenactment with him in Rochester, Indiana, 30 miles north of Wabash and 180 miles from Georgetown. But on cross-examination, Beaumont reviewed the answers Gary had given FBI agent Temples shortly after his brother's arrest. At that point, before Gary understood the significance of what he told Temples, he even volunteered the place where he and Larry first saw a handbill advertising the fateful Georgetown Revolutionary War reenactment. For those who knew the Hall family history, the most surprising defense witness may have been Gary's first wife. Despite a history of periodic estrangement from her ex-husband, she still showed up to confirm his alibi testimony, since he claimed to have brought their daughter with him. But some of the other friends who testified about Larry's presence at the Rochester reenactment were far from certain about the exact day they saw him and were easily shaken by the prosecutor. The alibi was shredded even further by shop owners who testified in rebuttal about Robert asking them to fabricate receipts, and Ross Davis, who produced a shipping receipt to prove he had had dinner with Larry a few nights after Jessica Roach's abduction, and not the night of her abduction as Larry claimed.

Another essential part of the defense was to show that everything in Larry's confession was contained in one of the articles he read or collected. But as Beaumont pointed out, no newspaper reported on strangulation as the cause of Jessica Roach's death or pinpointed the place where she was murdered, as Hall did on his map and in his statement. Also, when he confessed to Randolph about Reitler, Hall remembered that a barking dog had approached shortly after he seized her. At the time of the abduction, police in the area had received a complaint about a barking dog, which had never been reported in the press. Also, Hall had described Jessica's bike as having both curved handles and ten speeds, another detail he could not have read in the papers.

But more than anything, DeArmond's case hinged on how Larry's mental issues could make him unusually suggestible to the good-cop/bad-cop routine of Randolph and Miller. As DeArmond pointed out, the day after the deputy sheriff's first interview with Hall, Larry learned that he would be losing his counseling services at the local mental health clinic. DeArmond argued that Larry was then forced to pretend he might be a danger to the community so that his therapy would continue. He signed the statement from Randolph because he was eager to please and "suggestible." Indeed, he didn't even question the first line of the statement where Randolph accidentally wrote, "I, Larry DeWayne Daniels . . ."

To prove his point, for two hours DeArmond hammered away at Gary Miller about what information Hall had really volunteered and what Miller had suggested to him. Eventually, the cross-examination tried even the patience of the judge, who admonished the defense counsel in a sidebar. ("You are asking the same thing over and over again.")

Having observed DeArmond so often in the past, Miller knew exactly what Hall's lawyer was trying to do. "Basically his mission was to destroy my credibility and the credibility of the statement we took from Hall. But I don't think he caught me."

In addition to his cross-examination of Miller and Randolph, DeArmond planned to build much of his coercion argument around the testimony of Richard Ofshe, a professor at the University of California–Berkeley and an expert in the field of false confession. But Ofshe never personally interviewed Hall. Instead, he listened to a tape of Larry that DeArmond had made. The professor was also prepared to analyze the testimony Miller and Randolph gave during the trial. But in a hearing outside the presence of the jury, flinty Judge Harold Baker (the same judge who sentenced Jimmy Keene) dismissed the idea of Ofshe critiquing other testimony in the trial. He snapped, "You're asking this witness to judge the credibility of the witnesses and you usurp the function of the jury [to judge the witnesses' credibility] and I will not permit it." Judge Baker then dismissed Ofshe before he uttered a word to the jury.

The most crucial testimony on the state of Larry Hall's mind was therefore left to Larry Hall himself when he took the stand in his own defense—in every way the climax of a most dramatic trial. It was a bold move on DeArmond's part, but the confidence that Hall had in his lawyer was clearly mutual. Ironically, in meeting DeArmond's expectations for his performance, Hall may have performed too well.

In contrast to the defense testimony that he had a "low-average" IQ, Hall came off as articulate and well prepared on the stand. Like an actor in a play, he hit every mark that had been laid out for him during rehearsal, especially when DeArmond walked him through the convoluted reasons why he desired police attention. "It made me feel important that they wanted to talk to me," Larry told the court. "I was desperately trying to get—I don't know—you call it attention or whatever."

In a similar vein, he testified that he actually *wanted* to be arrested by the Gas City police. "I love the attention of when they would pull me over and they wanted to question me, and I would refuse the questioning and it made me feel important, like I knew something that they didn't."

He went on to claim that he had prepared a script about the Reitler abduction a few weeks before he was pulled over in Gas City. "I wrote out everything the way I wanted to tell him or tell whoever I was talking to."

Hall admitted he was not as eager to talk to Randolph and Miller, but that they held him in the Wabash station for too long a time. "I would have said just about anything for them to let me go home, which they told me [they would do] after the questioning was over."

If Larry's self-assurance seemed out of character during his direct examination, so, too, was his attitude during Beaumont's cross-examination. His responses were sharp and combative. When the prosecutor asked where he learned unpublicized information about Roach and Reitler, without hesitation he claimed that it had been divulged to him by the detectives who questioned him.

At times, in the heat of their exchanges, Larry could even be snarky. When Beaumont pointed to a dot on the map that marked where Jessica Roach's body was found, he asked, "Where did you get the precise location [to put that] dot?" Hall shot back, "How precise can you be on an Indiana state map?"

At another point Beaumont asked, "Is it possible that there was a great big bag of lime in your van?" Hall replied, "It is possible that there was a bag of lime in there, but I don't know about a great big bag of lime."

In both direct examination and cross-examination, Hall spent more time on the stand than he did when he was supposedly trapped in the Wabash police station, but he never cracked—the sort of fortitude that may not have played well with his jury. Beaumont could turn that feat into one of his strongest arguments. Although the defense psychologists had testified that Hall was "unduly suggestible," Beaumont argued, "On cross-examination, for an hour and ten minutes, I asked him nothing but leading questions, and he never agreed with me once. Not once."

The jury took fewer than three and a half hours to convict Larry Hall for the abduction of Jessica Roach. But behind the scenes of the Roach trial another battle had played out over the abduction of Tricia Reitler. Although Detectives Bender and Kay had been called by the defense to testify about Hall's confession to them and why they dismissed it, they were fairly circumspect about eliminating him entirely as a suspect. But out of the presence of the jury, Sergeant Darrell Himelick, chief investigator for Grant County, and Marion chief of police David Homer both named Tony Searcy as the prime suspect in the Reitler case. Because nothing else in evidence supported their theory, Judge Baker would not let them testify.

Although the Roach trial was effectively over, Larry Beaumont and his Illinois investigators had some unfinished business with Larry Hall and the Marion police. The one way, outside of court, to definitively prove Hall's guilt in the Tricia Reitler case was to find her remains using one of the maps pulled from Hall's van in Gas City. On it Hall had marked an X on the southeast side of Marion.

Three weeks after Hall's conviction, Assistant U.S. Attorney Beaumont was at that spot, on the edge of the Mississinewa River, and "waist-high in weeds," according to the *Chronicle-Tribune*. As he explained to the reporter, a lot was at stake in his search. Finding Reitler could influence Hall's sentencing for the Roach murder. It could also be the impetus for a homicide indictment from the state's attorney in Indiana, where Larry could get the death penalty, and it would continue the momentum for investigating more unsolved crimes associated with his notes and confession.

To help in this extraordinary expedition, Beaumont brought along a forensic anthropologist, cadaver dogs, divers, Marion detectives (including Lieutenant Kay), and FBI agents from Illinois and Indiana. Beaumont even arranged for an FBI plane with special cadaver-detecting heat sensors to fly overhead. But after a full day of looking with all of these high-tech resources, they had only a buried carpet to show for their efforts. Once again Kay pronounced Tony Searcy his prime suspect in the abduction of Tricia Reitler. Even more infuriating for Gary Miller, the Marion PD was joined in that assessment by Ken Ivan, the FBI agent working out of the office in Fort Wayne, Indiana, who had collected the evidence in Wabash and testified for the government during the trial.

A month later, Hall was sentenced, and during the hearing he continued to proclaim his innocence. He told the court, "I would just like to say to you, Judge Baker, and to God in heaven, that I did not commit this offense that I am charged for. I would like to say that I am very sorry for the loss of Jessica Roach to her family, and that I am in no way responsible for taking their child away from them; and I just pray to God that the truth be known that I am not guilty of this crime in no way. I just pray to God for help with my personal problems and that the truth be known eventually."

Judge Baker felt otherwise. "The jury found [Hall] guilty beyond a reasonable doubt and the court [namely, the judge himself] concurs in the finding of the jury." Baker disclosed a letter he'd received from Jessica's parents. "It's a statement of personal sorrow and heartfelt regret from the family and the void that has been created in their lives through the loss of their daughter. And the court takes that into consideration in disposition of the case." Soon after, Baker sentenced Larry Hall "for the term of his natural life without release." He added, "The court elects not to impose conditions of release. They would be pointless in this case."

However, the judge did not entirely dismiss all the testimony about the defendant's troubled mental condition: "It's the recommendation of the court that because of the personality disorders that the evidence show affect the defendant, that he be assigned, at least initially, at the correctional institution at Springfield, Missouri, to the psychiatric division for further evaluation and ultimate assignment. I think he is a vulnerable prisoner . . . and that appropriate caution should be taken in handling him."

As expected, DeArmond appealed the verdict; however, the decision of the notoriously unpredictable Seventh Circuit Court of Appeals was anything but expected—especially by Larry Beaumont. As Gary Miller sat through oral arguments in Chicago, he could see the wind was not blowing the government's way. He was particularly surprised by how testy the three judges on the panel were with Beaumont. Afterward the prosecutor assured the deputy sheriff, "They're always like that." But Miller did not like what he saw. "They're upset," he told Beaumont, "and I think we lost."

Miller was right, but the decision, issued in August 1996, did more than just throw out Hall's conviction. It was a stinging indictment of Beaumont's case, a condemnation of Judge Baker's decision making, and practically a brief for the defense. If anything, in writing the decision, Seventh Circuit judge Diane Wood summed up Hall's case better than DeArmond: "At the trial, Hall's entire theory of defense boiled down to a simple proposition: due to a personality disorder that makes him susceptible to suggestion and pathologically eager to please, he 'confessed' to a crime that he did not really commit, in order to gain approval from the law enforcement officers who were interrogating him."

The appeals court agreed with the defense argument that Gary Miller could have intimidated Hall into a false confession. "Some of the evidence indicated that Miller became upset with Hall's responses, moved closer to Hall, and started suggesting the 'right' answers as the questioning progressed," Wood wrote.*

Since the verdict hinged on Hall's state of mind during the confession, Wood argued, Dr. Ofshe's testimony would have gone "to the heart of Hall's defense." As a result, the Appeals Court found Judge Harold Baker to have acted too abruptly in dismissing him. "Properly conducted social science research often shows that commonly held beliefs are in error. Dr. Ofshe's testimony, assuming its scientific validity, would have let the jury know that a phenomenon known as false confessions exists, how to recognize it, and how to decide whether it fit the facts of the case being tried." If Hall was indeed capable of a false confession and was indeed suggestible, Judge Wood wrote, then the jury might have appreciated "the likelihood that the 'confession' added nothing to what the government already knew."

To add even more insult to injury for Beaumont, the Appeals Court disagreed with Judge Baker's ruling on issues related to the abduction of Tricia Reitler. Once again, Judge Wood questioned whether the government learned anything new about Tricia's case from Hall's confession. "The Reitler case had been discussed extensively in the press, and Hall's statement contained facts that could have been gleaned entirely from news reports. It offered nothing that

---

*Judge Wood, who has been mentioned as a candidate for the U.S. Supreme Court, appears to have misread the evidence, confusing Miller's first interview with Hall in the Wabash City Hall with the session in the Wabash City police department when he actually gave his confession. She also uses DeArmond's argument instead of the evidence to characterize the nature of Miller's first interview. None of the other detectives present—even Phil Amones—testified that Miller acted in an unprofessional or coercive manner.

could have been known only to the guilty party. The government presented no other evidence linking Hall to the Reitler murder."* Given the "potential unreliability of the confession," the Appeals Court found Judge Baker at fault for barring Chief Homer and Deputy Sheriff Himelick from stating their opinions about Tony Searcy. If Beaumont had wanted to keep them from testifying, Wood wrote, the prosecution should have concentrated exclusively on the Roach case without introducing "the massive prejudice that inevitably attends evidence suggesting Hall had committed three similar murders." In other words, the likelihood that a defendant might be a serial killer must be hidden from a jury so as not to prejudice it. This is the sort of judicial jujitsu that raises the bar even higher for prosecutors attempting to explain why a stranger would be motivated to suddenly rape and ritually kill a vulnerable young woman.

Although Judge Wood expressed regrets for dragging "all involved in this case through another trial," she almost predicted that Hall would be acquitted in a retrial when she concluded, "A jury with all the evidence before it might have convicted, but it might have concluded that Hall was a 'wanna-be,' and that the true kidnapper/murderer is still at large."

In August 1997, Beaumont retried the case against Hall—before a different judge, *without* any evidence related to Tricia Reitler, *without* the problematic testimony of the defendant, and *with* the testimony about false confessions from Professor Ofshe. This time the jury took fewer than four hours to convict. If Judge Wood had thrown down the gauntlet when her panel reversed the first conviction, Beaumont had certainly met the challenge by winning the second.

But the Appeals Court decision still did lasting damage to the overall Larry Hall investigation. No longer would state's attorneys

---

*Actually, the government did produce notes and memorabilia from Hall that related to Reitler as well as eyewitness testimony that Hall had been stalking in the area.

threaten him with trials in state courts where he could be sentenced to death. His case was not the slam dunk that it appeared to be when he was first arrested. Interest in his involvement with any other unsolved murders or missing persons waned from local investigators and reporters. When some of the victims' stories were dredged up again on five- or ten-year anniversaries after their death or disappearance, Larry's name had flaked off the list of suspects like old paint. Evidence such as Rayna Rison's birth control pill bottle was misplaced or destroyed. Some items, including women's clothing, were returned to Hall's family by the FBI office in Indiana.

No doubt the urgency of getting Hall convicted for another crime dissipated after he was sentenced again to a term of natural life. In contrast to his usually placid appearance, Hall heard the judge pronounce the punishment with his shirt torn and his hands cuffed, supposedly as the result of a tussle with the U.S. marshals when he warned them that he might lash out in court. DeArmond blamed the odd behavior on Larry's despair over losing again. He explained to a reporter that his client's "emotional state [had] gotten worse because he put a lot of hope in this second trial."

But this time, Beaumont was not rejoicing over the jury's verdict either. He still had to worry about the schizoid Seventh Circuit Appeals Court. When he pulled Jimmy Keene out of his Michigan prison in the summer of 1998, Hall's appeal on the second trial was still pending. Hall's defense team was once again seeking to get the conviction overturned on issues related to the expert testimony. Once again, they claimed that the judge had not given a fair hearing to their arguments about a coerced confession.

Meanwhile, the court of public opinion had considerable doubt that Hall was guilty of anything. In Wabash, old friends such as fellow reenactor Micheal Thompson and neighbor Bobby Allen, who had been so shocked at Larry's arrest, could now credibly believe that Larry had been no more than a wannabe who had, in the words of

Allen, been "railroaded" by the press and unscrupulous investigators from Illinois.

Meanwhile, in Marion, on the fifth anniversary of Tricia Reitler's disappearance, a TV reporter organized a billboard campaign that urged passersby to "Do the right thing" and call the police if they had any information about what had happened to her. Newspaper articles once again replayed the competing arguments about the likely culpability of Tony Searcy and Larry Hall, but a consensus had clearly grown among investigators that a third man was responsible. Lieutenant Kay had almost closed the door on Hall, explaining to a reporter that Larry had been "a psychiatric patient . . . which has diminished the credibility of his confession," but the detective still couldn't close the door completely, adding that Hall remained a suspect because "we've never been able to rule him out."

9.

The Falcon's Tale

BY NOVEMBER 1998, FOUR MONTHS since his arrival at Springfield, Jimmy Keene had to make his move. He no longer worried about getting access to Hall. "We had plenty of time to just sit in that cell every night and talk an hour or two before lockdown, and it was totally safe, because the mob guys were in a whole different wing from us. In the mornings I'd play my little charade about being a part of their group, and I'd go down to play boccie ball with them. At night, they didn't know where I was and they didn't care."

But even with all the time they spent together, Hall was no closer to telling Keene why he had been sentenced to prison. The closest they ever got to the subject was Beaumont. "It all came up naturally," Keene remembers. "We were talking about how close I lived to Indiana, and then he realized that we were both tried in the Central District."

"Who was your prosecutor?" Hall asked.

Jimmy had to catch himself before he answered. He couldn't tell Hall the truth, so he mentioned the name of another assistant U.S. attorney who operated out of the court.

"Have you ever heard of this guy named Beaumont?" Hall asked.

"I heard about him," Keene replied. "I heard he's real hard-nosed."

"Yeah, he's something else," Larry said. "That fucking guy, he was after me no matter what. Man, he was crazy."

Typically, Hall had little bad to say about anyone, but Beaumont was different. "He'd even make jokes about Beaumont," Keene says. "He might see some inmate strung out on drugs stumbling around and he'd go, 'Look at that guy, kind of looks like Beaumont.'

"Everybody hates their prosecutor. But Larry really hated Beaumont. You could see it in his eyes and the fear, too. That boy has nightmares about Beaumont."

Still, no amount of Beaumont bashing would get Larry to talk about the actual charges against him. "I had to find some other way to pry the lid off," Keene says.

"One day we were sitting in the library and I was watching him read his paper one page at a time when I suddenly got an idea." Later that night as they sat in Hall's cell, Jimmy asked, "Haven't we been hanging around each other long enough to tell each other the truth?"

Hall replied, "What do you mean?"

"Come on, Larry. You've been telling me all along that you had this weapons charge and you got forty years. But you're the same Larry Hall that lives in Wabash, Indiana, right?"

Hall nodded, but instead of looking confused, his eyes grew wide and then he looked away. "What are you trying to say?"

"I know all about your case, dude. You know my mom's from that state. The other day I told her about my new friend here, and when I mentioned your name, she said you were the one they accused of killing those girls. It's in all the Indiana newspapers."

"But it's not like they said. It's not like they said."

"Relax. It doesn't matter to me what you did, man. Look at all these crazy people in here. Whatever you did, you did for your own reasons. I just thought that you'd have leveled with me because we were friends. I didn't expect to hear this from my mother."

When Keene left Hall's cell, he began to second-guess himself and once again barely slept through the night. This time there was no doubt he had pushed too hard too fast. But he had finally reached the point where he was willing to accept the risk. In no way could he wait any longer for Hall to talk without going crazy himself. During breakfast the next morning, as he ate at the mob table, he could see Hall stealing looks at him from across the dining hall. Had he been up all night thinking, too?

Jimmy couldn't wait to find out. When they passed each other on the way out of the dining hall, he slapped Hall on the shoulder and said, "See you later in the library," as though nothing had happened the night before.

Hall looked back at him with visible relief, saying, "Yeah, sure."

With that one relieved look, Hall revealed what he most feared—that *Jimmy* would stop talking to *him* because of his crime. "He got really worried about offending my mom," Keene remembers. "He didn't want her to think that my new friend was this psycho killer that they were making him out to be in the papers."

That night while they were talking in his cell, Hall was not ready to go into detail about the charges, but he said, "It's not the way they made it sound. Everything your mother read in the papers came right from Beaumont's mouth."

Keene was careful to let these discussions come in snatches, and then he'd move on to a different subject, so he didn't sound too interested. But he had to introduce a name. "Back when I was in Ford County jail," Keene says, "Beaumont and the FBI told me to start with Roach, since it was only natural to talk about the one he had been convicted for killing."

One day, Keene finally just blurted out, "So who was this Jessica Roach girl?"

Hall immediately became defensive. "What do you mean?"

"That's one of the girls that they prosecuted you for, right? Didn't they say that you murdered her or something?"

"What do you mean?"

"Larry, come on, man."

"Well, you know, Jim, it's not like they say. Beaumont thinks he's got all the facts right, but it's not like he says."

This was always the endless loop with Larry, but Keene kept probing, "Well, what was it then?"

"Yes, I met this girl, but when I met her, it wasn't like they say."

"Were you dating the girl? Is that how you knew her?" Jimmy asked, trying to sound as ignorant as possible.

"No, but I could have dated her." For the next few minutes, Hall talked about Jessica Roach as if she had lived down the street or gone to school with him, how she was the kind of girl he had always wanted. How she was cute with long brown hair and how nice she seemed at first. This turn in the conversation relaxed Larry, and Keene realized that Hall still had vivid memories about his victims and extensive fantasies that he actually knew them for more than the few horrific moments of their actual encounters. But Hall still did not feel comfortable about discussing the actual murder.

If Keene was going to get him to talk, he says, "We had to take the girl bashing to a deeper level." It wasn't enough for Jimmy to feel sorry for Larry and the other guys who had been ignored or mistreated by women. Jimmy had to express rage at what the women in his own life had done to him.

But how could the experience of a man who had all the women he wanted—even a porn star—compare with that of a man who had none? At night, as Keene lay awake plotting how to get into Hall's head, he spent nearly as much time psychoanalyzing himself. A part of Keene did truly have regrets about his love life. He never had the long-term relationship he wanted: a woman he could marry and have children with. The closest he came was with April, the girl who lived with him the first time he was busted. After she had gotten rid of the drugs in the house and given the money to Big Jim, she and Jimmy decided it was best for her to leave town and live with relatives until Keene could settle the charges against him. But in months, she had met someone else and gotten pregnant. Even Jimmy's last girlfriend, Tina, who had worked so hard to get him out of prison, became unhappy when Keene abruptly left Milan and had to cut her out of the loop. In recent weeks he heard that she, too, had had a fling, gotten pregnant, then had an abortion.

Jimmy was as much to blame as the girlfriends for the failed relationships, if not more so, but in talking to Hall it was easy to work himself up about their betrayals. "I wanted Larry to understand that I've been hurt by women, too, and that was the risk I took by getting involved with them. He was hurt by women *not* wanting to get involved with him, but we could feel the same anger. I'd walk across the hall to his cell and say, 'Yeah, girls suck, man.'

"Once when we were talking like this, he asked if I had dreams about hurting women, which seemed pretty weird at first. I said no, but then I said, 'When I think about all the things I gave to April and then what she did to me, I could fucking kill her with my bare hands.' And Larry would look at me and start nodding. All of that talk finally pushed the door open for him to tell me what happened with Jessica Roach."

The most extended conversation started when Keene asked how Hall had met her. "I don't understand," Jimmy said. "If you didn't date her, then how did you get together?"

Hall told him about the nearby reenactment at the park near Georgetown. He slept that night in his van and the next day drove around looking for the car in *Auto Trader*. "I was driving down the road," he said, "and I seen her walking her bike."

He pulled up alongside and he got out of his van asking if he could help. "They make it seem like I just jump on these girls, James, and it's not true. They really wanted to talk to me."

Hall opened up the double doors to the van and showed her the bike he had inside and told her he liked cycling, too. "Then she got into the van. She really did. The trouble started when I went to kiss her and she wanted to get out."

He then explained how he had a rag ready with "chloroform." Keene says, "He never told me he made it out of starter fluid. He just said that if he put one hand around her neck and used the other to put the rag over her face, it would settle her down."

"If I didn't do it," Hall told Keene, "she would have kept on hitting me."

After she was bound in the back of the van, Hall drove away with her. "He said how he didn't know where he was going, but finally found a place where he could stop and then got in the back of the van with her." When she started to struggle, Hall would put the rag over her face to subdue her again.

"Did you have sex with her?" Keene asked.

Hall replied with a vacant look in his eyes, "I kind of had a blackout and then it was like a dream and I see myself beating on her and using the rag on her. Then I wake up and her clothes are off and my clothes are off, so I think we had sex together."

But his victim was now conscious as well. She was not just crying for help, Hall told Keene. "She was crying for her mother and I didn't like that." He put his clothes on, then led her naked out of the van and told her to sit with her back against a tree.

Keene says, "He showed me with his fingers how he would interlock two leather belts. He then got behind the tree, so he wouldn't have to see her face. He whipped the belts around her neck and used a stick to twist them like a tourniquet and kept turning and turning until he didn't hear her make another sound."

Jimmy shrugged his shoulders and nodded. "Well, I guess you had to do what you had to do," he said, but suddenly Keene felt as if he were choking, too. Until he heard Hall talk about whipping the belts around the tree, he never truly appreciated the horror of what Hall had done to the young girl. "I probably should have changed the subject and stayed around to shoot the bull, but I just had to get out of there."

When Keene returned to his cell, he says, "I was thinking, 'Man, if only I had a wire on.'" The Feds had briefly considered it, but a concealed tape recorder, no matter how small, is impractical for use in a prison where inmates are constantly searched, and it's highly dangerous for the informant if word ever leaks out about it. "But I still felt very good about what I had," Keene says. "I had a solid confession out of him, which was eighty percent of what they wanted from me."

Yet, along with his elation, another feeling as well clawed at any joy he felt about finally cracking Hall. "I went back to my cell and replayed in my head what he told me, and I kept seeing the pictures of Jessica Roach that Beaumont showed me in the Ford County jail— the ones of her body in the cornfield—and I kept thinking about her crying for her mother. And I told him, 'You had to do what you had to do.' It was part of the act, so he would talk to me. But later I felt so bad about that. Almost like I was guilty of killing her, too." From this night forward, that revulsion would become a ticking time bomb inside Keene. To keep it from blowing up would be one more unexpected challenge in completing his mission.

As always, with the dawning of the next day, Hall had regrets about his nocturnal admissions. "At breakfast," Keene says, "I could see him watching me from his table; like he was afraid I was going to turn on him. After the mob guys left, I walked right up to him, and I could see he was examining me. Then I said, 'Are we meeting down at the library today?' Again, he had that look of relief, and the next time we talked, I brought up an entirely different subject, telling him how out of shape he had gotten and what he could do to work out. I wanted him to see that what he told me the night before didn't change anything between us."

Although Keene could control his emotions around Hall, sometimes it wasn't so easy around other prisoners. "There were certain days when I felt unbelievably happy that I'd be leaving soon. It's like the cold, gray days of winter, and all around me are these guys shuffling along on medications and double life sentences. But here I am thinking that Beaumont's crazy plan is actually going to work out, and suddenly I would get giddy. I'd have to catch myself to bring myself down again. Otherwise someone could look at me and say, 'What the fuck are you so happy about, dude?' It could have blown my cover."

But at night, alone in his cell after another session with Hall, any happiness that Keene felt was mixed with equal amounts of dread. To hear about the killings from Hall's own lips made them more real than anything he had read on paper. As he listened to each new detail, he ultimately realized why he felt so guilty. "It wasn't that Hall was my ticket out. It was what he did—the number of victims he had and that they couldn't find them all. I was trying to help find Reitler, but the evil in this guy was helping me get an early release. I used to think, 'What if these girls didn't die? Or what if he didn't kill so many? I'd be rotting in prison another ten years.' The closer I got to accomplishing the mission, the more those thoughts started to eat at me."

After Hall told him how he killed Jessica Roach, Keene waited another few days before he broached the subject again. "That's pretty wild how that went down," he said. "So what was with this other girl they keep talking about, this Reitler girl?"

Once again, Hall assured Keene that the official version was not accurate: "It didn't happen that way." While it was true that he approached Reitler after she left the store, he did not immediately confront her with a knife. "Me and her were talking. She was friendly with me, James. She's one of the first girls that I ever talked to that was being nice to me."

"Well, that's cool."

"But they said I just jumped on her with a knife and that is not true."

Keene shrugged his shoulders and acted disinterested. "I just kind of let it be," he says, so Larry wouldn't get more upset. But the following night, Hall brought it up himself. In the statement that FBI agent Randolph took from Hall in the Wabash City Police Department, Larry reportedly said that Reitler tried to run away and he stabbed her with a knife and then had sex with her on a tarp outside the van.

Instead, Hall claimed that Reitler still had her clothes on when she got into the van with him. Keene remembers, "He made it sound like she went inside the van herself, but he admitted he had the knife, so you can't believe she was willing to be with him. And then he got bug-eyed and started talking like he was in a trance."

The dim light in Hall's cell that had once seemed so comforting had now become creepy. "It was like this little confession room for him and me alone," Keene says. "It was weird."

"When I tried to kiss her," Hall said, "she started like going crazy on me, and hitting me, and punching me, and wanting to get out of the van."

None of the girls had ever fought with him like that, and Hall was caught by surprise because she had seemed so nice. "I started choking her to make her stop. And honestly, James, that's the last thing I remember. It was like I blacked out again. When I woke up, I was lying next to her, and her clothes were all off. Then I looked at her and I knew that she was dead. I started feeling for a pulse but it wasn't there." Although Hall didn't say it directly, Keene assumed that in the van he might have stabbed her as well as choked her, since the clothes were found with bloodstains.

This wasn't how it went with the other girls, Hall told Keene, so he panicked. First he gathered up her clothes and shoes. He had pulled his van alongside a pocket park, and he put her things under a tree there. Then, he got behind the wheel of his van and drove directly back to his home twenty minutes away. He left the van in the street outside the house and went to his little room to gather his thoughts.

"I realized I had done it again," Hall said. "I was real panicky trying to figure out what I would do next, pacing back and forth."

"He buried her that night," Keene says, "in a place that was way out in the country." Once again, as Jimmy heard the details, he felt his blood run cold. While everything Hall told Jimmy brought him that much closer to freedom, it was also too much to bear. The first chance he could, he got up to say he was tired and went back to his cell.

He had the confessions, but that was still just part of the mission. He knew he would have to probe deeper to get a more precise location for where Hall had buried Tricia Reitler, but that wasn't going to be easy. It sounded as if he had taken her into the wilderness. What landmarks could Hall possibly give him to pinpoint an exact location in an area like that?

The next two nights when they met to talk, Keene tried to steer the conversation back to Reitler, but there really was no way to ask where she was buried—other than coming out with the question. "Once I got those two confessions out of him," Jimmy explains, "I just got incredibly antsy and impatient. I kept pacing all day long, all around the building as far as I could go, and I don't think I slept more than a few hours a night. Now when I looked at his cell, it was like torture. Getting out was so close and it was still so far away."

Finally, one night in January 1999, Keene decided to act. He found himself going back to the thoughts he had the first time he saw Larry Hall—that he could grab *him* by the throat and wring Reitler's burial place out of him. But six months later, he felt crazed enough to actually do it. Then the masquerade would be over. He wouldn't have to pretend to be Hall's friend, and if nothing else, Hall would finally get some of the rough justice he deserved. "Oh, I wanted to beat the hell out of the guy. Just mess him up real bad. I stormed into his cell, but it was empty," Keene remembers, "so I just started walking real fast to the little TV room. When I saw he wasn't there, I figured he could only be in the wood shop."

If Larry was in the Arts & Crafts center at some kind of class, Keene planned to wait outside the door and ambush him as he left, but when he arrived, no guard was at the door. Looking over at the wood shop area, he spotted Hall from behind, sitting in front of his workbench on a stool, hunched over a project. He stepped through the doorway and crept closer until he could see what Larry was working on.

"The first thing I saw," Keene says, "was that falcon. But then I saw that there wasn't just one, but ten or twelve of them—exactly alike." Hall had them lined up at the top of a big piece of paper that lay partly on the bench and partly in his lap. When Keene got close enough to look over Hall's shoulder, he saw it was a black-and-white photocopy map of Illinois and Indiana with several red dots scattered inside the borders.

"I was just behind him," Keene says, "when I said, 'Hey, Larry.'"

"He practically fell off his chair, but then he dove to put both shoulders over that map so I couldn't see it."

"What are you doing here?" Hall asked. "You shouldn't be here."

"He was just stunned that I was in there," Keene recalls. "And I said, 'The guard wasn't at the door, so I figured I could come in and take a look at what you're always working on.'"

As Larry folded up the map and pushed it to the side, Jimmy

reached over to pick up a falcon. They were all unpainted, but as Jimmy looked at one closely, he could see that its eyes and feathers were so carefully etched, they could have come from a machine.

"This is pretty cool," Jimmy told Hall. "Did you make all of these yourself?"

Hall reached out as though to grab the falcon away from him, but then extended a quivering hand, palm side down, and petted the head as though it were alive. "I'm sending them to my brother. Do you know what they're for, James?"

Keene shook his head.

"They watch over the dead." Hall kept petting the head, then asked, "Do you want one, James?"

Jimmy chuckled. "Uh, no thanks, Larry. What do I need something like that for?"

But Hall was totally focused on the falcon, and Keene handed it back to him. Jimmy says, "As he looked at it, he had big, buggy eyes—all red and wild—like he was in some kind of zone over the spiritual being of these little falcons."

Immediately Keene realized that he had stumbled onto the key to his entire investigation. "He was so protective of that map that I knew it had to mean something, but I got a good enough look at it before he rolled it up to see all the red spots on it." Jimmy assumed that each of the red spots had marked a place where Hall killed someone, like the maps in the Roach trial. Larry must have intended for his twin to put a falcon near each of the spots marked on the map.

Hall looked up at Keene with the falcon in his hand and repeated, "They watch over the dead, James. They will guard their spirits to make sure they're okay."

All the murderers that Jimmy ever knew wanted to get as far away from the scene of the crime as possible. Frank Calabrese, for one, probably had no interest in seeing the cornfield where they buried

Tony Spilotro after Frank helped to kill him.* But Keene could see that Hall wanted nothing more than to return to the places where he killed the girls, and while he was behind bars, the falcons would go in his place. "As I looked at him," Keene says, "all I could think was 'Dude, you sure are a nutcase. No doubt about it.'"

But now Jimmy was anxious to let his handlers know that he had finally cracked the case. If they seized the map before it got to Larry's brother, they might actually find out where he buried Tricia Reitler and some other missing victims, too. "Look, Larry," Keene said. "I got to get out before that guard comes back and catches me in here or I'll be in the hole for three days."

Keene slipped back out of the Arts and Craft center and ran to the nearest pay phone. First he called the emergency number he had been given by his visiting "girlfriend," Agent Butkus. Jimmy hadn't even told her that he was talking to Hall regularly, let alone that he was visiting his cell, because he was afraid she would rein him back. "I figured she'd be shocked to hear that I had the whole thing licked with the confessions and the map," Keene says, "but I couldn't wait. I wanted her to get that map from Hall before he put it in the mail the next day." Since it was so late at night, the operator at the FBI could not put him in direct contact with Butkus. Instead, he got her voice mail and left a long, breathless message. He would have preferred to talk to her in real time, but she'd always responded quickly when he or a member of his family had called her voice mail in the past.

Keene then put in a call to Big Jim—equally breathless and probably even more incoherent: "Dad, listen, I just went down to Hall's wood shop class and he's got a map just like the one that was in the back of his van when they caught him, and he also had all of these little birds that he carved out."

***

*That cornfield lay only a few miles from where Jimmy grew up in Kankakee.

After a moment of silence, Big Jim asked, "What are you talking about, Son?"

"Dad, just trust me. I've figured this thing out. I think I've got this thing conquered. I just want you to know so that you can finally get some peace of mind and relax about me being here."

Big Jim knew that inmate calls could be monitored, so he didn't ask any further questions. "Whatever you say, Son. I just hope it's true."

Keene practically flew back to his cell. It would all soon be over. He clattered around his shelves and locker to pull together his few belongings—the toiletries, the girlie magazines, the stupid headphones that almost got him killed—all crap that he'd probably dump the moment he got outside. Glancing across the hall, he saw Larry returning to his cell. With all the anxiety and sleeplessness of the last few days, he could not contain himself. He had some unfinished business with Larry Hall before he left.

Then Keene did something he's regretted ever since. He decided to give Larry Hall a piece of his mind. To this day, he does not exactly understand why he did it. Partly he was intoxicated with the belief that he had done the impossible—not only gotten Larry to confess to him, but found the body as well. But mostly he was driven by guilt. He felt guilty when he'd passively nodded as Hall explained how he killed the girls. He felt guilty for telling him, "You had to do what you had to do." And he felt guilty that his early release would come from the suffering of those girls and their families. "Before I left Springfield," he says, "I just had to tell Larry that I wasn't like him." He didn't see how it could hurt. Only minutes later, lights would go out and they would both be locked down for the night. Jimmy had no doubt that Janice Butkus would be as responsive as ever to his message. FBI agents would probably be waiting when the door opened for Hall in the morning.

As soon as Keene entered Hall's cell, he could see that Larry sensed something. There was none of the chumminess or cordial "Hi,

James." Instead he stayed in his chair and watched Jimmy quietly, almost reflectively.

"Yeah, Larry," Keene said. "Looks like I'll be going home pretty soon, now."

"What do you mean?"

"Just that a few things are working out pretty good for me."

Hall's face froze with fear—perhaps at losing his friend, but Jimmy didn't want him to think he was really his friend. "You know, Larry, those things that you did were some rotten shit, man. I don't see how you can live with yourself doing that."

Hall slid his chair back on the tennis balls halves, his eyes wider than ever. "Beaumont sent you, didn't he?"

"I don't know what you're talking about. I don't even know the guy," Keene lied. "I just know how fucked up you are."

But Hall knew the truth now and he kept repeating, "Beaumont sent you. It was Beaumont, Beaumont . . ."

"He was practically hyperventilating," Keene remembers. "Like he was having a panic attack." Keene backed out of Hall's cell and stepped into his own just as the doors were locked down. "And I figured we were both trapped for the night."

But Keene had forgotten one thing: Hall was not like the other inmates on the floor. He was let out at three in the morning for his maintenance job. Instead of remembering Larry's schedule, Jimmy fell into a deep, blissful sleep, daring to dream about freedom for the first time in months.

Keene slept as well that night as any he spent in prison. The next morning, he woke to the sound of keys rattling in his door. As he turned to the light, suddenly guard after guard piled into his cell. A short, squat woman in a white smock and pants suit hovered over his bed. She pointed a finger at him and shouted, "Who are you and what are you doing here?"

Jimmy was still wrapped in his blanket. "What do you mean?" He spun around and sat on the edge of the bed. "I'm James Keene and if you look at my medical file—"

"But I want to know who you *really* are," she said, cutting him off. "Why are you hassling my patient with all these questions about his cases and trying to get into his life?"

Her patient? Keene peered through the phalanx of guards in his cell, and he could see Hall watching from the corridor with a guard on either side, as though they were shielding him. "I don't know what you're talking about," Keene said. "You need to talk to my doctor."

But she kept barking at him. "Who sent you here? The government? The FBI? That prosecutor? Do they have you working undercover?"

Two guards grabbed Keene by each arm and dragged him out of bed. "You're going down into the hole until you decide to tell us the truth," she said. He was only in a T-shirt and boxer shorts, but they didn't even give him a chance to dress. They put on cuffs and shackles and pushed him outside in his bare feet. Still groggy from sleep, Jimmy stumbled forward as if he were in a dream. How could this be happening? As they shoved him down the hall, he looked back over his shoulder and saw the doctor and Hall walk off together in the opposite direction.

Keene was back in the hole again. He told himself it was just a misunderstanding. As soon as the FBI followed up on his message, they would come to set him free. But the day wore on and no one appeared as Jimmy shivered, barefoot with just his boxers and T-shirt.

Keene's only communication with the rest of the world came through the two slots in his steel door: the eye-level wicket, which the guard could slide open and shut, and a lower slot opening at knee level, just high enough for rubberized food trays or for the guard to reach through to secure cuffs. After he had been in the hole for a day, Jimmy tried reaching out to the guard on duty. When he heard him pass by, he kicked on the door and the upper wicket slid open. Keene put his face by the slot. "Officer, listen, I need to talk to you."

"I don't want to talk to you about nothing," the guard shot back. "Just do your time and shut up."

For Jimmy, the Special Housing Unit cell in the "Medical Center" was no different from solitary in any other prison he had been in. "It's just a damp, dark, nasty little hole," Keene says, "like all the other holes, but in Springfield they start you off with absolutely nothing. Maybe a few sheets of toilet paper and that's all." It took another day before he got clothes, and a few more after that before he got a blanket. "And they really hold out on the pillow.

"Even though they tell you they don't have enough stuff to go around, it's really an honor system that they have in that prison to make you behave," Keene explains. "But if you've got prisoners who are crazy to begin with, it only makes them crazier. All day and all night you hear unbelievable bitching and moaning: 'Let me out of this fucking place' or 'Give me a new pillow, I want a different pillow.' Over and over until you practically go crazy yourself."

After a few days went by and no one had tried to contact him, Jimmy couldn't keep silent any longer. "I felt very hyper because I knew I had a very limited time if Hall still sent the map and the falcons to his brother in the mail, so I had to explain what was happening as clearly as possible." When the day guard came by to deliver the tray, Keene was waiting by the opening. "Officer, now listen to me," Jimmy said when he bent down. "Just listen to me, okay? Don't think I'm trying to come up with some crazy, nutcase story. Just listen to me! I'm not just a regular prisoner. I'm working undercover with the FBI, and I'm down here on a case for them to investigate a serial killer. You need to go and talk to—"

But the guard cut him off. "Don't you ever say something as whacked-out as that again!" he hissed, then slammed the flap shut.

"Just listen to me," Keene screamed, "listen to me!" He kicked the door with his feet and pounded it with his fists, but then, he says, "It started to scare me that I was raising so much hell. I said to myself, 'If you act crazy, they're going to treat you like you're crazy.'" When Keene watched for the guard later as he passed his door, the guard intentionally turned away from him.

Keene says, "I realized what that guard saw when he looked through my slot. My hair was sticking all over my head and my eyes were bugging out. I must have looked the part of a crazy guy." Now the words of Big Jim kept echoing through his brain: "Lost in the system. Lost in the system." Did anyone even know where he was? By the time his father and his lawyer found out, would it be too late to help him?

All he could do was sit for hours on the metal bed or in a corner and replay his last conversation with Larry. It probably scared Hall enough to contact his shrink when they let him out for his early shift. He may have gone straight to the wood shop to destroy the map, too. For all Keene knew, after Hall's doctor threw Jimmy in the hole, she called the chief psychiatrist with some story about Keene threatening Larry.

"I started to think about every worst-case scenario imaginable," Keene recalls. "Like, since I've blown this investigation, the Feds are now going to treat me like a mental case and keep me locked down here forever." That was the nightmare he'd contemplated when the marshals first brought him to Springfield and what Big Jim had warned him about over and over. He says, "I almost expected it to happen."

As the days passed into weeks in Springfield's solitary, Keene could not help but obsess about other times in his life when he'd tried to do the right thing and it backfired. All the money he'd sunk into Big Jim's businesses never did either of them any good. Then there was his daring rescue of Nick Richards from Hector's mountaintop lair only to have Richards snitch on him a few years later. If only he had listened to Hector's admonition about knowing who his true friends were. "I'm telling myself, 'This is what happens when you work with the Feds. They feel I've blown this case, but I can't even contact anybody to tell them what I do know, anyway. Now they're going to think I'm a mental case, and they're just going to leave me locked down here forever.'

"At this point, I had a full beard and mustache going, and I hadn't seen daylight or had a shower for days. The fear that my dad put in my head about getting lost in the system was pumping through me. I couldn't think about anything else. I could barely sleep for more than a few hours at a time. I was so mad, I was going mad, too."

But no matter how justifiable his anger, Keene still had to calm down and act as normal as possible. He only had to look through the upper wicket at the cell across the hall to see what could happen if he didn't keep himself under control. The inmate there was a Mexican, who seemed harmless enough at first. "His name was Julio or something like it," Keene says, "and he would sing the same song over and over. I didn't understand the words, but I can still hear that melody to this day. He kept singing it louder and louder until the guard would come around. He'd smack the door with his stick and go, 'Keep it down in there.' And then Julio would say, 'Fuck you, man. I'm sitting here forty fucking years for selling marijuana.' As soon as the guard left, he would just break into a frenzy—kicking and hitting on his door. When he got exhausted doing that, he'd start singing his song again.

"And I thought to myself, 'He does have a point. If he really was just a dealer and not killing anybody, he certainly didn't belong in a place like this for forty years.' But as far as the guards were concerned, he was crazy, and they came around with a nurse to give him pills until he yelled, 'You guys ain't making me take that shit no more.' And the next thing you know, they busted in on him with a whole crew of the prison SWAT team—guards who wear helmets and pads. I could hear him screaming and thrashing around and the guards telling the nurse to inject him some more. Then someone yelled, 'Get the gurney,' and a little later they rolled him out into the hall strapped down to a cart which is shaped like a *T* on top for his arms and like a *V* on the bottom for his legs. He was still thrashing around, and the nurse had to inject him again, and he just went, 'Ughhh,' and conked out. For the next few days they left him out there where we all could see him as an example to us. He would piss on himself and defecate on himself and they took their time before they cleaned him up. It smelled horrible. But it sure did stop him from singing."

Keene decided he needed a new strategy and he would try it out with the night guard. "I knew I just couldn't unload everything on him at once," he says. "Instead I wanted him to see I was a normal person. When he took my tray away, I thanked him and we chatted about the weather."

Keene then waited until the early-morning hours when he knew the guard wouldn't be too busy and asked him to stop by for a minute. This time he delivered a capsule version of his situation in as calm a voice as he could muster. "I could see him giving me one of those wary looks like I might turn out to be another nutcase," Jimmy says, "so I told him, 'Look at my jacket and you'll see my doctor is the chief psychiatrist. Could you just let him know that I want to see him?' "

The guard gave Keene a noncommittal nod, but at 7:00 a.m. when his shift changed, he came back and rapped on Jimmy's door. "Hey, listen, I went down to talk to the doc," he said, "but he's on vacation. As soon as he gets back, I'll go talk to him. I'll tell him your story and we'll see what he says."

It was another week, but it felt like a month to Keene. "It's the uncertainty that makes you crazy," he says. "That's worse than any physical torture they could have given me. I had been in the hole before, but I knew why and when I was getting out. This was totally different. It was so unfair and so unjustified, it made me incredibly angry. All I could think about was how good I had it back in Milan and how my father knew best when he warned me not to go to Springfield. All these negative voices go around and around in your head when you have no one else to talk to. It doesn't take long before you really do become a whack job."

Finally the guard came back one morning to tell him, "I think the doctor is giving you a visit later today."

Only moments later, Keene heard a rap at his door, and when he looked through the eye slot, he saw the chief psychiatrist on the other side with an office chair. He sat down, lifted the lower flap, and put his face as close to the opening as he could. "Jim," he whispered, "what's going on? These guards are all telling me how angry you are and that you were kicking on the door. They also said you told them you work for the FBI. You're not supposed to say that."

"And you're not supposed to go on vacation," Keene shot back. "Look what that lady did to me."

Jimmy now had a full beard and had not had a shower in the two weeks he had been in solitary. From the look in the doctor's eyes, he could see how wild he must have appeared. "I don't think any of us thought you'd move so fast," he explained. "They wanted this to be a slow-developing thing."

"Yeah, and Hall's psychiatrist attacks me while you're gone. You were supposed to protect me," Keene hissed. "You never told me you were going on vacation. But the least you can do is get me out of here."

"Well, I don't know about that," the doctor said as he fumbled through Keene's file jacket. "It looks like this other doctor has you on an evaluation hold right now. And I'd have to cut through some red tape to get you out with that hanging over your head. Maybe I'll need the contacts at the FBI to help."

"I don't care what you do, Doc," Keene shouted. "You just get that FBI lady here—"

"Just settle down," the doctor shushed.

But Jimmy yelled louder until his voice echoed through the hall. "And you get her today or I'll let everybody know you're working with the FBI, too."

"That's enough. I'll get her here. I'll get her here. Just don't worry."

But later that day when Keene heard a rap on his door, he looked through the wicket and saw three guards. They rushed in, as if he had just been in a fight, and put him in cuffs and shackles. "Hey, hey," he shouted. "What's going on now?"

They shoved him through the door and dragged him down the hall. Only when he lifted his head and looked all the way down the long, long corridor did he see a blond woman surrounded by four men in dark suits. It was Janice Butkus.

"The guards didn't know what was going on either," Keene remembers. "They walked me down the corridor—totally handcuffed and shackled—and the first words out of her mouth were 'Jim, I am so sorry. I am so sorry.' I said, 'This is ridiculous. I thought you guys would get me out of here right away if something happened, but I've been rotting in this hellhole for weeks.' Then she looked at the guards and said, 'Please, get all of that stuff off of him.' And they did. They took everything off of me right on the spot. My hands, my feet, everything, and I was free."

Then, walking shoulder to shoulder with the FBI agents and the guards, Keene walked through the tunnels and corridors to the administrative building. On the way, they walked past clusters of startled prisoners, including identity thief Malcolm Shade, who watched the procession with his mouth hanging open—once again dumbfounded by Keene's mysterious change in fortunes. "I didn't have to say anything," Jimmy remembers. "They knew something big was going on because the suits wouldn't come in there unless something big was going on."

A few inmates started to follow the procession. "One of them was a little, scraggly guy I used to hang out with named John," Keene says. "He started yelling, 'Jim, Jim, what's going on, man? What's going on?' The guards had started pushing him away. I looked at him, and I said, 'Don't worry, John. I'm going home, man.' And he yelled back, 'Then can you help me? I want to get out of here, too, man.'"

The guards led them directly to the intake center—the same area where Jimmy first entered the Medical Center. "They had to give me back the clothes that I wore when I arrived," Keene explains, "and the guards who were watching this whole deal were as confused as the inmates. There was one guy in particular, a real fucking asshole, who made life difficult on me the whole time I was inside that prison, and you could have knocked him over with a feather. He looked at me and said, 'What's going on, James? Are you going home?' and I said, 'Yeah, dude, and guess what? You're stuck here for the rest of your life.'"

A van waited for them outside, and although the airstrip was eight miles away, Jimmy remembers it as being as close as the prison's backyard. When Keene asked Butkus about the falcons and the map, she deflected the question. "No one knew that you were in so deep with him," she explained. "When we stopped hearing from you, it was hard to take your call seriously." Keene had never confided in her that he was even talking to Hall, let alone that he was in his cell nightly.

The van drove him right to a sleek private jet waiting on the airstrip. When he got inside, a turkey dinner was waiting. It was nothing fancy, but it was far and away the best food he had eaten since the marshals took him to dinner near the Ford County jail six months earlier. "I literally ate like a wild animal," Keene remembers, "stuffing my face with food and scratching at my beard. But I was still livid and I kept yelling at Janice, 'This is really bullshit what you did to me.' And she kept apologizing and saying it was the doctor's fault for not keeping in touch with her and that her phone system had lost my voice mail. But I just kept raving with the turkey falling out of my mouth—kind of like a maniac myself."

Still, for all the shortcomings of the Feds, some of Jimmy's rage was also directed at himself. He had jumped the gun with Hall, and now he had no idea if he was really going home, as he'd bragged back at the Medical Center. "Without Tricia Reitler's body I did not complete my mission, and I didn't know what Beaumont was going to do about that."

His anger did not abate for another few hours until the plane circled to land in Chicago, and it finally dawned on him that at least he was out of Springfield and still had some chance that this could soon be over.

10.

Closure

DURING THE WEEKS FOLLOWING KEENE'S RELEASE from Springfield in January of 1999, his travels amounted to a fast-motion replay of his first ten months in the prison system. Butkus took him directly to Chicago's MCC from the airport, and after a mercifully brief stay, he was sent to Milan, Michigan, where Jimmy used a cover story about winning an appeal, and then, as abruptly as before, he was yanked back to Illinois, first to the MCC and then Ford County jail, where he was told he'd have to wait a few weeks for his sentencing judge, Harold Baker, to return from vacation.

As he lingered yet again inside a stinking Ford County jail cell, Jimmy could not help but worry. He may have gotten out of Springfield, but he continued to roil inside his own purgatory of remorse that he had not helped locate Tricia Reitler's body. His lawyer, Jeffrey Steinback, confirmed that the falcons and the map were not recovered, but he kept assuring Jimmy that the Feds were sure to provide some reward for his travails—especially after his unjustified stint in the hole. But who really knew how Beaumont and the judge would respond? They alone would decide his fate.

For his part, Keene was convinced that he had learned enough from Hall to become an important witness in any future prosecution. "I could get up on a stand and testify in all honesty that he did it," Jimmy says. "I know that jailhouse confessions are a dime a dozen. Prosecutors use cellie snitches to set up guys all the time. But I'm not saying that Hall like turned around one day and bragged to me how he killed those girls. It took weeks of slowly working him every night in the cell; and getting him to believe in me and believe we were friends."

Equally important in his conversations with Keene, Larry disputed key elements of the statement that was so hastily transcribed by FBI agent Randolph—especially in regards to the death of Tricia Reitler. What Hall told Jimmy was more consistent with other evidence and the victim's personality. For example, according to the statement, Larry forced her to undress in the park on the edge of the IWU campus, something her friends and parents don't believe she would ever have done without a struggle—even if threatened by a knife. It makes much more sense that she was stabbed and ultimately killed inside Hall's van, as he disclosed to Jimmy, and that Hall had neatly piled her clothes under the tree later.

The information that he gave Keene about returning home before he buried Tricia Reitler is also plausible. Unlike with Jessica Roach, he had much more time to think about disposing of her remains and to gather the tools necessary—shovel, lantern, gloves—to complete the job without leaving any evidence behind.

Suddenly one morning, without warning, the Ford County guards shackled Keene again and bundled him over to the courthouse thirty minutes away. At first he thought the judge had returned from his vacation, but instead of a holding cell, he found himself in Larry Beaumont's office.

The prosecutor—who once provoked such fear and loathing in Jimmy—now offered him a doughnut, which Keene politely refused

("I'd rather starve than eat junk food," he says), but then did something just as unexpected. He asked Keene to take a lie detector test.

"Do you have any objections to it?" Beaumont asked. "I can assure you that if everything comes out the right way, it will be in your best interest."

It was gut-check time. Beaumont could not just take Jimmy's word that Hall had confessed to him. He needed to know without a doubt.

"No, I have no problem with taking the test," Keene answered confidently. "None at all."

"Good," Beaumont said. He already had everything set up in the next room.

Jimmy had taken a polygraph before, but this equipment was nothing like the device he remembered. "They didn't just have a few wires wrapped around your fingers and biceps. Instead they had me pull off my shirt so they could attach electrodes to my chest and then they slipped some other things on my fingers and put a cap on my head. I must have looked like an alien."

Instead of running lines across a graph page, this machine had digital readouts and charts. But rather than watch the flashing lights, Keene looked out the window as the examiner began his test. "He started out asking me the most general questions. Like my favorite color or who was my first girlfriend," Jimmy remembers. "And then, out of nowhere, he hit me with a pinpoint question about Hall. What did he say and when did he say it? Did he talk about choking her first or using the rag? And then he went back to his general questions again."

It was a cold, sunny day, and Keene focused on a little sparrow that had perched on a branch just outside the window. "It was the dead of winter," he says, "and this little bird was still hanging around. I kept my eyes on it the whole time that I took the test, and I thought, 'It won't be long before I'm out there with you.'"

Beaumont was still huddling with the examiner when the U.S. marshals put the shackles back on Keene. But before they could march him out of the building, Beaumont pulled Jimmy aside. At first he glared, sending a shiver down Jimmy's spine. Then suddenly and unexpectedly his face broke into a smile. "Jimmy, you did wonderful. You passed it."

Still numb from the experience, Keene would not allow himself to be exhilarated by the news until he returned to the jail and was told to call his lawyer, Jeffrey Steinback. "I just talked to Beaumont," Steinback told him. "He is ecstatic about the results of that lie detector test. I think they're going to let you get out."

On February 23, 1999, Lawrence S. Beaumont, assistant U.S. attorney for the Central District of Illinois, filed what is known as a Motion for Reduction of Sentence Under Rule 35(B), stating, "Mr. Keene was placed in an undercover role at the Bureau of Prisons medical facility in Springfield, Missouri. He conducted this activity for approximately six months. He was able to gain specific information from the target of the investigation which may lead to the solving of a kidnapping and murder case from Indiana. During this time, Mr. Keene was placed in a facility in which he faced substantial danger."

The next day, Keene was taken to the courthouse. As opposed to his previous sentencing hearing before Judge Baker, this was mostly a procedural affair with little said in open court. But to go off the record, stern Judge Baker put his hand over the microphone. This time when he looked down again at Keene, it was not to admonish but to soothe: "Young man, I can tell you've been through hell and back. Just bear with me while we go through the formalities."

Papers were shuffled between Beaumont, the clerk, the judge, and Steinback. No formal thanks were offered one way or the other. The 35(B) motion to reduce Jimmy's sentence to time served—with a few months to spare—was granted. Judge Baker stated simply his reason for the ruling in the minutes of the proceeding: "Court finds defendant has rendered assistance."

Larry Beaumont is one lawyer who does not take polygraphs lightly. His own lie detector business helped put him through law school. If the federal government had not prevented polygraphs from being used as evidence in 1988, he would probably be in the field to this day. "They're not perfect," he says. "If it says you're lying, there's a ten percent chance it's wrong. But if it says you're telling the truth, you're telling the truth. You just can't beat it without several months of preparation."

Early in his career as a state's attorney, Beaumont put his belief in lie detectors to the test in the case of a botched kidnapping that ended with the death of a Kankakee media mogul. To spare his girlfriend, the man who was ultimately convicted for the kidnapping fingered a local criminal as his accomplice. "We grabbed that guy while he was eating breakfast and threw him in a jail cell," Beaumont remembers, "and he said, 'Hey, I'm a burglar and a car thief, but I sure as hell didn't kidnap anybody.' He claimed that at the time of abduction he was having sex with a girl and described in pretty graphic terms what they were doing. I polygraphed him and sure enough he passed. Before we let him out of jail, we next questioned the girl, and she corroborated everything he said—right down to the graphic details. From then on, he was no longer a suspect in the kidnapping. You could say that the polygraph ended up saving that guy a lot of time and expense—if not his life."

For Beaumont, Larry Hall's case is exactly the sort that proves the polygraph's value. Not only did Keene pass his battery of questions, but Hall failed *his* test when he took a polygraph soon after he arrived in Illinois. Although it was never publicized, Beaumont did grant Hall's request to take a lie detector test, which he made repeatedly to

FBI agent Randolph. "The FBI was dead set against giving him a polygraph," Beaumont says, but the prosecutor wanted to call Hall's bluff. "I just couldn't see how it would hurt us, so I arranged for him to get a polygraph from a state examiner." As he expected, Hall failed the test, and although the results could not be used against Larry in court, they did confirm for Beaumont and Miller that Hall really was a worthy suspect in both the Roach and Reitler cases. "I also watched a videotape of the examination," Beaumont says, "and Hall even looked deceitful."

Today in private practice, having retired from the Department of Justice in 2006, Beaumont has shaved off the beard that Jimmy Keene once found so fearsome and looks back on the Larry Hall case with few regrets. Beaumont does not deny that "competition" developed between his team and the Marion detectives during the investigation leading up to Hall's trial. "We were pretty sure [Hall] did Reitler, and there was kind of a fight between us and Marion [police] because they were so convinced that he didn't do it. Then, when they came out in that article before trial where they were quoted saying that [Tony Searcy was the prime suspect], that pissed us off even more."

Ironically, Beaumont had second thoughts about including Reitler in the first trial. He explains, "Because we didn't have any physical evidence with her case, it really could have looked like Hall was somebody who was just confessing to a lot of murders. But finally we did feel that we could not leave Reitler out, if for no other reason than to give her parents some closure. They really were not aware of all the evidence implicating Hall, and when that trial began, they still had no idea of what happened to their daughter. I have a little girl myself, and I can only imagine what that's like to have your daughter suddenly disappear."

Beaumont again tried to give the Reitlers closure when he conducted the search party to Marion and, after that failed, when he plucked Keene out of Milan and sent him to Springfield. The idea to choose Jimmy for the mission, Beaumont says, actually came from a DEA agent in the narcotics task force. "All I knew was that Jimmy Keene was a smart, wily kid who wasn't happy with the sentence we gave him. I figured he would jump at the opportunity to get out early."

As to the ultimate outcome, he says, "Well, we didn't find the body, and the goal of this investigation was to find the body. In fact, I had told Jim that unless we found the body, he ain't getting jack for it. But once he passed the polygraph about the statements he heard from Hall, I still had to ask the judge to give him credit. It was the only fair thing we could do because, after all, he did sit in the nuthouse with this guy."

Ironically, within days of Keene's passing the lie detector test, the Seventh Circuit released its decision on Hall's second appeal. This time the jury's guilty verdict was affirmed with the court finding that the judge acted appropriately in admitting and barring expert testimony for the retrial.

If nothing else, Beaumont had the satisfaction of knowing that Hall would spend the rest of his life in prison for the murder of Jessica Roach. But his attempt to tie him to Tricia Reitler's abduction or any other murders appeared to come to an official end with the motion to release Jimmy Keene.

In fact, the investigation was still far from over. Now Jimmy's story would accomplish what he himself could not. It would continue to play out in unexpected ways over the next nine years with allies and sources that Beaumont would never have anticipated in his wildest dreams.

Today, if there is any clearinghouse for the Larry Hall investigation, it resides in the boxes and file cabinets of Ron Smith's home office. When Smith retired five years ago from the Wabash City police department, where he served as both a patrolman and a detective, he started work as pastor for his church. At sixty-three, he is a big, expansive man with a brown brush mustache. "One thing about us ex-cops," he says, laughing, "We either turn to God or the bottle." But in the last few years, he has also devoted an increasing amount of his spare time to all of the various loose ends that the night janitor may have left behind.

"One of the first ones goes back to 1987," he says. "A sixteen-year-old girl." Although Smith is reluctant to provide the name, she has been identified as Wendy Felton by other investigators and lived just two miles from where Tricia Reitler was last seen. Although as with Reitler, Felton's body was never found, her likely abduction from a quiet road near the family farmstead bore similarities to that of Jessica Roach.

In 2007 Smith was again approached about Larry Hall by a state police trooper in Rochester, Michigan, this time regarding a woman found just a month before Hall confessed to Randolph and Miller. If Felton had been the first known victim, this older woman was probably the last. Police believed that she had been a prostitute. Like the other suspected Hall victims who had been found—Beck, Rison, and Roach—she, too, had been strangled. If Larry had really killed her, Smith says, he had reached a murderous frenzy where he was going after any vulnerable woman he could find, which may be why he even pursued the middle-aged jogger who lived up the street from him in Wabash.

In the winter of 2007, during a car trip to Florida, Smith made a stop in Butner, North Carolina—just outside of Durham—where Hall is currently incarcerated in a high-security hospital. Although Larry had to give him permission before he could visit, Smith found him to be barely coherent when he arrived. "I really didn't get him to respond to anything until I took out a picture [of Wendy Felton], and just like Gary Miller did, I laid it out in front of him and he couldn't take his eyes off of it. Then, out of nowhere, he said, 'Oh, yeah, I remember her.' I said, 'You do?' And he said, 'Yeah, she used to work in a restaurant. I was going in there to eat pretty frequently. And I bought her some jewelry and then she befriended me and I had to kill her.'" Of course none of the details applied to Wendy Felton, but something about her picture had touched off Hall's babble of free associations. For the retired detective, the sudden bits of confession were like the brief flashes of lucidity one hears from someone with dementia or severe schizophrenia.

"I never found out who he was really talking about," Smith says, "but the clinical psychologist who was watching about fell off his chair. He said, 'I've never even seen him talk to anybody like that.' I said, 'Well, I've known him for years.'

"I later found out that his mother found out I was coming and she tried to get him to stop from talking to me."

As far as Smith is concerned, all mysteries about Larry Hall begin and end with his brother, Gary. The twin fervently defended Larry during his trials and appeared to take the convictions especially hard. He later became chronically unemployed and needed treatment for substance abuse—at the same public facility where his brother received counseling in the year before he was arrested for murder. After their father, Robert, died in 2001, Gary stayed with their mother in a tiny house owned by his older half brother, who maintained steady employment at a local factory. But at times Gary was also seen by friends living out of a car. They have no doubt that his decline was due to Larry's crimes. "He keeps telling you, 'I'm not like my brother,'" says Ron Osborne, who knew the Halls back in high school when they cruised street rods together. "But I think somewhere deep down inside he's afraid he *could* be like him since he is his identical twin. And the truth is that Gary has not been emotionally or mentally stable since his brother [was arrested]."

Some of Larry's therapists believe that Gary may have played a much larger role in his twin's pathology than he ever thought or intended. They argue that when Gary moved out of the family household to live with and then marry his girlfriend, it fundamentally rearranged the furniture in Larry's psyche. None of them articulates this better than psychiatrist Arthur Traugott, who was a witness in Larry's defense. "I remember very distinctly when Larry was telling me about Gary's first marriage and how Larry just felt utterly abandoned," Traugott testified in the first trial. "As he was telling me about this during the interview, he broke into tears crying about how he felt left alone."

The hectoring voice in Larry's notes may have cropped up to take the absent twin's place. As one counselor points out, it is probably no accident that victims such as Jessica Roach and Tricia Reitler had the same hairstyle and body type of Gary's first wife, Catherine, who was sixteen when they first started dating.

But in the eyes of retired Wabash detective Ron Smith, Gary shares some more direct blame for his brother's homicidal behavior or at least in covering it up. Smith believes that may feed his guilt as well. During the years of Gary's downward slide, Smith reached out to him to see if he would be willing to come clean. When they met, it was only for short, sporadic sessions. "When he was living with his mom, you couldn't get anywhere near him," Smith says. "He would ask to meet you someplace and then would never show up. I probably spoke to him a total of three and a half hours over three years, and like Larry, he gave me stuff in bits and pieces—just enough to get me interested but not too much to make me think he was involved in what his brother did."

The twin confided in Ron about the road trip that he, Larry, and another friend took out West in 1984. According to Smith, Gary said, "We got this girl and we had our way with her." It's not clear exactly what Gary meant by this, and he has never been charged with any sexual assault, but Smith wonders whether that incident tripped a lust reflex inside Larry that led to the later rapes and murders.

Gary also told Smith about the reenactment and sightseeing vacation in Pennsylvania that the twins took with Gary's second wife and how the couple booted Larry out of their motel room. Smith says, "So [Larry] then took off in Gary's car. They didn't see him for a while, but when he came back, he went and got another room and took a shower for several hours. And when he came out of the motel room, he was all kind of roughed up with scuff marks on his face. And Gary is telling me this like he's finally put all the pieces together. He then said, 'I didn't think much about it until we were back home and all of a sudden my wife gave me all kinds of shit and wanted to know what female I had in my car, because she found a woman's earring underneath the front seat and it didn't belong to her.'"

Another time, Gary told Smith, Larry took him to a farmer's field by the Mississinewa reservoir where they could search for arrowheads. "He says, 'We were out walking all through there and we go by a gravel pit, and I see what I think is a hand sticking up, and when I said, 'Did you see that?' Larry grabbed my arm and brought me to the side and said, 'I don't think you want to go over there.'"

But most disturbing for Smith is what happened, according to Gary, after Larry was arrested by Deputy Sheriff Miller. From the jail in Marion, Hall called his father and told him to retrieve some items from his storage cars in Ross Davis's barn. When Robert returned, Gary told Smith, he saw him with a "big map" of Indiana with more than twenty "DB" marks all over it. Smith says, "I asked him, 'What's DB stand for?' and he answered, 'At the bottom [of the map] it said DB equals "dead body."'" And then he watched his dad burn that map into a trash can." Smith later talked to one of Robert's neighbors who saw him burning material in barrels for several days after Larry's arrest.

Ron Smith was not the only Wabash resident to hear these revelations about Larry Hall from his twin brother. In late 2007 Gary Hall dropped by Ron Osborne's house with Osborne's younger brother.

The two had met when they were both in the same drug treatment program. Since Ron Osborne has long worked at a Wabash foundry, his unemployed brother came to ask him for money and Gary tagged along. It had been years since Ron Osborne had seen Gary, and he says, "I didn't hardly recognize him. He looked pretty rough and his hair had some gray. He talks different now—like a robot really—and I think he was a little messed up that night, so it was pretty sad. Just to be polite, I asked him how his brother was doing, and he told me that Larry was in a prison for the criminally insane. And then he says, 'Because he killed twenty-two women.'

"And I was shocked. I asked, 'That many?' I didn't realize he had done that many. To be honest with you, I didn't really follow the case that closely in the newspapers. Then he sat there telling me details about how the first couple [of women] that Larry did, that he couldn't look them in the eye, so he pinned them up against a tree and he strangled them from the other side.

"He was telling me that and I was like, 'You've got to be kidding me.' And I asked him, 'How did you *not* know [Larry was doing these things]?' He said, 'Well, when we would go away to these reenactments, we'd have like a camp setup, and what he would do is sneak out of the tent after everyone was asleep and do whatever he did and come back.'"

Ron Osborne says he later told his younger brother, "I would rather you not bring him here again."

"I have problems with my memory," Larry Hall says. "I'm not sure why that is."*

---

*In August 2008, Hillel Levin had a phone conversation with Larry Hall that lasted a little more than an hour. Although they arranged to meet in person, the warden of Butner Correctional Center did not permit Levin further contact with him.

But during a brief telephone interview in the summer of 2008, Hall is nothing like the incoherent puddle of free associations that former detective Ron Smith encountered a year before. As Larry explains, his real problem then was sleep apnea—not schizophrenia as Smith thought. Since he's been using a mask at his bedside to assist with breathing, he's been getting full nights of sleep for the first time in his adulthood. Indeed, his responses to questions are quick and lucid, and his high-pitched voice sounds steady with just a slight warble at the end of his sentences. Despite the protest about his memory, he still remembers that he was blamed for breaking those store windows when he was fifteen and that they cost $500 to repair.

Most of the memories of his youth are sharp—the childhood playmates, his teachers in school, each and every car he owned, the Civil War battlefields he visited. When asked about his tendency to look away from cameras in all the photographs, he quickly replies, "I'm always afraid of breaking them. I never really liked the way I looked. Maybe that's got something to do with it."

He is equally candid about the solitary life he lived as a young man—still in his parents' house and working alone at night. "I didn't want to keep living my life the way I was living it," he says. "I wanted things to be different, you know, but I guess I didn't really do the right things and change the way my life was going."

When asked what his dream would have been if he had won the lottery, he replies, "Then I would have bought my mom and dad a nice new house. And bought myself one real close so I could, you know, watch over them and take care of them."

It is the answer of the good and kind son as his mother portrayed him in interviews with reporters. But something adolescent is in these wishes as well, and when asked what his dream job would have been, he also harks back to the passions of his teen years, saying, "[To] own my own street-rod shop, where I could fix up antique street rods."

As for girlfriends and family, he says of his life before prison, "I thought about getting married a couple different times, but it always kind of scared me off. I'm not sure why, but I was always afraid of not being able to handle a family. After I had seen what had happened to both my brothers being married twice and divorcing, having to pay a lot of child support, it kind of scared me off."

Larry has no contact with his nieces, although one lives near the prison in North Carolina, and he admits that he has not seen Gary in ten years. He explains, "It's a long travel distance from Indiana," but even though he calls his mother on the phone each week, he does not talk to Gary.

He seems resigned to living the rest of his life in the Butner prison, but misses Springfield, where he says he had several good friends. When asked about Jimmy Keene, he hesitates at first and then replies, "I became friends with James for a short while. As I remember it, when he found out what I was charged with, he kind of scared me off. I didn't really want to be around him anymore."

Hall then names the woman who was his "doctor" in Springfield and says, "She had [Keene] put in the hole because he said that he knew I was responsible for a bunch of people dying, and he was going to get it out of me. . . . I felt bad about him going to the hole, but I felt that he was sent [to Springfield] by the prosecutor. . . . I'm not sure why [Beaumont] acted the way he did towards me, but I felt that he had a lot of hate for me and I don't really understand why."

Larry's doctor certainly did not have that hate for him. Not only did she protect him from Keene and Beaumont, she also had him transferred to one of the most desired placements in the Bureau of Prisons—the medium-security facility in Oxford, Wisconsin. Set among rolling hills and dairy farms, it has a culinary vocational program and the best food in the federal prison system. "It's like a hotel in there," one frequent visitor told the *Chicago Tribune*. "It's clean and comfortable and quite quiet." As a result, it has become the destination of choice for Chicago's convicted mobsters and corrupt politicians.

If Hall's doctor truly believed he was a dangerous serial killer, it's unlikely that she would have sent him to a place with lower security than the Medical Center. But once a convict enters the Bureau of Prisons, no outside checks are made on his transfers within the system. His doctor can take the place of the sentencing judge, jury, and prosecutor. A law enforcement officer familiar with Hall's prison records says, "It's amazing how Larry brings out the maternal instincts in the women who have worked with him in prison, especially when you consider the crimes he committed against women on the outside."

But if Hall's Springfield doctor thought she was doing him any favors by transferring him out of the MCFP, she was wrong. He did not like Oxford at all and attempted suicide there.* Another factor contributing to Hall's depression may have been that when the Seventh Circuit court denied his second appeal, any flickering hope of leaving prison was snuffed out forever.

After the suicide attempt, Hall was sent to the BOP's hospital in Rochester, Minnesota, for intensive treatment, and then, in 2004, to the long-term psychiatric care center in Butner. By the summer of 2008 when he had the interview over the phone, Larry may have regained his senses with the treatment for sleep apnea, but he was not yet ready to concede that he had committed murder. Why then did he confess to so many different policemen? He replies, "I did confess to certain policemen that I had dreams that I did things."

And could those dreams be a window into actual things that the bad side of Larry Hall has done? After a few moments of silence, he says, "Yes, I've thought of that."

Only eight months later, in April 2009, Larry would not be so

---

*Psychologist Joel Norris writes, "Often serial killers who are not caught eventually kill themselves. This is the final act in a life of utter despair and hopelessness.... Most serial killers find a way to turn themselves in before they choose to commit suicide. They accomplish this by becoming too despondent to take the care to conceal their latest crime."

tentative. Instead, he swung back to making the sort of full confession that would be difficult—if not impossible—to deny later. Once again, his admission was prompted by two visiting law enforcement officers, but this time they were joined by none other than his twin brother, Gary.

The police were cold-case detectives from Indianapolis investigating the 1991 murder of twenty-one-year-old Michelle Dewey. She had been strangled at home in a quiet residential neighborhood known as Irvington. Her infant son had been left unharmed in the next room. Although the family always suspected that an old boyfriend committed the crime, the police were not so sure and could find no evidence to link him to the killing. The 2008 August issue of *Playboy*, with an article about Jimmy Keene's mission to Springfield, appeared nearly seventeen years after Dewey's death, but the story became especially timely for the cold-case detectives when they read about Tricia Reitler and Hall's forays to Marion—just eighty miles north of Indianapolis, up U.S. Route 69. When they contacted retired Wabash detective Ron Smith, he suggested that they go see Larry in Butner, North Carolina, and bring Gary Hall along.

If Jimmy Keene had become something of a substitute twin to Larry to get him to confess in Springfield, then the real twin would be the catalyst to keep him confessing in Butner. After briefly meeting with Gary, Larry agreed to speak with the Indianapolis police and admitted that he killed Michelle Dewey. As he did before with FBI agent Mike Randolph and Deputy Sheriff Gary Miller, Hall provided vivid details about the murder that were not generally known to the public. He was drawn to her neighborhood by his never-ending search for a vintage Dodge van advertised in the *Auto Trader,* and Michelle caught his attention as she lay sunbathing in her backyard. When he followed her into the house, he was startled by the cries of her baby and left soon after he strangled her, but took a record album with him as a souvenir.

According to Gary Hall, Larry did not just admit to the Dewey murder. He confessed to killing fourteen other young women as well. He continued talking with the detectives for five hours until visiting hours were over. They returned the following day and spent another eight hours with Larry before they were through.

Gary broke the news about his twin's confessions during a November 2009 interview on Indianapolis TV station WTHR. He no longer had the gray, haggard look that Ron Osborne had seen two years before. Instead his brushed-back hair was jet-black. With a tanned complexion and scruffy Fu Manchu, he appeared more Mexican than Midwestern, but his voice had the same high-pitched whine and warble of his brother's. "I believe Larry killed Michelle," he told the WTHR reporter. "I believe Larry killed a lot of young women, I'm sorry to say."

The victims, Gary revealed, were spread out across the country. In addition to Indiana, Illinois, and Wisconsin, he counted out California, Colorado, Missouri, and Wyoming on his fingers—states that had not previously appeared as places of suspected Larry Hall murders. He then added, "I don't believe he's making any of this up. He's got too many specific details."

When the reporter asked Gary why he was "coming forward" with the information about his twin brother, he replied, "We're searching for the truth," but then he echoed the sentiments expressed by both Jimmy Keene and Larry Beaumont in the *Playboy* article. "We want closure for the families," Gary said. "We want the victims all brought home—every last one of them."

He confirmed that those victims included Tricia Reitler. On the second day of their interview with Larry, the Indianapolis detectives brought him a map to show them where he buried her. Hall pinpointed a spot near 700 West *Old* Slocum Trail—the same address listed in his notes for "Frances Slocum Trail."

As the Indianapolis detectives have worked through the information they received from Hall, they have been careful to keep Garry and Donna Reitler abreast of the investigation. "We are very honored that they continue to focus on finding Tricia," Garry says. The Reitlers were not aware of all the evidence connecting Larry Hall to the abduction of their daughter until the *Playboy* article was published. In addition, the scenario that Hall disclosed to Keene makes much more sense to them than the statement originally taken by Deputy Sheriff Miller and FBI agent Randolph.

But knowing who murdered Tricia is not enough for her parents. "We just need to find Tricia," Donna says. "That immeasurable longing never ceases. The ache is still unbearable."

Given the sixteen years that have elapsed since Tricia's murder and the remote area where she was buried, it may still be a challenge to find her remains—no matter how accurately Hall marked the map. Garry Reitler remains hopeful and is anxious for the authorities to start looking again with cadaver dogs, but because of the dense wilderness in the area, searches must be limited to a few weeks before spring, when vegetation starts to flourish, or winter, when the ground freezes. If necessary, he believes Hall should be brought back to assist them. An important incentive could be a last chance to see his mother, since she has been too infirm to visit him in prison. But Garry adds, "Ideally we wouldn't need his help."

The Reitlers often think about a project they could pursue that would prevent other families from going through the same ordeal, which could be a living tribute to Tricia's memory. Garry says, "Maybe there could be a resource to help educate the police about serial killers, so if someone does confess, they know whether to take it seriously."

Meanwhile, Garry has no problem updating the Marion police with anything he learns from the Indianapolis cold-case detectives.

He bears Lieutenant Jay Kay and Detective Bruce Bender no ill will for dismissing Hall as a suspect in their daughter's case. "We know their hearts," he says, "and they are passionate about finding her—even if Larry ends up being the one to tell us where to look."

Ironically, if Jimmy Keene's mission to Springfield did not succeed in providing closure to one family—the Reitlers—it did for another: his own.

After he left Judge Baker's courtroom, Keene still had to bounce around the BOP like a pinball. First he had to go back to the MCC for processing, then again to Milan, where Jimmy expected his release would come in days. The first night there, he couldn't sleep, but since he was placed in a lower-security unit, he was permitted to watch television. When he first walked into the TV room, it appeared to be empty, lit only by the shimmering light of the television screen. But as he went to sit down, he noticed his old library coworker and former bank president, Frank Cihak, slumped in a nearby chair.

Keene went over to greet him. "Hey, Frank, how you doing?"

"Hey, Jim," Cihak said in a monotone. He barely looked up and kept staring at the television. When he spoke again, he asked, "So how's it going on your appeal?"

"Everything went really well," Jimmy replied. "Actually, I could be out of here in the next four or five days."

Cihak rocked backward and turned to fully face Keene. "That's some news, Jim. I'm really happy for you." Cihak then swallowed and added, "I finally lost my last appeal and I'm never getting out of here. I'm going to die in here."

Then, in the light of the TV set, Keene saw the tears running down Cihak's face.

Keene could only sit and watch. "I felt bad for the guy, but I really didn't know what to say to him."

When Jimmy finally met his caseworker at Milan, he discovered his own unpleasant news. To satisfy all the terms of his release, he needed one official meeting with the probation officer, and that could not happen for another few months. Meanwhile, Milan was too full for him to wait there, so he was bounced again, this time to the prison in Terre Haute, Indiana. The facility had similar levels of security as Milan, but with older, grungy facilities.

When he first arrived in Indiana, Keene was placed in solitary until his paperwork could be fully processed and a bed was found for him in the prison camp. "Every solitary unit is shitty," he says, "especially because you can smell the other guys there. It's beyond body odor. It's like death."

Terre Haute is the one federal prison with a death row, and a few weeks after Keene arrived, he watched what looked like a military division—complete with battle-helicopter gunships—bring in Oklahoma City bomber Timothy McVeigh, who would be executed there two years later.

When Jimmy did get his bed in a low-security prison-camp building, he discovered that another inmate in his wing would be B, the alphabet gangbanger who'd fought with him in Milan. "As soon as I saw him, I thought, 'You've got to be shitting me, man. This guy is going to be on my trail for the last few weeks before I get out of here.' It's so typical of the prison system that they would put us together without checking whether we had any problems."

But the two found a way to keep their distance. Jimmy says, "I just bought my time until it was over and I finally got out of there." It was August 1999, and practically a year had passed since the U.S. marshals had taken Keene to Springfield, but it could have been another lifetime.

To pick up Jimmy in Terre Haute, Big Jim drove a van for the three-hour trip from Kankakee and brought along Keene's brother and sister for the ride. After his stroke, he had recovered nearly all of his robust vitality, although one corner of his mouth still drooped slightly. Jimmy had already had one tearful reunion with his father in the MCC after he was released from Springfield. This time, there were no tears—just buoyant happiness. "We went and grabbed this gigantic meal and I had fish. Not the deep-fried crap they gave us in the prison chow halls, but something that was real fresh and tasted as good as any meal I ever had."

As they ate, Keene's sister teased him about how muscle-bound he had gotten after all those months of lifting weights in prison. "Look at your arms," she said. "You are getting way too big."

Big Jim disagreed. "I think it looks good on him. He looks like he used to look when he played ball." It was as if there had never been any drug dealing or prison sentence or failed business ventures. It was as if Big Jim's golden son had the chance to start all over again.

But from then on when father and son got together, they were no longer so focused on the obsessions of their earlier lives. Jimmy Keene says, "Before, if we saw each other, it was always about something else—the sports when I was a kid or the business deals when I was older—but after I left prison, we would just hang out. Go on his boat, maybe fish a little or do nothing more than sit around on a couple of lawn chairs. It was crazy, but after all I had been through, it wasn't so important that we get rich anymore. We just enjoyed each other's company."

On the night of November 28, 2004, five years after Jimmy got out of prison, James Keene died suddenly of a heart attack at the age of sixty-seven. If Jimmy had not accepted Larry Beaumont's mission to Springfield, he would still have been in the Milan correctional center.

I still can't believe my dad died. I think about him every day. There are times after something happens when I pick up the phone, ready to give him a call and tell him about it. I can never forget his voice—that deep, booming voice. I hear it like we just talked yesterday.

Once, we were driving around town together when I was fourteen or fifteen, and Dad pointed out the car window to a storefront and said, "Now that's a lucrative business, Son."

"What does lucrative mean?" I asked him.

He got a big laugh out of that. "You've got to be kidding me," he said. "What are they teaching you guys in school these days? I want you to go home and I want you to learn what the word lucrative means, and you come back and tell me when you know."

And he meant it, too. I couldn't just shrug it off and hope he'd forget about it. He really expected me to look that word up, and I did. I memorized the dictionary definition, and the next time we were together, I told him the meaning of lucrative without him having to ask me. He said, "That's very good, Son. Why aren't they teaching you those things in school?"

I heard that a lot from him. He wanted me to go to school and do well, but he always thought that life's lessons were the most important learning I could do. Now, when I look back on my mission to Springfield, I understand what that whole experience really taught me. Until that time, I don't think I fully appreciated life and the importance of just being around the ones I love. After my early release, the five years I had with my father meant more to me than all the money in the world. I'm sure the families of Larry's victims would say the same if they could bring those girls back.

Sometimes I wonder what would have happened if Beaumont didn't pull me out of Milan. I was pretty set in that prison with the mob guys, and if I had hung around with them for ten years, I would probably have gone to work for them once I was released. Who knows? I didn't have anything else going for me.

Now, I can't imagine doing anything that takes advantage of other people's weakness. Since I got out in 1999, I haven't had any trouble with the law, and everything I've done to earn a living has been honest. Lately, I've been working on some book and movie projects related to my experiences. If a movie about me does come along, that would be pretty ironic—especially with my *father's passing. After I got out of prison, nobody else believed that I would ever amount to anything. When I used to tell people I could make something of my story, they practically laughed in my face. But my dad was different. He never let me forget that I gave up a chance to go to Hollywood after I met Tom Cruise and Martin Scorsese. He actually thought I could move mountains and the best in life was yet to come. But I can hear him saying, in that big booming voice, "It's about time, Son. It's about time."*

Introduction

The jail dated back to the nineteenth century . . . Ford County Historical Society, *Atlas of the State of Illinois* (Mt. Vernon, IN: Windmill Publications, 1992), 11.

Notations at the bottom of the photo . . . Grant County, IN, Sheriff's Department, "Larry Hall Mug Shot" (November 16, 1994).

Beaumont added, "We think he's responsible for more than twenty other killings" . . . Associated Press, "Report: Hall linked to 20 murders," *Wabash (IN) Plain Dealer,* January 21, 1995.

His clients have ranged from . . . Maria Kantzavelos, "Profile: Jeffrey Steinback," *Chicago Lawyer,* November 13, 2008, http://www.chicagolawyermagazine.com/2008/11/13/profile-jeffrey-steinback/.

1. Fathers & Sons

"It's the judgment of the court . . ." United States of America v. James Keene (CD IL 1997), sentencing hearing transcript at 154.

"I know I did something wrong . . ." Ibid. at 152.

George [Ryan who] would also end up in prison . . . The other Illinois governors who preceded Ryan to prison were Otto Kerner in 1973 and Dan Walker (also from the Kankakee area and a friend of Big Jim's) in 1987. Ryan, who started out as a pharmacist, also served as Speaker of the House of Representatives, lieutenant governor, and secretary of state. Matt O'Connor, "Feds say Ryan is greedy, 2-faced—prosecutors tee off in closing arguments," *Chicago Tribune,* March 7, 2006, Chicago Final edition; Matt O'Connor, "Ryan gets 6½ years—ex-governor regrets conviction, but doesn't admit to wrongdoing," *Chicago Tribune,* September 7, 2006, Chicago Final edition; "Verdict is talk of the town where Ryan makes home," *Chicago Tribune,* April 18, 2006, Chicago Final edition.

But such was the Kankakee pedigree of power and corruption . . . Lennington "Len" Small was yet another Kankakee politician who went on to become governor and was indicted soon after his election in 1921. He was acquitted and served a second term, during which he commuted the sentences of thousands of prisoners— supposedly in return for a fee that he split with their lawyers. Among the men he let out were some of Capone's top henchmen. Mark Grossman, *Political Corruption in America: An Encyclopedia of Scandals, Power, and Greed,* 2nd ed. (Millerton, NY: Grey House Pub, 2008), 304–5.

Their team ultimately went all the way . . . "Keene in Control," *Kankakee (IL) Daily Journal,* November 6, 1980.

If Big Jim had any illusions . . . United States of America v. James Keene (CD IL 1997), Presentence Investigation Report at 12.

For nearly the next twenty-four hours . . . Ibid., 4–9.

It took another few weeks . . . Ibid., 3.

What Richards alone said he bought . . . Ibid., 10.

Jimmy's lawyer tried lamely . . . Keene sentencing hearing transcript at 150.

"It's well-known," he said . . . Ibid., 146–47.

2. On the Banks of the Wabash, Far Away

When the sister found it abandoned . . . United States of America v. Larry D. Hall (CD IL 1995), trial transcript 37–45.

Georgetown, Illinois (population) . . . U.S. Census Bureau, "Georgetown City, Illinois— Fact Sheet—American FactFinder," factfinder.census.gov, 2000.

When he called his chief investigator . . . Hillel Levin, Gary Miller interview, December 2007.

Miller, then forty-five . . . Margie Yee, "Deputy retires after 31 years," *Danville (IL) Commercial-News,* January 4, 2004.

At first, Miller had his hands full . . . Levin, Miller interview.

he came across [a report] about a man in a van . . . Hall trial transcript, 322–27.

On a hunch . . . Levin, Miller interview; Hillel Levin, Jeffrey Whitmer interview, February 2008.

The Miami, the native tribe . . . William Bright, *Native American Placenames of the United States* (Norman: University of Oklahoma Press, 2004), 537.

It is the longest river . . . "WabashRiver.us—History," WabashRiver.us, http://www.wabashriver.us; Mark Bennett, "Paul Dresser: Popular songwriter crafted state song," *Terre Haute (IN) Tribune-Star,* February 2, 2005, sec. Special Reports.

Despite the sentimental attachment . . . "Canal Society of Indiana—Impact on Indiana Geography," http://www.indcanal.org/Geography.html; "WabashRiver.us—History."

Nothing exemplifies that spirit . . . "A brief history of time (in Indiana)," *Indianapolis Star,* April 30, 2005, sec. Library Fact Files, http://www2.indystar.com/library/factfiles/history/time.

Police headquarters . . . Levin, Whitmer interview.

At first, Miller didn't know . . . Levin, Miller interview.

Miller asked first . . . Gary Miller, "Jessica Roach Death Investigation" (Vermilion County Sheriff's Department, November 2, 1994), 107–9.

3. Lost in the System

It held both antsy . . . Blair Kamin, "Jail a prisoner of ill-conceived renovation plan," *Chicago Tribune,* October 22, 2006, Chicagoland Final edition.

One of Green's codefendants . . . Matt O'Connor, "Noah Robinson Is Found Guilty Again in Retrial—4 High-Ranking El Rukns Also Are Convicted," *Chicago Tribune,* September 27, 1996, North Sports Final edition.

The prison's low-rise buildings sprawl . . . "BOP: FCI Milan," Federal Bureau of Prisons, September 24, 2009, http://www.bop.gov/locations/institutions/mil/index.jsp.

Cihak, who had another twenty years to serve . . . Among Cihak's frauds was an excessive loan he provided to Calumet Farm, one of the most successful breeders of thoroughbred racing champions. In return, Cihak was to receive a share of one of the stable's racehorses. Partly to repay the loan, Calumet's owners killed Alydar—thrice runner-up to Affirmed in the Triple Crown—to collect on the insurance. They, too, received prison sentences. Skip Hollandsworth, "The Killing of Alydar," *Texas Monthly,* June 2001; Associated Press, "Calumet Honchos Found Guilty—CBS News," http://www.cbsnews.com.

At sixty, Frank Calabrese Sr. . . . . During the Family Secrets trial in the summer of 2007, Calabrese was linked to thirteen murders. Both his younger brother and his son testified for the prosecution. He was convicted of ten of them. "He Killed 14 People. He Got 12 Years—Murder victims' families react in shock, but judge says that without hit man's testimony, mob bosses would still be free," *Chicago Tribune,* March 27, 2009, Chicagoland Final edition; "10 murders laid at feet of 3 in mob—some families wish verdict went further," *Chicago Tribune,* September 28, 2007, Chicago edition.

"Everybody thinks they were killed out in that cornfield . . ." "Setting Hollywood Straight— Spilotros lured to suburbs, killed," *Chicago Tribune,* July 19, 2007, Chicago edition.

Calabrese's younger brother confessed . . . "He Killed 14," *Chicago Tribune.*

For some of the media covering the trial . . . Tapes of conversations between Frank Sr. and Jr. were crucial evidence in the case against the father. "'Made' in the Chicago mob—undercover tape details Outfit initiation ceremony, and reputed mobster's son tells jurors why he decided to turn on his dad," *Chicago Tribune,* July 10, 2007, Chicagoland edition.

The problem, Beaumont explained, was that no federal prisoner . . . Hillel Levin, Lawrence Beaumont interview, January 2008.

4. Life in the Cemetery

Things never went better . . . Hillel Levin, Larry Hall interview, August 2008.

for the son of a housepainter . . . Roy Hall, Robert's father, reported himself to be self-employed as a "painter" when he registered for the draft in World War II. He described his occupation as "house moving" on his World War I registration card. "Draft Registration Cards—Roy E. Hall," Ancestry.com, 1942.

The Falls is one of the oldest independent cemeteries . . . Background on the cemetery and Wabash was provided by Ron Woodward, a former high school teacher, longtime board member of the Falls cemetery, and the official Wabash historian. Hillel Levin, Ron Woodward interview, January 2008.

For most of those who grew up in the neighborhood . . . Hillel Levin, Ross Davis interview, February 2008; Hillel Levin, Ron Osborne interview, December 2007.

When the boys were born . . . "Hospital News," *Wabash (IN) Plain Dealer,* December 12, 1962.

Robert was forty . . . U.S. Social Security Administration, "Social Security Death Index—Robert R. Hall," Ancestry.com, 2001.

Berniece thirty-three . . . U.S. Census Bureau, "1930 United States Federal Census— Wabash, Wabash, Indiana" (U.S. Government, 1930).

She already had a sixteen-year-old . . . Levin, Hall interview; "People Search & Directory Services—Eugene Cloe," Intelius.com, http://www.intelius.com.

Larry emerged from the womb looking blue . . . Levin, Hall interview.

A more recent diagnosis . . . Elizabeth M. Bryan, *Twins, Triplets, and More: From Pre-Birth Through High School—What Every Parent Needs to Know When Raising Two or More,* 1st ed. (New York: St. Martin's Press, 1999), 28.

Because of Larry's complications . . . "Hospital News," *Wabash (IN) Plain Dealer,* December 17, 1962.

Despite their modest means . . . Levin, Davis interview.

Some friends believe they were led into the mischief . . . Ibid.; Levin, Woodward interview; Levin, Osborne interview.

Wabash detective Ron Smith and his partner were assigned . . . Hillel Levin, Ron Smith, Phil Amones interview, January 2008.

Growing up, the twins were inseparable . . . Levin, Davis interview; Hall trial transcript at 1171.

While searching the woods and fields around Wabash . . . Levin, Davis interview.

Besides the name of Wabash itself . . . Stewart Rafert, *The Miami Indians of Indiana: A Persistent People, 1654–1994* (Indianapolis: Indiana Historical Society, 1996), 72–76.

Each year, reenactments . . . Mississinewa Battlefield Society, "Mississinewa 1812," mississinewa1812.com, 2009.

The government ultimately prevailed . . . Rafert, *Miami Indians,* 108–13.

She chose to remain . . . Ibid., 103–4.

In the 1960s, as if to further obliterate . . . The reservoir's most controversial collateral damage was to Miami burial grounds, particularly the grave site of Frances Slocum, whose body had to be disinterred and moved elsewhere. Ibid., 252–53.

The twins avidly read stories . . . Levin, Hall interview.

Little of the twins' curiosity . . . Levin, Woodward interview.

"We used to say our high school . . ." Levin, Davis interview.

From the time he was a little boy . . . Levin, Hall interview.

Allen has only fond memories of Larry . . . Hillel Levin, Robert Allen interview, January 2008.

The experience with Allen . . . Levin, Hall interview.

But for all of Larry's expertise . . . Levin, Osborne interview.

"Gary had a mouth on him . . ." Levin, Davis interview.

None of his friends remember him having a girlfriend—ever . . . Levin, Hall interview; Levin, Davis interview; Hillel Levin, Micheal Thompson interview, January 2008.

But with his long hair . . . Levin, Davis interview.

The twins could not share . . . Hall trial transcript at 1171.

It would get even worse in 1984 . . . Levin, Woodward interview.

Larry's bed was crammed into the tiny living room . . . Levin, Thompson interview.

after she became pregnant with a daughter born in 1985 . . . The birth year of their daughter, Kayla, puts her in the Wabash High School class of 2002. She is among the alumni that classmates seek to contact via posts on the Web. Natalie Graf, "Wabash County Class Reunions—Class of 2002," ingenweb.com, August 22, 2009, http://ingenweb.org/inwabash/reunion.html.

Although she was five years younger . . . "Wabash County Marriage Licenses—Gary Wayne Hall, Catherine Elaine Dome," July 6, 1987.

Despite the upheavals in the twins' relationship . . . Gary later described the trip to retired Wabash City detective Ron Smith. Levin, Smith, Amones interview.

Gary bounced among several different jobs . . . Hall trial, transcript at 778.

He was also employed by a janitorial service . . . Levin, Hall interview.

Despite the confidence he inspired in his employer . . . Levin, Thompson interview.

He may have been shy . . . Levin, Hall interview.

No wonder then, friends thought . . . Levin, Davis interview.

By the late eighties, another diversion . . . Levin, Hall interview.

Known for their distinctive high "Hardee" hats . . . Lance J. Herdegen, *The Men Stood like Iron: How the Iron Brigade Won Its Name* (Bloomington: Indiana University Press, 1997), 11.

Most of the Iron Brigade reenactments . . . Levin, Thompson interview.

For Larry, the events were a welcome break . . . Levin, Hall interview.

True to form, Gary made himself so popular . . . Ibid.; Levin, Thompson interview.

The Nineteenth Indiana looked so authentic . . . Ann Calkins, "Area men in 'Glory' battle scenes," *Marion (IN) Chronicle-Tribune,* February 3, 1990, sec. Living.

and Gettysburg . . . Levin, Thompson interview.

Gary is briefly visible . . . Levin, Hall interview.

Glory, *though not nearly as lavish* . . . Levin, Thompson interview.

The moviemaking turned out to be more exciting . . . Calkins, "Area men in 'Glory.'"

The filming for Gettysburg . . . Levin, Thompson interview.

Although he had divorced . . . "Wabash County Marriage Licenses—Gary Wayne Hall, Deaitra Sue Ward," January 18, 1991.

A few nights before Thompson arrived . . . This story was related to Ron Smith by Gary. Levin, Smith, Amones interview.

Although Thompson didn't know about the incident . . . Levin, Thompson interview.

It would be the twins' last extended road trip together . . . Levin, Hall interview.

Looking at photographs from this period . . . "Hartford City Civil War Days Photograph," Micheal Thompson personal collection, June 1990.

By October of 1990 . . . "Noblesville, IN, Civil War Event Photograph," Micheal Thompson personal collection, October 1990.

He wanted to portray General Ambrose Burnside . . . Levin, Hall interview.

His neighbors, says his high school . . . Levin, Osborne interview.

He even went to Revolutionary War events . . . Levin, Miller interview.

After listening to Hall blurt out his dreams . . . Ibid.

Hall, they insisted, was harmless . . . Ibid.; Levin, Whitmer interview; Levin, Smith, Amones interview.

As Miller drove back home . . . Levin, Miller interview.

On Tuesday, November 15, 1994 . . . Levin, Whitmer interview.

Whitmer took him to the old station house . . . Hall trial transcript at 151.

Miller sat waiting with Mike Randolph . . . Levin, Miller interview.

Randolph matter-of-factly explained . . . *United States of America v. Larry D. Hall: Hearing on the Motion to Suppress* (CD IL 1995), transcript at 138.

Miller practically jumped out of his seat . . . Levin, Miller interview.

But Randolph was going for more than a refusal . . . Hall trial transcript at 152.

Both men spoke softly . . . Levin, Miller interview.

FBI agent Randolph would later testify extensively . . . Hall trial transcript at 152–54.

Hurrying back to the interview room . . . Levin, Miller interview.

Instead, from what he recalled of Larry's confession . . . Hall: Motion to Suppress, 157–58.

Since Miller wanted to record his conversation . . . Gary Miller, "Jessica Roach Death Investigation" (Vermilion County Sheriff's Department, November 15, 1994), 110–11.

Throughout the day . . . Levin, Whitmer interview.

5. Breakfast with Baby Killers

Trained to kill by the Marines . . . Ron Davis, "The Most Dangerous Man," *Springfield News-Leader*, December 17, 1989.

Once in the civilian correctional system . . . In denying Fountain's appeal, the Seventh Circuit judges described his assault on the guards as a "mad dog attack." They also cite testimony from his trial that had him taunting other guards soon after the attack by asking them if they "would scream like the other bitches screamed." *United States of America v. Clayton Fountain et. al.*, 768 F.2d 790 (7th Cir. 1985);

Pete Earley, *The Hot House: Life Inside Leavenworth Prison* (New York: Bantam Books, 1993).

The media dubbed Fountain . . . Davis, "Most Dangerous Man."

Far from state-of-the-art, Springfield is a relic . . . A. E. Miller, "U.S. Medical Center for Federal Prisoners," *Bulletin of the Greene County Medical Society,* September 1982.

when it was the first medical facility in the federal prison system . . . Docia Karell, "Government's Battle to Reclaim 'Lost Men' at Medical Center Here Holds Interest of Entire Nation," *Springfield Leader and Press,* July 28, 1935.

If it is known for anything . . . Mike Penprase, "Many Infamous Men Pass Through Medical Center," *Springfield News-Leader,* June 11, 2002.

even in the operating room, handcuffs are not removed . . . Randy H. Greer, *Echoes of Mercy,* 1st ed. (Leathers Pub, 1998), 122.

But in addition to medical patients . . . Miller, "U.S. Medical Center."

Some can erupt . . . Greer, *Echoes,* 27–31.

As a result, the MCFP has developed a wide array . . . Julie Westermann, "10 Building: From Illness to Acceptance," *Springfield Leader and Press,* June 14, 1983.

Fountain's MCFP treatment plan . . . Davis, "Most Dangerous Man."

Although no household name like Leavenworth . . . Penprase, "Many Infamous."

Although no prisoner has ever escaped . . . Greer, *Echoes,* 85–92.

within its walls there can be remarkable freedom . . . Hillel Levin, James Keene interview, November–December 2007.

Meanwhile, the treatment of other inmates . . . Westermann, "10 Building."

The Medical Center's split personality . . . Karell, "Government's Battle."

The doctors clearly called the shots . . . Chicago Curt Teich & Company, "U.S. Federal Hospital, Springfield, Mo.," http://thelibrary.springfield.missouri.org.

What made it most attractive . . . Dirk Vanderhart, "Federal prison major employer for city," *Springfield News-Leader,* March 2, 2008.

Nothing is more surprising . . . "Greatest Triumph in History of City Nets $142,000 Fund," *Springfield Daily News,* April 1, 1931.

In this and other reporting . . . "$100,000 hospital contract to Carthage firm," *Springfield Leader and Press,* April 12, 1932; "May ask city to help build U.S. Hospital; Official considers plan to speed construction work here," *Springfield Leader and Press,* August 31, 1931; Henry Hahn, "Hospital Site: Test borings preparatory to construction work to be made soon," *Springfield Leader and Press,* July 29, 1931.

Neighbors did not get their first look . . . Karell, "Government's Battle."

by today's standards for a federal prison . . . Mary F. (Francesca) Bosworth, *U.S. Federal Prison System*, 1st ed. (Sage Publications, 2003), 36.

Staffing aside, Karell describes . . . Karell, "Government's Battle."

But despite these "impregnable" defenses . . . "Two Escape U.S. Prison Here," *Springfield Leader and Press*, November 16, 1933.

a few more guards were immediately hired . . . "More Guards Hired as 2 Flee Hospital," *Springfield Daily News*, November 17, 1933.

Karell may have best summed up . . . Karell, "Government's Battle."

The life in the complex that she goes on to describe . . . Docia Karell, "Get Up! Whistle Signals Round of Activities," *Springfield Leader and Press*, July 29, 1935.

In this early period . . . "Southeast Spotlights on Faculty—Mary Virginia Moore Johnson," Southeast Missouri State University, http://www.semo.edu/spotlights/faculty_6461.htm.

But just three years later in 1938 . . . Westermann, "10 Building."

But the degree of difficulty increased . . . Ibid.

As Springfield's prisoner population . . . "Now, This Is the Guards' Story," *Springfield Leader and Press*, February 27, 1944.

It was precipitated by a band of Socialist conscientious objectors . . . Associated Press, "To Sift Brutality Charge; Biddle Acts on Complaint from Federal Medical Center," *New York Times*, February 10, 1944.

Charging that the guards tortured prisoners . . . "Recommend inquiry on prisoner charges," *New York Times*, March 2, 1944.

An undercurrent of clashing cultures . . . "Guards' Story," *Springfield Leader and Press*.

Within days after the guards talked to reporters . . . "Inmate Stages Break from Center," *Springfield Leader and Press*, February 25, 1944; "Alert Citizen Finds Fugitive," *Springfield Leader and Press*, February 26, 1944.

10 Building erupted again . . . "Guards Quell Riot at Medical Center and Prevent Break," *Springfield Leader and Press*, March 7, 1944.

Upon their departure . . . "Tough Inmates to Be Scattered to Other Prisons," *Springfield Leader and Press*, March 12, 1944.

The 1944 riot did serve one institutional purpose . . . "Medical Center Charges Called Hallucinations," *Springfield Leader and Press*, March 16, 1944.

Despite the expulsion of the "tough guys" . . . Associated Press, "Prison Hospital Quells Uprising," *New York Times*, June 24, 1959.

Using clubs—in a haze of tear gas . . . Greer, *Echoes*, 72.

The farming, once seen as so therapeutic . . . Cultivation stopped in 1966. Vanderhart, "Federal prison."

The hospital staff's families moved . . . Hillel Levin, Mary Virginia Moore Johnson interview, April 2008.

In the early seventies . . . "Status of U.S. Prison Hospital Poses Problems, Director Notes," *Springfield Leader and Press,* April 24, 1974.

But it left some stubborn prisoners . . . Lesley Oelsner, "Jails Chief Backs Behavior System," *New York Times,* February 28, 1974.

But by then Springfield, like the psychiatric hospitals on the outside . . . Greer, *Echoes,* 32.

Supervision at the top of the facility . . . "Non-Doctor 11th Warden at Hospital," *Springfield Leader and Press,* January 22, 1979.

Mobsters from Mickey Cohen . . . "Can't Regain Health at MC, Cohen Claims," *Springfield Leader and Press,* July 10, 1970.

to John Gotti . . . "Lawyer Critical of Treatment for John Gotti: U.S. Medical Center Officials Say Mob Boss Hasn't Made Formal Complaints," *Springfield News-Leader,* October 7, 2000.

so, too, did deposed Panamanian dictator Manuel Noriega . . . "Med Center Monitoring Policy Unchanged by Noriega Stir," *Springfield News-Leader,* November 14, 1990.

Larry Flynt, who needed special treatment for his paralysis . . . Penprase, "Many Infamous."

During the porn magnate's stay . . . Traci Bauer, "Springfield vs. Larry Flynt: A Movie and Book Prompt Memories of the 5 Weeks the Porn Publisher and Ozarkers Had to Put Up with Each Other," *Springfield News-Leader,* December 27, 1996.

Blind sheikh Omar Abdel Rahman . . . Associated Press, "Sheik, Calling Imprisonment Humiliating, Seeks Support," *New York Times,* June 24, 1996.

Throughout the federal prison system . . . "Guards' Story," *Springfield Leader and News.*

an enormously ungainly eight-hundred-pound cocaine dealer . . . "800-Pound Cocaine Dealer Hauled to Springfield on Special Plane," *Springfield News-Leader,* February 17, 1989.

various crackpot con men . . . Among the most famous was Oscar Hartzell, who gulled thousands of Depression-era Midwesterners into paying him to gain access to the lost fortune of Sir Alfred Drake. Richard Rayner, "The Admiral and the Con Man," *New Yorker,* April 22, 2002.

Putative presidential assassins . . . "Med Center Takes Would-Be Assassin," *Springfield News-Leader,* August 12, 1995; "Man Found Guilty of Assassination Threat," *Springfield News-Leader,* March 28, 1990.

116 psychotic Cubans from the Mariel boatlift . . . "Med Center Gets 116 Cubans from Chaffee," *Springfield Leader and Press,* January 26, 1982.

While he tries to put the MCFP in the best light . . . Greer, *Echoes,* 23–27.

Although Greer confronted violent prisoners . . . Ibid., 30.

It was "gloomy" . . . Bosworth, *U.S. Federal Prison System*, 304.

But even that word was too kind . . . Elliot Goldenberg, *The Hunting Horse: The Truth Behind the Jonathan Pollard Spy Case* (Amherst, NY: Prometheus Books, 2000), 58.

like Sheikh Rahman . . . Joseph Fried, "U.S. Moves Convicted Sheik to Missouri Medical Center," *New York Times*, October 3, 1995.

the BOP claimed the MCFP . . . Goldenberg, *Hunting Horse*, 58.

Her real name was Janice Butkus . . . Butkus was still working for the FBI in 2008, but did not return messages left on her voice mail. Her participation was confirmed by former assistant U.S. attorney Lawrence Beaumont. Levin, Beaumont interview.

She had gone to some length . . . Levin, Keene interview.

Then seventy years old, he had been the leader . . . Selwyn Raab, "Vincent Gigante, Mafia Leader Who Feigned Insanity, Dies at 77," *New York Times*, December 19, 2005, sec. Obituaries.

6. "I can't see the faces, but I can hear the screams"

After Larry Hall signed his statement . . . Levin, Miller interview.

To book and hold Hall . . . Robert Bryan, "Wabash man may be murder suspect," *Wabash Plain Dealer*, November 16, 1994.

Miller stayed the night in a Wabash motel . . . Levin, Miller interview.

The media onslaught had been touched off . . . Bryan, "Wabash man."

When Jessica Roach first disappeared . . . Levin, Miller interview.

Almost as soon as he was settled . . . Hall: Motion to Suppress, 147–50.

No matter how much Hall dismissed . . . Levin, Miller interview.

Hall had spoken to Miller of a steel bridge . . . Miller, "Jessica Roach Death Investigation", 112.

Hall talked about heading east . . . DeLorme, *Indiana Atlas & Gazetteer*, 3rd ed. (DeLorme Publishing, 2001), 36.

At last, he said, he took a paved road . . . Miller, "Jessica Roach Death Investigation," 112.

Miller was able to pinpoint . . . Levin, Miller interview.

As Hall freely admitted . . . Hall trial transcript at 585.

As Whitmer drove over to the Hall house . . . Levin, Whitmer interview.

It was up to the FBI to lead the way . . . "FBI searches Hall home; no new charges filed," *Wabash Plain Dealer*, December 9, 1994.

the Evidence Response Team . . . Robert Bryan, "Hall indicted in kidnapping," *Wabash Plain Dealer,* December 22, 1994.

Earlier they had seized his two vans . . . Hall: Motion to Suppress, 284–88.

Since he drove the Dodge to work . . . Hall trial transcript at 581.

But upon further examination, chilling evidence . . . Ibid., 572–75.

Her name was also found . . . Ibid., 564.

Less sensational but even more compelling . . . Ibid., 590–92.

Hall confirmed that the maps . . . Hall: Motion to Suppress, 151.

Other writing was found . . . Hall trial transcript, 562–72.

While Larry sat in his Danville jail cell . . . Alan Miller, "Hall's parents talk of 'kind' son," *Marion Chronicle-Tribune,* November 18, 1994.

It took those parents a day to respond . . . Ibid.

Those sentiments were echoed by the friends . . . Levin, Allen interview.

Micheal Thompson, the fellow foot soldier . . . Levin, Thompson interview.

A reporter for the Wabash Plain Dealer . . . Jennifer McSpadden, "Neighbors express shock, sympathy," *Wabash Plain Dealer,* November 17, 1994.

They would come to light in the same article . . . Miller, "Hall's parents."

For people in Wabash and Gas City . . . Alan Miller, "Agonizing day for the Reitlers," *Marion Chronicle-Tribune,* November 20, 1994.

In fact, the Marion police . . . Tammy Kingery, "Towns wait for word on investigations," *Marion Chronicle-Tribune,* November 17, 1994.

The Marion police felt they had a much more likely suspect . . . Craig Cairns, "The Reitler Riddle," *Marion Chronicle-Tribune,* May 28, 1995.

Next to the mobster, if any type of criminal has won . . . Internet Movie Database (IMDb), http://www.imdb.com/.

Amazon has more than twenty-two thousand books . . . Amazon.com, http://www.amazon.com/.

In the words of criminologist Steven Egger . . . Steven A. Egger, *The Killers Among Us: An Examination of Serial Murder and Its Investigation* (Upper Saddle River, NJ: Prentice Hall, 1998), 85.

Despite all the fascination with serial killers . . . "Linkage Blindness: A Systemic Myopia," in Steven A. Egger, *Serial Murder: An Elusive Phenomenon* (New York: Praeger, 1990), 164–65.

As opposed to fictional villains such as Hannibal Lecter . . . Egger writes, "Serial killers are frequently not captured until they have killed a number of victims. This is a law enforcement problem and not due to some special skills that allow the killer to elude the police." Egger, *Killers Among Us,* 12.

The failings of local police aside . . . Ibid., 88.

Although crime writers often refer . . . "The Aftermath of the Yorkshire Ripper: The Response of the United Kingdom Police Service," in Egger, *Serial Murder,* 110–11.

In the United States, the friends and relatives of the missing . . . The Pennsylvania State Police Web site does not have a link for "Missing Persons," but lumps them under an "Investigations" link for each of the state's sixteen troops. An example from Troop R: "Missing Person—Kathryn Margaret VanDine," Pennsylvania State Police, http://www.portal.state.pa.us.

As for the vaunted FBI profiles . . . Malcolm Gladwell, "Dangerous Minds," *New Yorker,* November 12, 2007.

According to criminologist Egger . . . Egger, *Killers Among Us,* 88–89.

Instead, he writes, "The identification of a serial murderer . . ." Ibid., 178.

Egger writes that typically "police do not exchange investigative information . . ." Ibid., 180.

Ironically, one of the items seized . . . Mark Starr, "The Random Killers," *Newsweek,* November 26, 1984.

Werewolves held particular fascination for Larry Hall . . . Hillel Levin, confidential interview, 2008.

Stories of men who switch back and forth . . . Sabine Baring-Gould, *The Book of Werewolves* (Cosimo Classics, 2008), 85.

Like werewolf hunters in fairy tales . . . Joel Norris, *Serial Killers,* 1st ed. (New York: Anchor Books, 1989), 226.

Of the twenty-one psychosocial "patterns" identified by Norris . . . Those that would have applied to Hall include ritualistic behavior; masks of sanity; compulsivity; search for help; severe memory disorders; suicidal tendencies; deviate sexual behavior; head injuries or injuries incurred at birth; alcohol- or drug-abusing parents; victim of physical or emotional abuse or of cruel parenting; products of a difficult gestation period for the mother; interrupted bliss or no bliss of childhood; symptoms of neurological impairment; feelings of powerlessness or inadequacy. Ibid., 222–23.

Hall's out-of-body experiences and inability to distinguish dreams from reality . . . Ibid., 123.

Citing the research of neuropsychologists . . . Ibid., 185.

During the acts of violence . . . Ibid., 186.

For those who rape and murder . . . Starr, "Random Killers."

But with men like Hall . . . The strange affection that killers have felt for their mothers was noted in a 1921 landmark study by Swedish lawyer and psychologist Andreas

Bjerre, who wrote, "Time after time during my studies among murderers I was struck by the fact that just the most brutal criminals—men who . . . had a stereotyped incapacity to conceive their fellow creatures as anything but dead matter or as the means to the satisfaction of their animal lusts . . . were nevertheless frequently attached to their mothers by bonds which seemed even stronger than those which one ordinarily finds between mother and son." Andreas Bjerre, *The Psychology of Murder: A Study in Criminal Psychology* (Da Capo Press, 1981), 81.

(who would call Berniece "darling" . . . Levin, Smith, Amones interview.

the mother's dominance leads to "inadequate socialization" . . . Egger writes, "Theories regarding inadequate socialization or childhood trauma are frequently cited in the homicide literature and often referred to regarding the serial murderer." "Serial Murder: A Synthesis of Research and Literature," in Egger, *Serial Murder,* 20.

To assume Norris's "mask of sanity" . . . Norris, *Serial Killers,* 226–29.

According to Norris, these extracurricular activities . . . Ibid., 231.

"Many killers have extraordinarily high mileage . . ." Ibid., 233.

The "megamobile" killer, such as Bundy . . . Egger, "Serial Murder," 26.

Whether a serial killer is "stat" or "mobile" . . . Researchers believe that some of these classifications of serial killers may be the result of "hindsight bias" exacerbated by "a small sample size." Katie A. Busch and James L. Cavanaugh, "The Study of Multiple Murder: Preliminary Examination of the Interface Between Epistemology and Methodology," *Journal of Interpersonal Violence* 1, no. 1 (March 1, 1986): 15.

As Norris writes, because the serial killer's homicidal behavior . . . Norris, *Serial Killers,* 19.

Norris compares serial killers to "wild animals" . . . Ibid., 18.

Even after the burial, he explains . . . Ibid., 88.

Hall's return to the scene of the crime . . . Hall trial transcript at 250.

what the police later described as "an abduction kit" . . . Jennifer McSpadden, "New trial ordered for Hall," *Wabash Plain Dealer,* August 29, 1996.

Again, this is in line with Norris's research . . . Norris, *Serial Killers,* 231.

On the bottom of one defaced magazine pinup . . . Hall trial transcript at 585.

In fact, Hall meant "Samhain" . . . "The Myth of Samhain: Celtic God of the Dead," Religious Tolerance, http://www.religioustolerance.org/hallo_sa.htm.

he is also what FBI profilers would call both "disorganized" and "organized" . . . Busch and Cavanaugh, "Study of Multiple Murder," 14–15.

no physical evidence . . . Hall trial transcript at 36.

Get one . . . Find one . . . Find one now . . . Ibid., 562, 567.

"Trolling or cruising activity . . ." Norris, *Serial Killers,* 233.

Seen several singles . . . Hall trial transcript at 567.

The notes instruct him to find a plate . . . Ibid.

He must always remember . . . Ibid., 579.

Take 300 to 500 *[Bradford Pike]* east into Jay Line . . . Ibid., 562.

Take out east wilderness . . . Ibid., 567.

His directions repeatedly refer to the "Jay Line" . . . DeLorme, *Indiana Atlas & Gazetteer,* 27, 34.

Things to have done for trips . . . Hall trial transcript at 579.

He includes the following on one list . . . Ibid.

Next to another reminder about covering the rear of the van . . . Ibid., 562.

Now, I know it's hard . . . Ibid.

Here, too, a Marsh supermarket is a few blocks . . . Ibid., 569.

The early-evening walkers . . . Ibid., 562.

Ready end of February? . . . Ibid., 567.

Some of the evidence was as explicit . . . Michael Bayer, "Evidence could tie area man to slayings," *Fort Wayne (IN) Journal-Gazette,* December 14, 1994.

Within days after Hall's extradition . . . Cathy Kightlinger, "Probe of Wabash man continues," *Marion Chronicle-Tribune,* November 19, 1994.

Two weeks later, the same group . . . Cathy Kightlinger, "Wabash man may face Illinois grand jury," *Marion Chronicle-Tribune,* December 13, 1994.

By the end of December, a federal grand jury in Illinois . . . Bryan, "Hall indicted in kidnapping."

word . . . finally reached a crescendo . . . Associated Press, "Report: Hall linked to 20 murders," *Wabash Plain Dealer,* January 21, 1995.

By the state line with Illinois . . . Katherine Skiba, "Serial killing suspect wrote about Depies," *Milwaukee Journal Sentinel,* January 20, 1995.

Two miles from where Tricia Reitler . . . Stacey Lane Grosh, "Some missing persons cases linger for years," *Marion Chronicle-Tribune,* March 29, 1998.

The third cluster was in central Wisconsin . . . Skiba, "Serial killing suspect."

Looking back on those heady days . . . Levin, Miller interview.

7. America's Most Wanted

Keene peered up at the window . . . According to the *Springfield News-Leader,* Gotti was transferred from the Super Max in Marion, Illinois, to Springfield for his diagnosis of cancer in 1996 and then again for surgery on September 13, 1998. "Medical

Center Housing Mob Boss: John Gotti's Health Is Being Evaluated During Incarceration in Springfield," *Springfield News-Leader,* December 27, 1996; Rick Veach, "John Gotti in Center for Throat Surgery," *Springfield News-Leader,* September 24, 1998; "Elusive Don Left 'Family' in Ruins," *Springfield News-Leader,* June 11, 2002.

As Keene later learned, "that thing" was surgery for cancer . . . Selwyn Raab, "John Gotti Dies in Prison at 61; Mafia Boss Relished the Spotlight," *New York Times,* June 11, 2002, New York edition, sec. A.

What Jimmy never knew . . . Selwyn Raab, "With Gotti Away, the Genoveses Succeed the Leaderless Gambinos," *New York Times,* September 3, 1995.

where they kept the most unmanageable psychiatric prisoners . . . Westermann, "10 Building."

8. Innocence

Through most of Gary Miller's career . . . Levin, Miller interview.

Emboldened by his attorney . . . Gannett News Service, "Hall: FBI framing me," *Marion Chronicle-Tribune,* February 4, 1995.

Between Hall's remarks to reporters and motions filed by DeArmond . . . Robert Bryan, "Hall's lawyer plans alibi defense," *Wabash Plain Dealer,* January 31, 1995.

Miller had no doubt who really orchestrated the interviews . . . Levin, Miller interview.

As the Hall family went around town enlisting witnesses . . . Levin, Davis interview.

When Garry Reitler thinks about his daughter Tricia . . . Hillel Levin, Garry and Donna Reitler interview, August 2008.

She stood out on the conservative Christian campus . . . Tammy Kingery, "Friends remember Tricia," *Marion Chronicle-Tribune,* March 30, 1994.

A bubbly free spirit, she could take two aerobics classes . . . Linda Renken, "Missing student's friends still waiting," *Marion Chronicle-Tribune,* July 4, 1993.

According to a journal entry . . . Tammy Kingery, "A Test of Faith," *Marion Chronicle-Tribune,* March 29, 1994.

Her freshman year at IWU had been tough on Garry, too . . . Levin, Reitler interview.

Tricia had entered IWU as a psychology major . . . Hillel Levin, Donna Reitler interview, October 2009.

She returned to memories of her family in an essay . . . David Nelson, "Missing student makes university nervous, worried," *Marion Chronicle-Tribune,* April 2, 1993.

Two weeks after she submitted her essay . . . Levin, Donna Reitler interview.

By the time Donna and Garry reached IWU on Wednesday . . . Nelson, "Missing stu-

dent makes university nervous"; David Nelson, "IWU in state of vigil until Reitler returns," *Marion Chronicle-Tribune*, April 3, 1993.

Earlier that morning, they had discovered the clothes . . . Linda Renken, "Woman last
seen near Reliable Drug store," *Marion Chronicle-Tribune*, April 4, 1993.

Although it was not initially reported . . . Kingery, "A Test of Faith."

In all the horror of this information . . . Ibid.

If there was any comfort in the midst of the Reitlers' nightmare . . . Cindy Losure, "Search
team looking for volunteers," *Marion Chronicle-Tribune*, April 3, 1993.

A *literally iconic poster . . .* Susan Schramm, "Skull found in Marion isn't of missing
student," *Indianapolis Star*, March 25, 1994.

As much as the town focused on the missing girl . . . Linda Renken, "Law officers keep
noses to grindstone to find missing girl," *Marion Chronicle-Tribune*, April 6, 1993.

But the first night in Marion, Donna and Garry also remember . . . Levin, Reitler interview.

They did the best they could to be helpful . . . Linda Renken, "Few clues turn up in
search for student," *Marion Chronicle-Tribune*, April 5, 1993.

The Reitlers tried to rally the search parties . . . Levin, Reitler interview.

A week after they arrived in Marion . . . Linda Renken, "Missing IWU student's parents return to Ohio," *Marion Chronicle-Tribune*, April 7, 1994.

They had left him and his two older sisters . . . Levin, Reitler interview.

there would be more massive search parties of hundreds . . . Traci Miller, "150 seek clues
in disappearance," *Marion Chronicle-Tribune*, April 18, 1993.

Two weeks after her disappearance . . . Tammy Kingery, "Parents say hope fading,"
Marion Chronicle-Tribune, April 11, 1993.

Still, for the Reitlers, the mission could never be complete . . . Jennifer Hamilton, "'I
want a place to put flowers,'" *Marion Chronicle-Tribune*, March 29, 1997.

A few weeks later they even took to the national airwaves . . . Tammy Kingery, "Reitlers
to tell their difficult story on TV," *Marion Chronicle-Tribune*, May 25, 1993.

It would start eight months after her disappearance . . . "Marion police interested in
body," *Marion Chronicle-Tribune*, November 10, 1993.

A few tantalizing days would pass . . . "Found body not Reitler's," *Marion Chronicle-
Tribune*, November 11, 1993.

The next year, more heartbreak followed . . . "Skull not Reitler's, police say," *Marion
Chronicle-Tribune*, March 25, 1994.

Each time a call came . . . Levin, Reitler interview.

In retrospect, the most important development . . . "Police won't connect Reitler with La
Porte case," *Marion Chronicle-Tribune*, April 29, 1993.

common to many victims of serial murder . . . Richard N. Kocsis, *Serial Murder and the Psychology of Violent Crimes,* 1st ed. (Humana Press, 2007), 125.

The local newspapers were quick to see a possible connection . . . "Police won't connect," *Marion Chronicle-Tribune.*

From the start no one became more closely associated . . . Caryn Shinske, "Probe never far from Kay's mind," *Marion Chronicle-Tribune,* March 29, 1996.

"I can't even tell you my feelings for Jay" . . . Associated Press, "Family losing hope in search for missing college student," *Fort Wayne Journal-Gazette,* March 30, 1997.

Posters of Tricia, aerial photographs of the campus, and diagrams . . . Shinske, "Probe never far."

Unlike most local detectives, Kay reached . . . "Police won't connect," *Marion Chronicle-Tribune.*

In Rison's case, the most obvious target for investigation . . . Scott Squires, "Waiting for Justice," *The La Porte County Herald-Argus,* April 4, 2008.

In Marion, detectives were convinced that they already had the culprit . . . Cairns, "Reitler Riddle."

copper secretions in the liver of a corpse . . . Tung-Pi Chou and William H. Adolph, "Copper metabolism in man," *Biochemical Journal* 29, no. 2 (February 1935): 476–79.

But for Marion police, nothing about Searcy . . . Craig Cairns, "Searcy: One man under suspicion," *Marion Chronicle-Tribune,* May 28, 1995.

On the one-year anniversary of Tricia's disappearance . . . Kingery, "A Test of Faith."

That afternoon, in the neighboring town of Gas City . . . Hall: Motion to Suppress, 4–9.

Detective Bruce Bender took the call . . . Hall trial transcript at 838.

He had been assigned to the Reitler case . . . Hall: Motion to Suppress, 280.

Bender called Kay at home . . . Ibid., 61.

Hall would later charge that Pence's commanding officer . . . Hall trial transcript at 1020.

While a few Gas City officers guarded Larry . . . Hall: Motion to Suppress, 40–49.

Just as alarming was a newspaper story . . . Ibid., 67.

By this time, Gas City police headquarters had completed a check . . . Ibid., 10–13.

After Patrolman Pence issued the ticket . . . Ibid., 839.

Kay stayed behind to sort through the items . . . Ibid., 51.

Larry Hall remained in the custody of the Marion police detectives . . . Hall trial transcript at 1038.

He spent much of the time with Bender . . . Ibid., 1028–35.

Instead of booking Hall or even holding him . . . Ibid., 1038.

Marion PD's quick dismissal of Hall's confession . . . Miller, "Hall's parents."

In his eyes the memorabilia about Reitler . . . Hall: Motion to Suppress, 275.

"Marion PD was never going to let Hall become the suspect" . . . Levin, confidential interview.

Deputy Sheriff Gary Miller admits that serial killers are the UFOs . . . Levin, Miller interview.

In their defense, the Marion detectives were not the only ones . . . Hall: Motion to Suppress, 272.

But the next time Marion detectives heard from Amones . . . Ibid., 226.

the Marion detectives picked up Hall from the Wabash police station . . . Ibid., 246–49.

When they deposited him at the Grant County jail in Marion . . . Ibid., 274–77.

Although Lieutenant Kay continued to call Searcy the "prime suspect" . . . Cathy Kightlinger, "Officials look for Reitler," *Marion Chronicle-Tribune,* July 1, 1995.

Other Marion officers working on the investigation . . . Cairns, "Reitler Riddle."

For example, he refers to the Marsh supermarket . . . Hall trial transcript at 569.

But most telling is an entry . . . Ibid., 571.

Just as intriguing are the final lines . . . Ibid.

Many different roads in the area . . . Google Maps lists a Frances Slocum Trail, an Old Slocum Trail, and a Slocum Boulevard—all with directional variants. Google Maps, http://maps.google.com/.

Elsewhere in the notes he reminds himself . . . Hall trial transcript at 567.

two young women recognized Hall and came forward to testify . . . Ibid., 130–33.

a guard soon spotted the van as well . . . Ibid., 143–44.

For Beaumont and his investigators . . . Levin, Beaumont interview.

When looking back at how the law enforcement agencies . . . Levin, Miller interview.

When he produced a list of the defendant's witnesses . . . Hall trial transcript index.

On May 23, 1995, when the curtain lifted . . . Ibid., 18.

John O'Brien, then a seasoned court reporter . . . Hillel Levin, John O'Brien interview, December 2007.

First he established how Jessica suddenly disappeared . . . Hall trial transcript, 37–79.

Beaumont next presented eleven witnesses . . . Ibid., 129–42, 253–311, 322–33.

discovered, jurors learned, by a farmer . . . Ibid., 338.

He was followed to the stand by a parade of forensic experts . . . Ibid., 341–84.

To place Hall in the area at the time of Jessica's disappearance . . . Ibid., 522–52.

Monte Cox, a gas station attendant returning from a late shift . . . Ibid., 612–15.

he waited two months before he called Crime Stoppers . . . Ibid., 614–15.

his vague memories of both Hall and his van . . . Ibid., 622–31.

The two government witnesses who spent the most time on the stand . . . Ibid., 82–92, 171–82, 389–416.

Beaumont's case culminated with . . . Ibid., 561–79, 592–94, 599–603.

"You may not like Larry Hall," he told the jurors . . . Ibid., 26.

As he explained, "[My client] suffers from a number . . . Ibid., 29.

As DeArmond admitted, it was hard to understand . . . Ibid., 28.

his most persuasive argument pointed out what the prosecution lacked . . . Ibid., 36.

Leading off these witnesses was a stooped Robert Hall . . . Ibid., 747–53.

He was followed by Larry's twin, Gary Hall . . . Ibid., 785–87.

Beaumont reviewed the answers Gary had given FBI agent Temples . . . Ibid., 796.

For those who knew the Hall family history . . . Ibid., 853–54.

But some of the other friends who testified . . . Ibid., 769, 828.

The alibi was shredded even further by shop owners . . . Ibid., 1220, 1223.

Ross Davis, who produced a shipping receipt to prove . . . Ibid., 1245.

But as Beaumont pointed out, no newspaper reported on strangulation . . . Ibid., 1343–44.

As DeArmond pointed out, the day after the deputy sheriff's first interview . . . Ibid., 33–34.

Indeed, he didn't even question the first line of the statement . . . Ibid., 176.

Eventually, the cross-examination tried even the patience of the judge . . . Ibid., 471.

Having observed DeArmond so often in the past . . . Ibid.

DeArmond planned to build much of his coercion argument around the testimony of Richard Ofshe . . . Ibid., 912–13.

But Ofshe never personally interviewed Hall . . . Ibid., 918.

But in a hearing outside the presence of the jury . . . Ibid., 928.

Judge Baker then dismissed Ofshe . . . Ibid.

In contrast to the defense testimony that he had a "low-average" IQ . . . Ibid., 1178.

especially when DeArmond walked him through the convoluted reasons . . . Ibid., 1024.

In a similar vein, he testified that he actually wanted to be arrested . . . Ibid., 1014.

He went on to claim that he had prepared a script . . . Ibid., 1031.

Hall admitted he was not as eager to talk . . . Ibid., 1114.

When the prosecutor asked where he learned unpublicized information . . . Ibid., 1140.

When Beaumont pointed to a dot on the map . . . Ibid., 1142.

At another point Beaumont asked, "Is it possible . . ." Ibid.

Beaumont argued, "On cross-examination . . ." Ibid., 1341–42.

The jury took fewer than three hours to convict Larry Hall . . . They left the courtroom at 11:25 a.m. and returned at 2:18 p.m. for another look at a video of the cornfield scene taken shortly after Jessica Roach was found. They left the court at 3:28 and then returned thirty-two minutes later with the verdict. Ibid., 1408, 1418–19.

Although Detectives Bender and Kay had been called by the defense . . . Ibid., 838–52, 857–70.

But out of the presence of the jury, Sergeant Darrell Himelick . . . Ibid., 973, 976.

Because nothing else in evidence supported their theory . . . Ibid., 974, 977.

The one way, outside of court, to definitively prove Hall's guilt . . . Kightlinger, "Officials look for Reitler."

A month later, Hall was sentenced, and during the hearing . . . *United States of America v. Larry D. Hall* (CD IL 1995), sentencing hearing transcript at 16.

Judge Baker felt otherwise . . . Ibid., 17.

Baker disclosed a letter he'd received from Jessica's parents . . . Ibid., 16.

Soon after, Baker sentenced Larry Hall . . . Ibid., 17.

However, the judge did not . . . Ibid., 17–18.

As Gary Miller sat through oral arguments in Chicago . . . Levin, Miller interview.

It was a stinging indictment of Beaumont's case . . . *United States of America v. Larry D. Hall*, 93 F.3d 1337 (7th Cir. 1996).

In August 1997, Beaumont retried the case against Hall . . . John O'Brien, "Hall's 2nd trial opening today," *Champaign News-Gazette*, August 18, 1997.

without the problematic testimony of the defendant . . . Associated Press, "Hall defense rests; jury to get case," *Wabash Plain Dealer*, August 28, 1997.

with the testimony about false confessions from Professor Ofshe . . . Associated Press, "False confession possible, witness says," *Wabash Plain Dealer*, August 27, 1997.

This time the jury took fewer than four hours . . . Associated Press, "Guilty again: Jury convicts Hall in kidnapping case," *Wabash Plain Dealer*, August 29, 1997.

When some of the victims' stories were dredged up again . . . Sharon Dettmer, "Police still searching for Rayna Rison's killer 10 years later," *South Bend Tribune*, March 26, 2003.

Evidence such as Rayna Rison's birth control pill bottle . . . Levin, Smith, Amones interview.

No doubt the urgency of getting Hall convicted . . . Gannett News Service, "Hall again draws life sentence," *Marion Chronicle-Tribune*, December 3, 1997.

Hall's defense team was once again seeking to get the conviction overturned . . . *United States of America v. Larry D. Hall*, 165 F.3d 1095 (7th Cir. 1999).

In Wabash, old friends such as fellow reenactor Micheal Thompson and neighbor Bobby Allen . . . Levin, Thompson interview; Levin, Allen interview.

Meanwhile, in Marion, on the fifth anniversary of Tricia Reitler's disappearance . . . Marc Lazar, "Reitlers revive their search," *Marion Chronicle-Tribune*, February 12, 1998.

10. Closure

For example, according to the statement, Larry forced her to undress in the park . . . Hall trial transcript at 179.

On February 23, 1999, Lawrence S. Beaumont . . . *United States of America v. James Keene* (CD IL 1999), Motion for Reduction of Sentence.

The 35(B) motion to reduce Jimmy's sentence . . . *United States of America v. James Keene* (CD IL 1999), Amended Judgment: Minute Order.

His own lie detector business helped put him through law school . . . Levin, Beaumont interview.

When Smith retired five years ago . . . Levin, Smith, Amones interview.

He later became chronically unemployed . . . Levin, Woodward interview; Levin, Thompson interview.

needed treatment for substance abuse . . . Levin, Osborne interview.

After their father, Robert, died in 2001, Gary stayed with their mother . . . Levin, Smith, Amones interview.

But at times Gary was also seen by friends . . . Levin, Woodward interview; Levin, Thompson interview.

"He keeps telling you, 'I'm not like my brother'" . . . Levin, Osborne interview.

None of them articulates this better than psychiatrist Arthur Traugott . . . Hall trial transcript at 1171.

As one counselor points out, it is probably no accident . . . Levin, confidential interview.

But in the eyes of retired Wabash detective Ron Smith . . . Levin, Smith, Amones interview.

In late 2007 Gary Hall dropped by Ron Osborne's house . . . Levin, Osborne interview.

"I have problems with my memory" . . . Levin, Hall interview.

Set among rolling hills and dairy farms . . . E. A. Torriero, "No fences, no violence, no privacy—Oxford camp lacks cellblocks and offers inmates a walking track, culinary classes," *Chicago Tribune*, November 7, 2007, Chicago edition.

A law enforcement officer familiar with Hall's prison records . . . Levin, confidential interview.

He did not like Oxford at all and attempted suicide there . . . Levin, Hall interview.

when the Seventh Circuit court denied his second appeal . . . Hall second appeal, v. 165.

After the suicide attempt, Hall was sent to the BOP's hospital in Rochester . . . Levin, Hall interview.

Only eight months later . . . John Caniglia, "Tricia Reitler disappearance draws fresh interest from Indiana investigators; inmate questioned," *Cleveland Plain Dealer*, April 26, 2009.

Instead, he swung back to making the sort of full confession . . . Scott Swan, "Who killed Michelle Dewey?—WTHR," WTHR.com Eyewitness News, November 23, 2009, http://www.wthr.com/Global/story.asp?S=11562020.

The police were cold-case detectives . . . Jack Rinehart, "Detectives Pursue New Leads in Cold Case Killing—Indiana News Story—WRTV Indianapolis," IndyChannel .com, August 25, 2009, http://www.theindychannel.com/news/20552712/detail .html.

She had been strangled . . . Swan, "Who killed Michelle Dewey?"

The 2008 August issue of Playboy . . . Hillel Levin, "The Strange Redemption of James Keene," *Playboy*, August 2008.

When they contacted retired Wabash detective Ron . . . Hillel Levin, Ron Smith interview, April 2009.

After briefly meeting with Gary, Larry agreed to speak . . . Swan, "Who killed Michelle Dewey?"

He continued talking with the detectives for five hours . . . Caniglia, "Tricia Reitler disappearance draws fresh interest."

Gary broke the news about his twin's confessions . . . Swan, "Who killed Michelle Dewey?"

detectives brought him a map to show them find where . . . Hillel Levin, Garry Reitler interview, April 2009.

As the Indianapolis detectives have worked through the information . . . Ibid.

Oklahoma City bomber Timothy McVeigh, who would be executed there two years later . . . Rick Bragg, "McVeigh Dies for Oklahoma City Blast," *New York Times*, June 12, 2001.

Bibliography

Books

Edith Abbott. *The one hundred and one county jails of Illinois and why they ought to be abolished.* Juvenile Protective Association of Chicago, 1916.

Sabine Baring-Gould. *The Book of Werewolves.* Cosimo Classics, 2008.

Andreas Bjerre. *The Psychology of Murder: A Study in Criminal Psychology.* Da Capo Press, 1981.

Mary F. (Francesca) Bosworth. *The U.S. Federal Prison System.* 1st ed. Sage Publications, 2002.

———. *U.S. Federal Prison System.* 1st ed. Sage Publications, 2003.

William Bright. *Native American Placenames of the United States.* Norman: University of Oklahoma Press, 2004.

Elizabeth M. Bryan. *Twins, Triplets, and More: From Pre-Birth Through High School—What Every Parent Needs to Know When Raising Two or More.* 1st ed. New York: St. Martin's Press, 1999.

Maria G. Cattell and Jacob J. Climo. *Social Memory and History: Anthropological Perspectives.* AltaMira Press, 2003.

DeLorme. *Illinois Atlas and Gazetteer.* 5th ed. DeLorme Publishing, 2000.

———. *Indiana Atlas & Gazetteer.* 3rd ed. DeLorme Publishing, 2001.

Pete Earley. *The Hot House: Life Inside Leavenworth Prison.* New York: Bantam Books, 1993.

Steven A. Egger. *Serial Murder: An Elusive Phenomenon.* New York: Praeger, 1990.

———. *The Killers Among Us: An Examination of Serial Murder and Its Investigation.* Upper Saddle River, NJ: Prentice Hall, 1998.

Ford County Historical Society. *Atlas of the State of Illinois.* Mt. Vernon, IN: Windmill Publications, 1992.

Lisa Gitelman. *Scripts, Grooves, and Writing Machines: Representing Technology in the Edison Era.* Stanford, CA: Stanford University Press, 1999.

Elliot Goldenberg. *The Hunting Horse: The Truth Behind the Jonathan Pollard Spy Case.* Amherst, NY: Prometheus Books, 2000.

Randy H. Greer. *Echoes of Mercy.* 1st ed. Leathers Pub, 1998.

Mark Grossman. *Political Corruption in America: An Encyclopedia of Scandals, Power, and Greed.* 2nd ed. Millerton, NY: Grey House Pub, 2008,

Lance J. Herdegen. *The Men Stood like Iron: How the Iron Brigade Won Its Name.* Bloomington: Indiana University Press, 1997.

Richard N. Kocsis. *Serial Murder and the Psychology of Violent Crimes.* 1st ed. Humana Press, 2007.

Moira Martingale. *Cannibal Killers: The History of Impossible Murders.* 2nd ed. New York: Carroll & Graf, 2000.

Karl A. Menninger. *The Crime of Punishment.* New York: Viking Press, 1968.

Stephen G. Michaud. *The Evil That Men Do: FBI Profiler Roy Hazelwood's Journey into the Minds of Sexual Predators.* New York: St. Martin's Press, 2000.

Joel Norris. *Serial Killers.* 1st ed. New York: Anchor Books, 1989.

———. *The Killers Next Door.* Rev. and updated by William J. Birnes. New York: Kensington Publishing Corp., 2002.

Stewart Rafert. *The Miami Indians of Indiana: A Persistent People, 1654–1994.* Indianapolis: Indiana Historical Society, 1996.

Nancy L. Segal. *Entwined Lives: Twins and What They Tell Us About Human Behavior.* New York: Dutton, 1999.

Jon C. Teaford. *Cities of the Heartland: The Rise and Fall of the Industrial Midwest.* 1st ed. Bloomington: Indiana University Press, 1994.

"The Aftermath of the Yorkshire Ripper: The Response of the United Kingdom Police Service." In Steven A. Egger, *Serial Murder: An Elusive Phenomenon.* New York Praeger, 1990.

"Linkage Blindness: A Systemic Myopia." In Steven A. Egger, *Serial Murder: An Elusive Phenomenon.* New York: Praeger, 1990.

"Serial Murder: A Synthesis of Research and Literature." In Steven A. Egger, *Serial Murder: An Elusive Phenomenon.* New York: Praeger, 1990.

Government and Legal Documents

Grant County, IN, Sheriff's Department, "Larry Hall Mug Shot." November 16, 1994.

Illinois Criminal Justice Information Authority. "A Profile of the Ford County Criminal and Juvenile Justice Systems." May 2004.

National Archives & Records Administration. "Draft Registration Cards—Roy E. Hall." Ancestry.com, 1942.

United States of America v. Clayton Fountain et. al., 768 F.2d 790 (7th Cir. 1985).

United States of America v. Larry D. Hall: Hearing on the Motion to Suppress (CD IL 1995).

United States of America v. Larry D. Hall: Report of Proceedings (CD IL 1995).

United States of America v. Larry D. Hall: Final Disposition (CD IL 1995).

United States of America v. Larry D. Hall: Appellate Decision, 93 F.3d 1337 (7th Cir. 1996).

United States of America v. Larry D. Hall: Appellate Decision, 165 F.3d 1095 (7th Cir. 1999).

United States of America v. James Keene: Presentence Investigation Report (CD IL 1997).

United States of America v. James Keene: Final Disposition (CD IL 1997).

United States of America v. Larry D. Hall: Appellate Decision, 165 F.3d 1095 (7th Cir. 1999).

United States of America v. James Keene: Motion for Reduction of Sentence (CD IL 1999).

United States of America v. James Keene: Amended Judgment in a Criminal Case (CD IL 1999).

U.S. Census Bureau. "1930 United States Federal Census—Wabash, Wabash, Indiana." U.S. Government, 1930.

U.S. Social Security Administration. "Social Security Death Index—Robert R. Hall." Ancestry.com, 2001.

Vermilion County Sheriff's Department. "Jessica Roach Death Investigation." Gary Miller, November 2, 1994.

Vermilion County Sheriff's Department. "Jessica Roach Death Investigation." Gary Miller, November 15, 1994.

"Wabash County Marriage Licenses—Gary Wayne Hall, Catherine Elaine Dome." July 6, 1987.

"Wabash County Marriage Licenses—Gary Wayne Hall, Deaitra Sue Ward." January 18, 1991.

Interviews by Hillel Levin

James Keene, November–December 2007.

Ed Eckhaus, November 2007.

Gary Miller, December 2007.

Ron Osborne, December 2007.

John O'Brien, December 2007.

Confidential interview, Larry Hall counselor, 2008.

Confidential interview, 2008.

Micheal Thompson, January 2008.

Robert Allen, January 2008.

Ron Woodward, January 2008.

Lawrence Beaumont, January 2008.

Ron Smith, Phil Amones, January 2008.

Jeffrey Whitmer, February 2008.

Ross Davis, February 2008.

Mary Virginia Moore Johnson, April 2008.

Larry Hall, August 2008.

Garry and Donna Reitler, August 2008.

Garry Reitler, April 2009.

Ron Smith, April 2009.

Donna Reitler, October 2009.

Journal and Magazine Articles

Katie A. Busch and James L. Cavanaugh. "The Study of Multiple Murder: Preliminary Examination of the Interface Between Epistemology and Methodology." *Journal of Interpersonal Violence* 1, no. 1 (March 1, 1986): 5–23.

Tung-Pi Chou and William H. Adolph. "Copper metabolism in man." *Biochemical Journal* 29, no. 2 (February 1935): 476–79.

Malcolm Gladwell. "Dangerous Minds." *New Yorker,* November 12, 2007.

Skip Hollandsworth. "The Killing of Alydar." *Texas Monthly,* June 2001.

Maria Kantzavelos. "Profile: Jeffrey Steinback." *Chicago Lawyer,* November 13, 2008. http://www.chicagolawyermagazine.com/2008/11/13/profile-jeffrey-stein-back/.

Hillel Levin. "The Strange Redemption of James Keene." *Playboy,* August 2008.

A. E. Miller. "U.S. Medical Center for Federal Prisoners." *Bulletin of the Greene County Medical Society,* September 1982.

Richard Rayner. "The Admiral and the Con Man." *New Yorker,* April 22, 2002. http://archives.newyorker.com/?i=2002-04-22#folio=150.

Mark Starr. "The Random Killers." *Newsweek,* November 26, 1984.

"Serial-murder; Aftershocks—Call for Help." *Newsweek,* August 12, 1991.

Newspaper Articles

Associated Press. "To Sift Brutality Charge; Biddle Acts on Complaint from Federal Medical Center." *New York Times,* February 10, 1944.

———. "Prison Hospital Quells Uprising." *New York Times,* June 24, 1959.

———. "Report: Hall linked to 20 murders." *Wabash (IN) Plain Dealer,* January 21, 1995.

———. "Sheik, Calling Imprisonment Humiliating, Seeks Support." *New York Times,* June 24, 1996.

———. "Family losing hope in search for missing college student." *Fort Wayne (IN) Journal-Gazette,* March 30, 1997.

———. "False confession possible, witness says." *Wabash (IN) Plain Dealer,* August 27, 1997.

———. "Hall defense rests; jury to get case." *Wabash (IN) Plain Dealer.* August 28, 1997.

———. "Guilty again: Jury convicts Hall in kidnapping case." *Wabash (IN) Plain Dealer,* August 29, 1997.

Art Barnum. "Dugan sends letter to *Tribune* on Nicarico plea." *Chicago Tribune,* August 28, 2009.

Traci Bauer. "Springfield vs. Larry Flynt: A Movie and Book Prompt Memories of the 5 Weeks the Porn Publisher and Ozarkers Had to Put Up with Each Other." *Springfield (MO) News-Leader,* December 27, 1996.

Michael Bayer. "Evidence could tie area man to slayings." *Fort Wayne (IN) Journal-Gazette,* December 14, 1994.

Mark Bennett. "Paul Dresser: Popular songwriter crafted state song." *Terre Haute (IN) Tribune-Star,* February 2, 2005, sec. Special Reports.

Rick Bragg. "McVeigh Dies for Oklahoma City Blast." *New York Times,* June 12, 2001.

Robert Bryan. "Wabash man may be murder suspect." *Wabash (IN) Plain Dealer,* November 16, 1994.

———. "Hall indicted in kidnapping." *Wabash (IN) Plain Dealer,* December 22, 1994.

———. "Hall's lawyer plans alibi defense." *Wabash (IN) Plain Dealer,* January 31, 1995.

Craig Cairns. "The Reitler Riddle." *Marion (IN) Chronicle-Tribune,* May 28, 1995.

———. "Searcy: One man under suspicion." *Marion (IN) Chronicle-Tribune,* May 28, 1995.

Ann Calkins. "Area men in 'Glory' battle scenes." *Marion (IN) Chronicle-Tribune,* February 3, 1990, sec. Living.

John Caniglia. "Tricia Reitler disappearance draws fresh interest from Indiana investigators; inmate questioned." *Cleveland Plain Dealer,* April 26, 2009.

Roger Daniels. "'Any information will help us.'" *Marion (IN) Chronicle-Tribune,* March 29, 1996.

Monica Davey. "In Mob Sweep, Feds Hope to Send Up the Clown." *New York Times,* April 26, 2005.

Ron Davis. "The Most Dangerous Man." *Springfield (MO) News-Leader,* December 17, 1989.

Sharon Dettmer. "Police still searching for Rayna Rison's killer 10 years later." *South Bend (IN) Tribune,* March 26, 2003.

Joseph Fried. "U.S. Moves Convicted Sheik to Missouri Medical Center." *New York Times,* October 3, 1995.

Gannett News Service. "Hall: FBI framing me." *Marion (IN) Chronicle-Tribune,* February 4, 1995.

———. "Hall again draws life sentence." *Marion (IN) Chronicle-Tribune,* December 3, 1997.

Stacey Lane Grosh. "Some missing persons cases linger for years." *Marion (IN) Chronicle-Tribune,* March 29, 1998.

Henry Hahn. "Hospital Site: Test borings preparatory to construction work to be made soon." *Springfield (MO) Leader and Press,* July 29, 1931.

Jennifer Hamilton. "'I want a place to put flowers.'" *Marion (IN) Chronicle-Tribune,* March 29, 1997.

Jack Jillson. "Springfield's U.S. Medical Center for Federal Prisoners." *Springfield!,* April 1995.

Blair Kamin. "Jail a prisoner of ill-conceived renovation plan." *Chicago Tribune,* October 22, 2006, Chicagoland Final edition.

Docia Karell. "Government's Battle to Reclaim 'Lost Men' at Medical Center Here Holds Interest of Entire Nation." *Springfield (MO) Leader and Press,* July 28, 1935.

———. "Get Up! Whistle Signals Round of Activities." *Springfield (MO) Leader and Press,* July 29, 1935.

Cathy Kightlinger. "Probe of Wabash man continues." *Marion (IN) Chronicle-Tribune,* November 19, 1994.

———. "Wabash man may face Illinois grand jury." *Marion (IN) Chronicle-Tribune,* December 13, 1994.

———. "Officials look for Reitler." *Marion (IN) Chronicle-Tribune,* July 1, 1995.

Tammy Kingery. "Parents say hope fading." *Marion (IN) Chronicle-Tribune,* April 11, 1993.

———. "Reitlers to tell their difficult story on TV." *Marion (IN) Chronicle-Tribune,* May 25, 1993.

————. "A Test of Faith." *Marion (IN) Chronicle-Tribune,* March 29, 1994.

————. "Friends remember Tricia." *Marion (IN) Chronicle-Tribune,* March 30, 1994.

————. "Towns wait for word on investigations." *Marion (IN) Chronicle-Tribune,* November 17, 1994.

Marc Lazar. "Reitlers revive their search." *Marion (IN) Chronicle-Tribune,* February 12, 1998.

Joel Levin. "An unequal justice—why commuting former Gov. George Ryan's sentence would be unfair." *Chicago Tribune,* December 2, 2008, Chicagoland Final edition.

Cindy Losure. "Search team looking for volunteers." *Marion (IN) Chronicle-Tribune,* April 3, 1993.

Jennifer McSpadden. "Neighbors express shock, sympathy." *Wabash (IN) Plain Dealer,* November 17, 1994.

————. "New trial ordered for Hall." *Wabash (IN) Plain Dealer,* August 29, 1996.

Alan Miller. "Hall's parents talk of 'kind' son." *Marion (IN) Chronicle-Tribune,* November 18, 1994.

————. "Agonizing day for the Reitlers." *Marion (IN) Chronicle-Tribune,* November 20, 1994.

Traci Miller. "150 seek clues in disappearance." *Marion (IN) Chronicle-Tribune,* April 18, 1993.

David Nelson. "Missing student makes university nervous, worried." *Marion (IN) Chronicle-Tribune,* April 2, 1993.

————. "IWU in state of vigil until Reitler returns." *Marion (IN) Chronicle-Tribune,* April 3, 1993.

John O'Brien. "Hall's 2nd trial opening today." *Champaign (IL) News-Gazette,* August 18, 1997.

Matt O'Connor. "Noah Robinson Is Found Guilty Again in Retrial—4 High-Ranking El Rukns Also Are Convicted." *Chicago Tribune,* September 27, 1996, North Sports Final edition.

————. "Feds say Ryan is greedy, 2-faced—prosecutors tee off in closing arguments." *Chicago Tribune,* March 7, 2006, Chicago Final edition.

————. "Ryan gets 6½ years—ex-governor regrets conviction, but doesn't admit to wrongdoing." *Chicago Tribune,* September 7, 2006, Chicago Final edition.

Lesley Oelsner. "Jails Chief Backs Behavior System." *New York Times,* February 28, 1974.

Mike Penprase. "Many Infamous Men Pass Through Medical Center." *Springfield (MO) News-Leader,* June 11, 2002.

Selwyn Raab. "With Gotti Away, the Genoveses Succeed the Leaderless Gambinos." *New York Times,* September 3, 1995.

————. "John Gotti Dies in Prison at 61; Mafia Boss Relished the Spotlight." *New York Times,* June 11, 2002, New York edition, sec. A.

————. "Vincent Gigante, Mafia Leader Who Feigned Insanity, Dies at 77." *New York Times,* December 19, 2005, sec. Obituaries.

Linda Renken. "Woman last seen near Reliable Drug store." *Marion (IN) Chronicle-Tribune,* April 4, 1993.

————. "Few clues turn up in search for student." *Marion (IN) Chronicle-Tribune,* April 5, 1993.

————. "Law officers keep noses to grindstone to find missing girl." *Marion (IN) Chronicle-Tribune,* April 6, 1993.

————. "Missing student's friends still waiting." *Marion (IN) Chronicle-Tribune,* July 4, 1993.

————. "Missing IWU student's parents return to Ohio." *Marion (IN) Chronicle-Tribune,* April 7, 1994.

Susan Schramm. "Skull found in Marion isn't of missing student." *Indianapolis Star,* March 25, 1994.

Caryn Shinske. "Probe never far from Kay's mind." *Marion (IN) Chronicle-Tribune,* March 29, 1996.

Katherine Skiba. "Serial killing suspect wrote about Depies." *Milwaukee Journal Sentinel,* January 20, 1995.

Scott Squires. "Waiting for Justice." *La Porte County (IN) Herald-Argus,* April 4, 2008.

E. A. Torriero. "No fences, no violence, no privacy—Oxford camp lacks cellblocks and offers inmates a walking track, culinary classes." *Chicago Tribune,* November 7, 2007, Chicago edition.

Dirk Vanderhart. "Federal prison major employer for city." *Springfield (MO) News-Leader,* March 2, 2008.

Rick Veach. "John Gotti in Center for Throat Surgery." *Springfield (MO) News-Leader,* September 24, 1998.

Julie Westermann. "10 Building: From Illness to Acceptance." *Springfield (MO) Leader and Press,* June 14, 1983.

Margie Yee. "Deputy retires after 31 years." *Danville (IL) Commercial-News,* January 4, 2004.

"Greatest Triumph in History of City Nets $142,000 Fund." *Springfield (MO) Daily News,* April 1, 1931.

"May ask city to help build U.S. Hospital; Official considers plan to speed construction work here." *Springfield (MO) Leader and Press,* August 31, 1931.

"$100,000 hospital contract to Carthage firm." *Springfield (MO) Leader and Press,* April 12, 1932.

"Two Escape U.S. Prison Here." *Springfield (MO) Leader and Press,* November 16, 1933.

"More Guards Hired as 2 Flee Hospital." *Springfield (MO) Daily News,* November 17, 1933.

"Inmate Stages Break from Center." *Springfield (MO) Leader and Press,* February 25, 1944.

"Alert Citizen Finds Fugitive." *Springfield (MO) Leader and Press,* February 26, 1944.

"Now, This Is the Guards' Story." *Springfield (MO) Leader and Press,* February 27, 1944.

"Recommend inquiry on prisoner charges." *New York Times,* March 2, 1944.

"Guards Quell Riot at Medical Center and Prevent Break." *Springfield (MO) Leader and Press,* March 7, 1944.

"Tough Inmates to Be Scattered to Other Prisons." *Springfield (MO) Leader and Press,* March 12, 1944.

"Medical Center Charges Called Hallucinations." *Springfield (MO) Leader and Press,* March 16, 1944.

"Hospital News." *Wabash (IN) Plain Dealer,* December 12, 1962.

"Hospital News." *Wabash (IN) Plain Dealer.* December 17, 1962.

"Can't Regain Health at MC, Cohen Claims." *Springfield (MO) Leader and Press,* July 10, 1970.

"Status of U.S. Prison Hospital Poses Problems, Director Notes." *Springfield (MO) Leader and Press,* April 24, 1974.

"Non-Doctor 11th Warden at Hospital." *Springfield (MO) Leader and Press,* January 22, 1979.

"Keene in Control," *Kankakee (IL) Daily Journal,* November 6, 1980.

"Med Center Gets 116 Cubans from Chaffee." *Springfield (MO) Leader and Press,* January 26, 1982.

"800-Pound Cocaine Dealer Hauled to Springfield on Special Plane." *Springfield (MO) News-Leader,* February 17, 1989.

"260 Pounds Lighter." *Springfield (MO) News-Leader,* June 18, 1989.

"Man Found Guilty of Assassination Threat." *Springfield (MO) News-Leader,* March 28, 1990.

"Med Center Monitoring Policy Unchanged by Noriega Stir." *Springfield (MO) News-Leader,* November 14, 1990.

"Police won't connect Reitler with La Porte case." *Marion (IN) Chronicle-Tribune,* April 29, 1993.

"Marion police interested in body." *Marion (IN) Chronicle-Tribune,* November 10, 1993.

"Found body not Reitler's." *Marion (IN) Chronicle-Tribune,* November 11, 1993.

"Discovery raises serial killer fears." *Gary (IN) Post-Tribune,* November 14, 1993.

"Skull not Reitler's, police say." *Marion (IN) Chronicle-Tribune,* March 25, 1994.

"FBI searches Hall home; no new charges filed." *Wabash (IN) Plain Dealer,* December 9, 1994.

"Med Center Takes Would-Be Assassin." *Springfield (MO) News-Leader,* August 12, 1995.

"Medical Center Housing Mob Boss: John Gotti's Health Is Being Evaluated During Incarceration in Springfield." *Springfield (MO) News-Leader,* December 27, 1996.

"Lawyer Critical of Treatment for John Gotti: U.S. Medical Center Officials Say Mob Boss Hasn't Made Formal Complaints." *Springfield (MO) News-Leader,* October 7, 2000.

"Elusive Don Left 'Family' in Ruins." *Springfield (MO) News-Leader,* June 11, 2002.

"A brief history of time (in Indiana)." *Indianapolis Star,* April 30, 2005, sec. Library Fact Files, http://www2.indystar.com/library/factfiles/history/time.

"Verdict is talk of the town where Ryan makes home." *Chicago Tribune,* April 18, 2006, Chicago Final edition.

"'Made' in the Chicago mob—undercover tape details Outfit initiation ceremony, and reputed mobster's son tells jurors why he decided to turn on his dad." *Chicago Tribune,* July 10, 2007, Chicagoland edition.

"Setting Hollywood Straight—Spilotros lured to suburbs, killed." *Chicago Tribune,* July 19, 2007, Chicago edition.

"'There's nothing to smile about'—prosecutors begin closing arguments." *Chicago Tribune,* August 28, 2007, North edition.

"Outfit case goes to jury—deliberations set to begin Tuesday." *Chicago Tribune,* August 31, 2007, Chicago edition.

"5 guilty in Outfit trial—'Family Secrets' jury to begin deliberating on murder charges against 4." *Chicago Tribune,* September 11, 2007, Chicagoland edition.

"Jury hears about killings—defense tries to cast doubts on top witness." *Chicago Tribune,* September 12, 2007, Chicago edition.

"10 murders laid at feet of 3 in mob—some families wish verdict went further." *Chicago Tribune,* September 28, 2007, Chicago edition.

"Ryan's gone. Who's next?" *Chicago Tribune,* November 7, 2007, Chicago edition.

"He Killed 14 People. He Got 12 Years—murder victims' families react in shock, but judge says that without hit man's testimony, mob bosses would still be free." *Chicago Tribune,* March 27, 2009, Chicagoland Final edition.

"Brooklyn—history proves elusive in the place where the greatest basketball player ever was born." *Chicago Tribune,* September 10, 2009, Chicagoland Final edition.

"Inmates' Artwork a Source of Pride, Satisfaction: A Sale Saturday at the Medical Center for Federal Prisoners Will Help Needy Families." *Springfield (MO) News-Leader* October 23, 1998.

Photographs

"Hartford City Civil War Days Photograph." Micheal Thompson personal collection, June 1990.

"Noblesville, IN, Civil War Event Photograph." Micheal Thompson personal collection, October 1990.

Web Sources

Associated Press. "Calumet Honchos Found Guilty—CBS News." http://www.cb snews.com/stories/2000/02/07/sports/main157964.shtml.

Chicago Curt Teich & Company. "U.S. Federal Hospital, Springfield, Mo." Image. http://thelibrary.springfield.missouri.org/lochist/postcards/medical_center_1.cfm.

Natalie Graf. "Wabash County Class Reunions—Class of 2002." ingenweb.com, August 22, 2009. http://ingenweb.org/inwabash/reunion.html.

Mississinewa Battlefield Society. "Mississinewa 1812." mississinewa1812.com, 2009.

Jack Rinehart. "Detectives Pursue New Leads in Cold Case Killing—Indiana News Story—WRTV Indianapolis." The IndyChannel.com, August 25, 2009. http://www.theindychannel.com/news/20552712/detail.html.

Scott Swan. "Who killed Michelle Dewey?—WTHR." WTHR.com Eyewitness News, November 23, 2009. http://www.wthr.com/Global/story.asp?S=11562020.

U.S. Census Bureau. "Georgetown City, Illinois—Fact Sheet—American FactFinder." factfinder.census.gov, 2000.

"BOP: FCI Milan." Federal Bureau of Prisons, September 24, 2009. http://www.bop .gov/locations/institutions/mil/index.jsp.

"BOP: MCC Chicago." Federal Bureau of Prisons, September 24, 2009. http://www .bop.gov/locations/institutions/ccc/index.jsp.

"Canal Society of Indiana—Impact on Indiana Geography." http://www.indcanal.org/ Geography.html.

"Missing Person—Kathryn Margaret VanDine." Pennsylvania State Police. http://www .portal.state.pa.us.

"The Myth of Samhain: Celtic God of the Dead." Religious Tolerance. http://www .religioustolerance.org/hallo_sa.htm.

"People Search & Directory Services—Eugene Cloe." Intelius.com. http://www.intelius
.com/search-summary-out.php?ReportType=1&qf=Eugene&qmi=&qn=Cloe&
qs=&trackit=74&focusfirst=1.

"Quality Report for U.S. Medical Center for Federal Prisoners." http://www.quality
check.org/qualityreport.aspx?hcoid=1825.

"Southeast Spotlights on Faculty—Mary Virginia Moore Johnson." Southeast Missouri
State University. http://www.semo.edu/spotlights/faculty_6461.htm.

"Wabash County Class Reunions." http://ingenweb.org/inwabash/reunion.html.

"WabashRiver.us—History." WabashRiver.us. http://www.wabashriver.us/history/in
dex.htm.

Amazon.com. http://www.amazon.com/.

Google Maps. http://maps.google.com/.

Internet Movie Database (IMDb). http://www.imdb.com/.

George Georgiou

JAMES KEENE is the son of a former police officer who went from high school football star to convict. Besides working on a book and movie about his life, he is also involved in producing, writing, and consulting for other film and book projects.

HILLEL LEVIN has been an investigative reporter for *The Nation, New York* magazine, *Metropolitan Detroit, Playboy,* and editor for *Chicago* magazine. He is the author of *Grand Delusions* and coauthor of *When Corruption Was King.*